M000237741

"Since the beginning of Youth With A ⟨...⟩ been woven into the core fabric of who ⟨...⟩ *God?* which has been read by millions and translated into more than 140 languages worldwide, is really just YWAM's story of learning to hear God's voice in the place of prayer. It's not surprising that Nick and Rozanne have been called to multiply that message in the most unlikely places! You will be challenged and inspired as you read the Savocas' journey of seeing Prayer Stations established to encounter people in their times of greatest need with *Five Little Words* that have changed lives and eternity!"

Loren and Darlene Cunningham
Co-founders of Youth With A Mission (YWAM)

"I have known Nick and Rozanne since the early days of their ministry with my brother David Wilkerson through the Teen Challenge ministry. From there they went on to work in Youth With A Mission (YWAM). This book *Five Little Words* reads like a George Muller-type of ministry in which miracle answers to prayers became a regular part of their missionary journey. Their story after story of God's divine intervention and answers to their missionary challenges and ministry is utterly amazing. The greatest tool of evangelism that has come out of their ministry has been Prayer Stations; one of the most remarkable street outreaches in modern times. Read how this Prayer Evangelism ministry had spread worldwide beginning in New York City. This life story of missions work, as told in this book, can serve as a Missions Manual for present and future workers called to reach the lost. May many more YWAM-ers and others hopefully follow in the Savocas' footsteps of faith, sacrifice, risk-taking, and as prayer warriors to 'rescue the perishing and care for the dying.'"

Don Wilkerson
Co-founder of Teen Challenge, Inc.
President Emeritus, Teen Challenge At Brooklyn, NY Center

"Nick and Rozanne Savoca's Prayer Stations, have been connecting needy people with a loving God using the biblical principle called 'Prayer Evangelism.' From palaces to prisons and street corners to penthouses, prayer evangelism is empowering ordinary people to do extraordinary deeds by connecting heaven to earth with five simple words. I pray Nick and Rozanne's story will become your story."

Ed Silvoso
Founder, Transform Our World
Author, *Prayer Evangelism* and *Ekklesia: Rediscovering God's Instrument for Global Transformation*

"I have known Nick for decades and his ministry. I have confidence that God will use this book and urge you to get more than one copy so you can give one to a friend."

George Verwer
Founder of Operation Mobilization

"We are so privileged to know Nick and Rozanne Savoca and we count them as some of our dearest friends. We wholeheartedly endorse *Five Little Words*. This intriguing title holds the key to life transformation so in reality these five words could be some of the most important ever spoken.

"This book portrays the heart of God, and as you read it, you will be built up in your faith. Trust in your loving heavenly Father will be affirmed and confirmed. This book is authentic to the core—the 'real deal'—the Savocas live what they say. The heartfelt illustrations are inspirational—adversity is overcome by victory time and time again. One cannot help but break into worship at the kindness of God in providing all that was needed over the years during the many challenging situations that were faced with courage.

"Thought-provoking quotes, testimonials and teaching with Scripture call the reader to deep soul-searching and action. When we take time to pray for others, the impossible becomes the possible and lives, including our own, are changed by the power of God. Yours will be too as you read this amazing account of God's faithfulness, a family's unconditional obedience, and the many who spoke these five words from the heart while working at Prayer Stations all over the world."

David and Linda Cowie
Co-founders—Marine Reach
www.marinereach.com

"Nick and Rozanne Savoca have a compelling story to tell—a story that will thrill your heart and infuse you with hope. You will laugh and probably cry as they unpack the riveting saga of God's unfailing faithfulness and present-day miracles. The unfolding story of the Prayer Stations and their global impact will challenge and inspire you to expect great things from God. Once you begin reading, you'll find this book hard to put down. After you've read this book, may you employ those five little words that can fling open doors of opportunity and change lives forever."

David Shibley
Founder and International Representative
Global Advance

"The great evangelist D.L. Moody was once criticized for his methods of evangelism which to his critics seemed unorthodox. His pithy reply was, 'I like the way I'm doing it better than the way you're NOT doing it!' This came to my mind as I read through Nick and Rozanne Savoca's captivating book *Five Little Words*, which chronicles Nick and Rozanne's nearly 50 years of DOING IT in the trenches of evangelism and prayer!

"I first met the Savocas in the early '80s in Hawaii where we worked together on the Year of the Bible (which became the YEARS of the Bible!) while YWAM's Mercy Ship, the *Anastasis* spent over a year in Honolulu installing its sprinkler system.

"I have followed their exploits from a distance for many years since then, reading regular reports of the fruit of the Prayer Stations that they pioneered in New York City which have now spread worldwide. Only eternity will reveal the fruit that they and their kids have borne for the kingdom of God.

"During that season, in addition to evangelizing Honolulu's red-light district every Friday night alongside Nick, those of us in YWAM-Honolulu also had the privilege of having Rebecca (their daughter) serve with us here in Hawaii for a season.

"*Five Little Words* was also captivating to me as an evangelist not only by the wealth of quotes from evangelistic saints throughout church history, but Nick's teaching gift is on display challenging the reader to stay on fire for a lifetime of effective evangelism.

"Guaranteed if you read *Five Little Words* you will be motivated to the triad of activities Nick and Rozanne have consistently modeled for half a century: Prayer, Obedience and Evangelism."

Danny Lehmann
Director, YWAM Hawaii

"For decades Youth With A Mission has had a history of doing new things in new ways. Nick and Rozanne Savoca are no exception to that.

"The story of the Prayer Stations adds to that YWAM history. You, too, can learn to live like the Savocas. The secret lies in their ability to listen to Jesus and obey. I highly encourage you to take their stories seriously and ask yourself what does God want me to do to impact the world in a way that perhaps it has never been impacted before?

"Knowing Nick and Rozanne, this story is not finished. There is more to come."

Paul Hawkins
Founder, Schools of Intercession Worship, and Spiritual Warfare

"In 1974, in Lausanne Switzerland I was invited to be a part of Billy Graham's Congress on Evangelization. That is when I sat down with Loren Cunningham and told him YWAM needed to have a separate school called the Discipleship Training School (DTS). I called Nick, about running a DTS. This is important because Nick and one other leader ran the very first DTS programs in the world. The DTS then became the port of entry for staffing YWAM.

"Nick and Rozanne, I have always had a high regard for you. I think a scriptures that fits you both well is 2 Timothy 2:2 about "entrusting to faithful men." You both have been so faithful and have not swerved in your commitment to the Lord at all. Your book, *Five Little Words*, could not have had a better theme. I agree with you that effective work for God must be bathed with prayer."

Leland Paris
President
Youth With A Mission Tyler, Texas
Past YWAM America's Director

"I read the book, penned by my friend Nick Savoca and his wife Rozanne, in one sitting. I could not put it down. It is an amazing story of their personal history and ministry with YWAM in New York City my home town, and throughout the globe. You will be filled with joy as you read and marvel at the mighty works of God accomplished through our brother and sister, in the power of the Holy Spirit. I especially enjoyed the book as I was part of the early story and was around for the early days of the Prayer Station ministry, including the events of 9/11. I saw firsthand what God could do through the ministry of prayer, love and personal concern shown for people through prayer and conversation. I cannot even imagine how many hours of zealous prayer was offered to God in heaven through the staff and volunteers, led by Nick and Rozanne.

"I praise God for the impact they had on my life and ministry among the Jewish people and in one way or another we continue to utilize a very similar strategy in our public ministries in reaching the Jewish people in New York City and across the globe.

"Blessings to you Nick and Rozanne, and thank you for taking the time to rehearse this incredible testimony of personal experiences with the Lord in service for Him through the Prayer Stations. May He continue to fill you with His joy and strength for many more years of direct evangelism, intercessory prayer and in mentoring new leaders in the Body of our Blessed Messiah Yeshua Hamashiach.

"Thank you for your focus on evangelism and your personal example as evangelists, bringing the Good News of the Messiah to a broken and needy world."

With admiration and love,
Dr. Mitch Glaser
President, Chosen People Ministries

"Nick and Rozanne Savoca have always been willing to pioneer, serve and reach out in new ways and difficult places. This has taken courage, sacrifice, knowledge of and trust in the character of God, and perseverance. The goal has always been to spread God's love and salvation to all. The stories and teachings of this book will build your faith, refire your prayer life and challenge you to new levels of involvement with the needs of people."

Dean Sherman
Dean of the College of Christian Ministries for the YWAM University of the Nations. Respected international Bible teacher, pioneer and leader in YWAM, and author of *Spiritual Warfare* and *Relationships*

"No matter whether you are an unbeliever, angry at God, backslidden or daily walking closely with Jesus, God will meet you personally through these remarkable prayer stories told by two hearts bound together as one, Nick and Rozanne Savoca.

"In 2005-6 this Prayer Station ministry had a direct and significant impact in the formative years of God's call on our lives to Igniting Prayer Action. Whatever you do in life as you experience the reality of God through this high adventure dual narration you, like me, will be convicted that we need more of God in our lives every day. Reading this book will validate the fact that the more you pray for others the more you will experience the manifested presence of our living God. Then the more you experience His presence the more your life will be a Prayer Station for others.

"Let us PRAY NOW: 'Oh Lord God, I commit to ask Nick and Rozanne's *Five Little Words* of at least two people every day. In Jesus name I pray, amen.'

"I say *ChkkChirrrrrrr* which is the shrill trill call of joy of the woodland kingfisher from my home country in Zimbabwe. This is how excited I am to recommend this book for you to read. Start today then pray, pray, pray."

Colin Millar
Founder of Igniting Prayer Action, Chief Prayer Officer for Global Media Outreach 2010-2020, Prayer Advocate for Global Alliance for Church Multiplication (GACX) 2015-present

Five Little Words

to change a life.

Foreword by John Dawson

Five Little Words

to change a life.

Nick & Rozanne Savoca

YWAM PUBLISHING
Seattle, Washington

YWAM Publishing is the publishing ministry of Youth With A Mission (YWAM), an international missionary organization of Christians from many denominations dedicated to presenting Jesus Christ to this generation. To this end, YWAM has focused its efforts in three main areas: (1) training and equipping believers for their part in fulfilling the Great Commission (Matthew 28:19), (2) personal evangelism, and (3) mercy ministry (medical and relief work). For a free catalog of books and materials, call (425) 771-1153 or (800) 922-2143. Visit us online at www .ywampublishing.com.

ISBN: 978-1-64836-076-3 (paperback)
ISBN: 978-1-64836-077-0 (e-book)

Cover art: Ron Setran

First printing 2022

Printed in the United States of America

Dedication

To our children and grandchildren.
Thank you for giving us joy in our journey.

Table of Contents

Foreword by John Dawson. 15

Introduction. 17

Chapter 1 – A God Idea. 21

Chapter 2 - The Day That Changed Everything 31

Chapter 3 - Long Ago and Far Away 45

Chapter 4 - The Pastor and the Missionary. 61

Chapter 5 - No Title, No Salary, No Guarantees 71

Chapter 6 - God's Frozen Chosen. 83

Chapter 7 - Where the People Are . . . . · 95

Chapter 8 - "Coming Home". 105

Chapter 9 - And Then There Were Four. 113

Chapter 10 - Old Roots with New Shoots 127

Chapter 11 - "Follow" 141

Chapter 12 - The Great Commission 149

Chapter 13 - Motivation for Evangelism 177

Chapter 14 - Purpose for Pentecost 195

Chapter 15 - House of Prayer. 215

Chapter 16 – Sold Out. 227

Chapter 17 – "Understanding the Times". 245

Chapter 18 - Five Little Words. 255

Foreword

By
John Dawson

Do you want to come up to speed? Do you want a handbook and guide that clearly tells you what you need to know? This is it. As I follow the Savocas' amazing story, I found myself thinking *This is the book I want every young Christian leader to read, especially the next generation of YWAM leaders.*

People are fascinated by New York stories. Think of Mario Puzo *The Godfather*. Nick and Rozanne's story is even more dramatic. It also stretches from Sicily to America but goes on to encompass the ends of the earth. However, this is not a tale of violence and superstitious darkness. This story is an inspiration and a revelation. This *true* story is a cosmic perspective on New York, a view from the throne of God.

Why is that relevant to your life? Right now, you are wondering about your future. You have many obstacles to overcome. You are summoning what courage you have, but looking for hope and resources.

Read this book. Take your time. Immerse yourself in it. I especially enjoyed the way that Nick and Rozanne take turns writing. We see two intimate views of the same surprising events. A boy and girl, American and New Zealander, husband and wife, companions of the heart, in tragedy and triumph. You will be lifted to new heights, your feet set in a place where the view of your future looks really promising.

This is the journey of a dynastic family, discovering the wonders of God, but it is not a pious exhortation. I found myself laughing and weeping in response to Nick and Rozanne's frank honesty. These are some of the noblest people I know, yet it was the confession of their weaknesses and failures that most gave me hope and guidance for my own future as I seek to know God and make Him known. There is also a profound simplicity to what God asked them to do. Any one of us can follow in their footsteps.

John Dawson
President Emeritus, YWAM International

Introduction

Five Little Words

"I will give thanks to you, Lord, with all my heart;
I will tell of all your wonderful deeds."

Psalm 9:1

The story you are about to read is a narrative of our lives from the early years on opposite sides of the world through more than 50 years of ministry together.

This pilgrimage has led our family to many locations around the world allowing us the privilege of discipling, equipping and mobilizing others for missionary service.

Five Little Words relates some of the life messages God has taught us and that have become the foundation of our ministry. It traces from its inception God's vision for Prayer Stations, a ministry that has become one of the most effective tools for evangelism in our time.

This is the story of two very ordinary people who learned early in our lives to hear God's voice and simply obey His direction. When that happens great and powerful outcomes occur.

This story is honest and forthright, not just about the wonderful things God has done, but also about the cost of the call. No one in ministry is without battle scars, but through the battles we learn our God is trustworthy, He never fails. He's there when our faith is strong and when it's not. His love is unwavering, and His compassion beyond comprehension.

It is our hope that as you read these pages you will be inspired and empowered to not only find and understand God's specific calling for your life, but also be energized with a new passion for Jesus and a love for the lost of this world

With Thanks

We want to begin by honoring and thanking our parents and family for their love, patience, prayers, and support of two crazy "kids." We know we left you shaking your heads sometimes, but you always supported us and prayed for us.

We honor our girls, Anita, Rebecca and Melissa who were part of our journey, and filled it with love, joy and lots of laughter. Each of you have continued to walk your individual path of faith, serving Jesus with all your hearts, and loving and honoring your "old folks." We are so grateful for Ron, Dan, Erik and our nine grandchildren. Each of you enrich our lives immeasurably.

We thank our spiritual mentors, Sunday School teachers, Bible College professors, YWAM leaders, fellow colleagues in ministry and loving compassionate pastors, who taught us the ways of God and gave us guidance and specific words of encouragement when we so desperately needed them.

We want to give special honor to those we affectionately and gratefully call our Support Team. These are dear friends and family, many from the early days, who have believed in us, prayed for us, encouraged us, and invested financially in our family and ministry. You are so dear to our hearts!

Pastor David Wilkerson once preached a sermon at Times Square Church entitled "A salute to those who stayed with the stuff." Pastor Dave tells the story found in 1 Samuel 30:23-25, speaking to those who were returning with him from the frontlines of battle, "David replied, the share of the man who stayed with the supplies is to be the same as that of him who went down to the battle. All will share alike. David made this a statute and ordinance for Israel from that day to this."

Some of our supporters have been with us from the beginning, and some have jumped in with both feet along the way. We are a team. You have prayed, given, encouraged, and stood with us through the good times and the difficult seasons. We would never have wanted to do this without you! We take this opportunity to thank you for the important role you, our Support Team, play in allowing us to live out God's call, for trusting us with your care, resources, prayers, phone calls, care packages, and on occasion, for sharing your homes and meals with us. We love doing ministry with you! Thank you from the depths of our hearts! The "spoil" of all God has given is as much yours as it is ours.

Nick's Special Tribute

For more than 20 years family, friends and colleagues have encouraged me to write this book. In 1974 I worked with Dick Schneider, senior editor of *Guideposts* magazine, to write "Roadblock to Moscow." Dick did the writing while I did the reporting. It tells of a mission God allowed me to be a part of in 1973—an attempt to share the gospel on Red Square in Moscow during the Brezhnev era of the old Soviet Union. We didn't make it to Moscow but we had quite an adventure along the way.

English, although it is my first language, has never been my strong suit. When God gave me my helpmate, he gave me a talented writer of both prose and poetry. Rozanne edits almost everything I write: letters, emails, posts, and sometimes even my sermons. She usually reads what I write, tells me, "I love it," and then changes everything for the better.

For the past 20 years I have been paralyzed with the thought of beginning this book. I searched for ghost writers unsuccessfully. Our ministry board encouraged me to get the story written, but I felt incapable. Rozanne had never written a book, but the thought of asking her to help me kept going through my mind. When I did, she was also overwhelmed, feeling completely inadequate for the task.

One morning, as we entered the dark COVID tunnel in early 2020, Rozanne turned to me and said, "Honey, I think God gave me the beginning of the book." She sat at her computer and I marveled at the anointing God gave her, she so inspired me. "OK, I got you started," she said, "Now take it from here." That helped, but it soon became apparent that this was not going to be MY book, but OUR book.

I am grateful that what you are about to read is the story of our life experiences, told from both of our perspectives. It is amazing how two people can go through the same thing but see it so differently.

Without Rozanne's involvement and commitment, I would never have endeavored to accomplish this task. For this reason, I want to give her the credit she is due and my heart full of thanks for endless hours spent prayerfully at her computer to make this all possible.

Thank you, my darling!

Nick

Chapter 1

A God Idea

We were cut off! All tunnels and bridges were closed! The only way off Long Island was by boat, and we didn't have one. Our city was under attack, and according to the news reports other targets were also being hit!

Earlier that beautiful September morning we had gathered as a staff to pray, a normal occurrence on a weekday at Youth With A Mission (YWAM) Metro New York. In the midst of our prayers, we received word that a plane had flown into the World Trade Center. Rushing to the TV we watched in horror as another plane hit the second tower, and soon the towers were falling.

It didn't take long for calls and emails to begin pouring in from YWAM leaders all over the world.

"What can we do?" "How can we help?"

I realized I had no idea. I was still in shock, trying to wrap my mind around what was happening in our city, along with Pennsylvania and Washington DC. I cried out to the Lord and His answer was immediate and clear;

"Use what I have already put in your hands."

My thoughts rushed back to 1992....

YWAM Metro New York was only six years old then. During the first few years my focus had been to build relationships with New York pastors and ministry leaders. I remember asking some of them if there was a forum where we could meet together regularly to share, pray and strategize. Most looked at me strangely saying nothing like that existed and they didn't believe it would work, due to doctrinal and other diversities. Being the "new kid on the block" I presumed it wouldn't bode well for me to keep pushing my idea.

One day however, I received a call from one of the leaders of Jews for Jesus in Manhattan, suggesting he might invite various ministry leaders to come together. We could see what would happen from there. Soon after I was encouraged to receive an invitation to the first meeting. Not knowing many of those attending, I was unaware that I was sitting next to a prominent pastor and ministry leader, a gentleman who was by no means a charismatic. Turned out we got along great, and so began a beautiful friendship.

This became a regular monthly meeting. We spent time sharing, praying, encouraging one another, and to my surprise, even strategizing how we might partner together. We eventually moved our meetings to the New York Bible Society where Chuck Rigby was our host and helped us all find common ground. Many of the ministries represented were outreach oriented and oh, how this blessed my evangelist heart!

I particularly remember coming to one meeting in January of 1992. Chuck shared a vision he had for us to work on an outreach to the city at New Year's, which is a big deal in New York. People come from literally all over the globe to be in the city for the holidays, and especially to watch the ball drop in Times Square on New Year's Eve.

Chuck had a plan that sounded both doable and effective. We would offer people free hot chocolate, which is always appreciated on a bitterly cold New Year's in the city, and then take the opportunity to share the gospel with them. Chuck encouraged us all to pray and seek God's specific vision for our ministry.

I began to pray. Immediately I felt that we needed to make this more than just a New Year's Eve outreach. Teams should arrive on Boxing

Day (December 26th) and be involved in ministry in the city from then through New Year's Eve. I asked God for clarity on exactly what He would want us to do?

God's response was clear; "Pray for people on the street."

"But Lord, we always incorporate prayer into our evangelism. What specifically do You want us to do?"

"Make prayer your up-front strategy."

Prayer and Evangelism. Those two words have always been an important part of my Christian life. If I were to choose which aspects of Christianity have meant the most to me and motivated me to action more than anything else, it would be prayer and evangelism. There was a strong sense that God was bringing these dynamics together in a way I had never imagined before.

During the months that followed I continued to pray for under-standing. Slowly God began to birth an idea in my heart, one I had never ever heard of anyone else doing. It seemed to me to be not only quite revolutionary, but very much an early church, book of Acts scenario.

I began to imagine placing a table on the street. Bibles, Gospels of John and salvation tracts were spread across it. We needed to identify what we were attempting to do. Perhaps we could put a banner over the table, but what should the banner say?

"PRAYER STATION" was the clear and powerful response.

"Yes! That says it plain and simple," I thought.

If New Yorkers want to catch a subway, they go to a train station. If they want gas for their cars, they go to a gas station. If they want and need prayer why not go to a Prayer Station?

Each time I prayed God revealed more details.

I envisioned two people standing about 20 feet on either side of the Prayer Station. They were handing out written invitations that could be read at a glance. The flier would encourage people to stop for prayer and also give suggestions as to prayer requests they might have: Their health, a job, their family or friends, or because it was the holidays, per-haps a prayer for the New Year. The remainder of the team would stand in front of the Prayer Station and back up the written invitation with a spoken one, just 5 little words, *"May I pray for you?"*

Somewhere I could recall hearing a teaching on the two basic needs everyone has in common, a Felt Need and a Real Need. The felt need could be dozens of things: health issues, loss of employment, finances, relationships, disability, a child, a marriage, etc.

As I searched the gospels and the book of Acts, I saw that Jesus and His followers would often pay attention first to an individual's felt need, and then share the gospel with them. For instance, Jesus was traveling down the Jericho Road when He heard Bartimaeus call out to him, "Jesus, Son of David, have mercy on me!" (Mark 10:46-52). Jesus stopped, called Bartimaeus over and prayed for him. Bartimaeus was instantaneously healed. The scripture then continues, "He followed Jesus down the road." Our first focus should be the person's felt need, and then their Real Need, a personal relationship with Jesus!

It all seemed to be coming together in my mind and heart, but the question was, would it work? Would cynical New Yorkers actually allow us to pray for them on a public street? Everyone knows that New Yorkers are a tough crowd! I contemplated all of this for several weeks and then decided to share the vision with my evangelistic buddies and find out what they thought of this strategy.

At the very next meeting I shared what God had laid on my heart and waited with bated breath for their response. I wanted to hear, "Wow, Nick, that's a great strategy. Why don't we build a Prayer Station and go out and see how the public receives it?"

Instead, they told me they thought it was a great idea, then added, "Why don't you experiment with it and come back and let us know how it worked?" They were being "politically correct" and I knew it. I left the meeting somewhat discouraged and wondered whether I had really heard from God, or if this whole vision was a New Yorker's "pizza dream."

Weeks passed. As the holidays drew closer and the 1992 New Year's Outreach loomed on the horizon, I could not forget or ignore the vision God had given to me. It just pounded in my chest, and I knew this must be God!

Finally, I asked Dave VanFleet, one of my YWAM leaders, if he would build two Prayer Stations. After I explained to him what I felt it should look like, Dave went to work and produced our first two prototypes just before the holiday season began. There was no opportunity to test the strategy ahead of time. All I had was the concept and a deep assurance that this was God's vision, not mine.

December 26th arrived and a number of YWAM and church teams gathered from Illinois, Tennessee, New Hampshire and other locations. On the first day, during the orientation time with the leaders, I shared my vision for Prayer Stations and was honest with them,

"Hey guys, I don't know if this will work, but I want to ask if you would be willing to experiment with me, and see?" They were all stoked and voiced their excitement, saying they would be happy to do it. Phew! Finally, some encouragement!

The following day I took two teams to midtown Manhattan. I set up the first team from YWAM Nashville on 34th Street between Sixth and Seventh Avenues, just across from the famous Macy's department store. I gave the team some quick instructions on what to do and how to do it. Having never actually experienced it myself, my hope and trust was that this was a God vision and we were simply being obedient. They seemed keen to go for it, so I put Steve Tackett, the YWAM leader from Nashville, in charge, and headed down to Seventh Avenue to set up the second team from Salem, New Hampshire. Having given their pastor instructions, I started back to 34th Street to see how the Nashville team was doing.

As I walked that short distance, fear gripped my heart. What would I find?

I imagined the team standing in front of the Prayer Station, arms folded, with discouraged looks on their faces. They were probably thinking, "This is the last time I ever experiment with you, Savoca. No one is stopping for prayer; people are laughing at us. This is just not working."

I passed several subway entrances and thought briefly about disappearing down into one of them. But I knew I had to face the music sooner or later, so I headed back to the team. I admit to attempting to hide behind people walking in front of me. I'm 6 feet, 6 inches tall, so that was not an easy feat!

Eventually I spotted Steve and noticed that he had a smile on his face from ear to ear. "Well," I thought to myself, "guess it can't be that bad."

"How are things going?" I asked.

Never will I ever forget his response.

"How are things going? Why, this is the best thing since sliced bread! Just a few minutes ago we had people standing in line waiting to be prayed for!"

My joy knew no bounds! I immediately joined the team and soon found out two very basic things about this strategy.

First, prayer is very disarming.

For years as a street evangelist, I had asked people if I could share my faith with them. This is, I often described as, "rejection city." Now I was discovering that when you asked, *"May I pray for you?"* the response was often very different. Many people gave an immediate, "Yes, please." People who did not consider themselves to be Christian or religious, were open to receive prayer. It was like people were saying, "Hey, I need all the help I can get, why not prayer?"

Second, witnessing following prayer comes naturally.

I discovered that when you pray with someone regarding their felt need and then begin to talk with them, they are much more receptive. They are grateful for prayer, barriers have been broken down, a measure of trust has been built, and the transition to their real need is natural, not forced.

That first day was such a faith builder! We had the opportunity to pray with a large number of people and many made the decision to commit their lives to Christ.

Connie Hughes was a member of the Nashville team. She came originally from London, Kentucky, a small town with a population of approximately 8,000. This wonderful Christian grandmother felt blessed to be a part of the short-term mission team. Connie had never been in a big city before, let alone New York City, and she was a little intimidated by its size and complexity. Her job at the Prayer Station that first day was to give invitation fliers to those who passed by. Connie loved God and had a real burden for people who didn't know Him.

In midtown Manhattan people walk down the streets in waves. A subway train arrives at the station and a wave of people emerge from the underground. Often there is a lull in pedestrian traffic until the next train arrives and the process is repeated. During one such lull, Connie spied a scruffy-looking man handing out his own fliers.

Connie had an inspired idea. She approached the man, and introduced herself, adding, "If you take one of my fliers, I'll take one of yours." He gave her a typical cynical New York look, grunted and turned back to what he was doing. Connie was persistent, so finally he took one of her fliers. Scanning it quickly, he said, "OK, lady, thank you," obviously hoping she would walk away.

Connie however, reminded him of their bargain. "Now let me have one of your fliers." He was very reluctant to do this, but eventually, with his back turned to her, he handed her one. Connie could not believe what she was seeing. He was advertising the newest pornography shop on the street!

"This is terrible! You shouldn't be doing this!"

"Hey lady, give me a break. This is the only job I could get," he responded in his New York slang.

Connie smiled, "Please, come over here. I want to pray for you that God will give you a decent job."

Now how can you turn down a grandma who wants to pray for you, even if it is on the street? Connie prayed that God would give the man suitable employment.

Just about the time Connie said, "Amen," her leader called. "Team, it's time for us to pack up and head back to our base. We'll be here again tomorrow." Connie asked the gentleman if he would be at the same location too. He said he would. "Good, I want to talk with you some more," she said.

The following day the Nashville team again set up their Prayer Station on 34th Street.

The same man came running down the street yelling, "Where's the lady from Kentucky?" The team pointed him to Connie.

Breathlessly he called to her. "Hey lady, you'd never believe it! This morning I found a decent job!" Connie smiled and asked if they could talk. She began to share the gospel with him and he made a decision right there in the midst of the hustle and bustle of 34th Street, to receive Christ into his life as Lord and Savior.

Later that year we heard that Connie had set up a Prayer Station at the Walmart in London, Kentucky and was instrumental in leading many young people to Jesus.

After 1992, the New Year's Eve outreach experiment became a regular part of our YWAM schedule. More and more teams began to come, and soon we graduated from two Prayer Stations to 25. Mission teams gave exciting testimonies as people on the street were blessed, encouraged, healed, found employment, and made the all-important, life-changing decision to follow Jesus.

YWAM Metro New York was a magnet for short-term teams coming to do urban outreach in the "city that never sleeps."

I will never forget the day I was in prayer and heard the Lord say, "Nick, why don't you use Prayer Stations year round with the many teams that come to do short-term missions in New York City?" Up until that time we had used it only as a strategy for New Year's.

My immediate thought was, "Duh." I realized I should have thought of that long ago.

"Of course, Lord, why not!"

During the years our ministry was in full operation in New York, we hosted more than 70,000 short-termers. We took teams all over the city, often to some of the most under resourced areas. Popular sites were 125th Street in the heart of Harlem, the South Bronx, downtown Brooklyn, various ethnic neighborhoods of Queens, and many locations in Manhattan as well as Long Island. They came to spend anywhere from a few days to two weeks doing outreach. They were involved in many types of ministry but their favorite was always Prayer Stations.

One particular March, a team came for spring break. Sharon, one of our international staff members, was in charge of this particular team.

The Lord laid it on her heart to take them down to 34th Street, just across from the Empire State Building, the same area where we had set up a Prayer Station during the New Year's Eve Outreach three months earlier.

As the team began their ministry the first day, a woman approached them with great excitement. "I have been looking all over town for you guys! I stopped at a Prayer Station three months ago, and someone asked if I had anything they could pray with me about. I said, 'Yes; I am a model and I have been unsuccessfully looking for a job for weeks.' They prayed with me and the next morning I found a modeling job! I've had that position for three months now, and I wanted to thank you for your prayers and find out more about this Jesus you pray to."

So many times God would give us what I call "divine encounters" with people who were at the end of their rope and needed help desperately.

A Prayer Station team in Spanish Harlem, stopped a woman walking down the street to ask, *"May we pray for you?"* She responded, "Are you people angels? I left work early today to go home and take my life." She gave her life to Christ and went home rejoicing!

Kevin, a short-termer, shared his story. "A man came up to me and said, 'I need to change my life.' We talked about the changing power of Christ, and he accepted the Lord. As we were praying, he started weeping. A woman walking by heard us and saw the man crying, and she joined us in prayer and then told the man of the power of Jesus in her life. I knew the Lord had prepared his heart for us that morning."

Now many years later, as we all huddled around the TV in the staff lounge at YWAM Metro New York in 2001, contemplating the reality of towers falling, lives being lost, and our world completely irreparably altered in a single moment of time, the weight of those fallen buildings seemed to be crushing our hearts with grief. But, I knew that God, as He said, had already prepared us and placed His tool in our hands, for such a time as this.

Chapter 2

The Day That Changed Everything

No sooner had God spoken on September 11, than I received a call from a pastor friend in Queens. His words were simple, but profoundly affirming. "Nick, if this city ever needed Prayer Stations, it needs them now!" I thanked him for reinforcing God's word to me.

God laid these verses on my heart:

> Grace to you and peace [inner calm and spiritual well-being] from God our Father and the Lord Jesus Christ. Blessed [gratefully praised and adored] be the God and Father of our Lord Jesus Christ, the Father of mercies and the God of all comfort, who comforts and encourages us in every trouble so that we will be able to comfort and encourage those who are in any kind of trouble, with the comfort with which we ourselves are comforted by God (2 Corinthians 1:2-4 AMP).

The unthinkable had happened in our beloved city. As Mayor Giuliani put it, the number of lives lost would be "more than any of us could bear."

By the next day Dave VanFleet was located close to the rubble of the towers with a Prayer Station. He and a revolving team of volunteers ran two 12-hour shifts, going 24/7, serving, feeding and praying for an average of 2,000 firefighters, police, and volunteers per day!

Within a few days, Bob Lungren came to visit me at my office. Bob was a retired NYC firefighter and the leader of a ministry called Firefighters for Christ. He asked if I would give him a Prayer Station, explaining that as a retired firefighter he would be allowed access into Ground Zero. I gratefully gave Bob a Prayer Station and boxes of literature and Bibles.

The rules as to who was allowed into Ground Zero changed by the day. After Bob's first day of ministry, he heard that if he left for any reason, he would not be allowed back in. That night he slept under the Prayer Station amid the rubble. Early the next morning as he was getting everything ready for another day of ministry, former President Bill Clinton and his daughter Chelsea, walked by. They both stopped at the Prayer Station and encouraged the retired firefighter to keep up the good work. Bob had the privilege of praying for Chelsea.

After the Clintons passed by, the Secret Service Officer assigned to them approached Bob and asked why he looked so discouraged. "It's just that I have run out of literature and if I leave the Prayer Station, I won't be able to come back into Ground Zero. I have actually called the American Bible Society at Columbus Circle. They have literature for me but I can't go get it." The Secret Service agent told Bob he would pick up the literature and bring it to him, which he did![1]

Just 11 days after 9/11 our YWAM ministry was scheduled to launch a new Performing Arts Discipleship Training School (PADTS) alongside a classic DTS. Twenty-nine students, both American and international, were expected but now the question on our minds was, would any of them come? Would parents actually allow their young people to come to the city that had just been attacked?

1. With great sadness we report that Bob Lungren passed away on October 3, 2017 from complications due to being at Ground Zero.

The Performing Arts DTS was the dream of our middle daughter, Rebecca, and her husband, Dan. Both are talented in the arts and passionate for their generation. After the tragic 1999 Columbine High School massacre in Colorado, a tragedy that changed our nation, Rebecca and Dan's hearts were broken for the youth in our middle and high schools. Around that time, they also read *The Wounded Spirit* by Frank Peretti, and God began to pour a vision into their hearts.

Under the leadership of Dave and Tammy Adams, co-workers with us since 1978, God inspired Rebecca and Dan to write a musical to perform in high schools and middle schools. They now planned to teach the musical to our students in this upcoming PADTS. Our staff made phone calls to each student, and in the end every single one of them showed up and had a life-changing experience!

With only a handful of our staff not specifically committed to helping with our two schools, how could I possibly launch what I knew would be a huge Prayer Station outreach? Where could we house incoming volunteer teams? Our YWAM facility was located in Smithtown, Long Island, 49 miles east of Manhattan, and it was already at capacity.

We also lacked the finances to build the 25 Prayer Stations we knew would be needed, purchase literature, and cover the myriad of other expenses that would be essential to support such an outreach.

By this time Rozanne and I had served more than 28 years in Youth With A Mission. We always lived by the principle that when God speaks and asks us to take on something we think is impossible, our response should not be dictated by anything other than the Word of the Lord.

So many times, we had said, "Yes" to God when He asked us to do something that was way beyond our abilities or resources. He had always come through in miraculous ways.

One day shortly after 9/11, I was driving and listening to a news broadcast on the radio. The man being interviewed headed up a nonprofit agency that had responded to the Oklahoma City bombing at the Alfred P. Murrah Federal Building in 1995. The interviewer asked the nonprofit leader what he had learned from that experience. The man's response changed everything for me. He said that any agency that intends to help in a time of crisis needs to make a minimum commitment to continue their work for at least one year.

In that instant I heard the Lord say to me, "Are you willing to make a one-year commitment to this outreach?" I swallowed hard and answered. "Yes Lord!"

Within a few weeks God provided:

— A strategic mobilization location, free of charge, just half a block from the center of Times Square, where we could gather our teams each day before heading to Ground Zero.

— The funds to build 25 Prayer Stations, given by World Vision.

— An empty brownstone on the Upper East Side of Manhattan, also free of charge, to house teams coming into the city from around the country and the world.

— Literature and Bible portions, donated by the American Bible Society and Campus Crusade for Christ.

— Specifically crafted, free-of-charge literature, Bibles, DVDs, and music CD's, given by a host of ministries around the country, to attract passersby to stop, browse and receive prayer.

Domestic and international mission teams from YWAM, local churches, and other ministries began to contact us, sharing their desire to come and help reach out to the people of our city.

New York was no longer the city we had known and worked in for so many years. It was quiet. Self-assured New Yorkers rushing from place to place, peddling their wares, hailing cabs, crowding streets, buses and subway cars, were hardly recognizable. Many had lost someone they knew, someone they worked with or someone they loved. Others had lost jobs. Everyone was feeling vulnerable and shaken.

There was also a new and very profound respect and desire for prayer. One Prayer Station team member reported to the media that the people he encountered on the street, "practically begged us to pray for them."

Never before had I seen such openness as when I approached someone and shared those five simple words: ***"May I pray for you?"***

One day Rozanne, along with veteran YWAMers Tammy Adams and Linda Cowie stepped out of a car in Manhattan, all wearing "Fallen but not Forgotten" tee shirts. Two girls who had been walking by fell into their arms crying. Rozanne, Tammy, and Linda had the beautiful opportunity to share and pray with them right there on the sidewalk. Passersby did not seem to find the scene at all unusual.

Another time, I took a team down Broadway just across from Ground Zero. A Wall Street executive stopped and began to talk to me about how he should have been in the North Tower on that fateful day. He had been delayed and didn't get there until after the tragedy had taken place. He began to weep with a mixture of grief for the loss of his friends and coworkers and a sense of guilt that he was somehow spared. This type of brokenness and sensitivity was unusual for a Wall Street executive, but in these painful days it was becoming the norm.

Our city was in mourning, and many people were finding the comfort that God wanted to give them. One woman from Queens, upon viewing the World Trade Center ruins for the first time, said she felt better after the impromptu prayer session at a Prayer Station. "I did find it very comforting to know that people do care, even though some of them don't even live in New York."

Members of our Prayer Station teams reported back with their stories.

Jana—"As I was finishing lunch, a lady sat by me and asked about my Prayer apron. I told her we were helping at the Prayer Station. She proceeded to tell me that she was an EMT who had been on duty on 9/11. Her unit received a cell phone call from one of eight people who were stuck in an elevator between floors in Tower 2. They told her that they could only get the door of the elevator to open a crack. She then broke down crying as she shared that her unit was not able to reach the people and get them out. I prayed with her and asked God to help heal the guilt she was carrying over not being able to rescue those precious lives. The lady then turned to her husband and told him I was an angel sent by God, just to pray for her."

Mark—"I prayed for the brother of one of the first firefighters found deceased."

Cindi—"I prayed for a man named Henry who lost his son in the World TC. He was angry and so sad. His son had only been a firefighter for six weeks before he died."

Charlotte—"I prayed with a woman who lost her husband in the WTC."

Jonathan—"We prayed for a Ground Zero construction worker whose sister died at the WTC."

Reuben, 15 years old—"I prayed for someone who had been stuck in traffic on 9/11 and arrived at the WTC just as the first plane hit. He lost his whole company."

Candice—"One young man lost his entire family on 9/11. They all worked at the WTC. He had just accepted the Lord and needed some more prayer and care."

Fear was rampant in the hearts of many New Yorkers: fear of going to work, riding the subway, or leaving their families, even for a few hours.

One team member shared, "I saw a businessman on the subway who looked at me with such sad, pleading eyes, as if he wanted to start a conversation with me. I asked him if he knew anyone who was lost in the World Trade Center. He opened up about how his company had lost a number of officers and workers in the towers. He said he was afraid of going back to work in the city in any capacity. I could smell alcohol on his breath. I told him all we could do at times like this was to go to God. He began to break down. We both just sobbed on the subway. There was so much brokenness."

We encountered very few people who either claimed to be atheist or who were mad at God for what happened. Most were extremely receptive and appreciative of our efforts to bring much needed and desired prayer to the street. Many people felt the comfort that God was wanting to give them.

We didn't just pray for people who had some sort of a Christian background, but for people of many religions, including Jews, Muslims, Buddhists, Hindus, agnostics and so many others.

Eighteen-year-old Amy shared her experience, "I started talking to a man from Pakistan. He was a Muslim so he was familiar with a lot of scriptures. I showed him through 'Steps to Peace with God' by Billy Graham, how Christ was the only way we could be made righteous before God, and I was surprised when he wanted to pray for salvation. He repeated a prayer for salvation, and you could see in his face that God had done something in his heart. I was blown away that God would use a clay jar like me to lead a Muslim man to Christ."

———————

Later on, I was contacted by Peter Jennings's staff from ABC's *World News Tonight*. Peter Jennings was interested in featuring Prayer Stations on his program on January 28, 2002. We invited the ABC crew to film us just one block from Ground Zero. This was not the first secular media interview we had done; we had already received coverage from other TV stations as well as radio and newspapers. Generally, the crews would interview us, then leave within about 15-20 minutes. The ABC crew stayed for three hours! They stopped almost every person we prayed for and asked how they felt about the experience. They asked questions like, "Did they push religion down your throat or in any way attempt to aggressively proselytize you?"

It became evident that they were attempting to find a disgruntled individual, apparently hoping to report something negative. After three hours they gave up and presented a very positive segment on Prayer Stations that aired worldwide.

We marveled at how God was putting things together on an almost daily basis. Six days a week there were anywhere from one to 14 Prayer Station teams strategically positioned all over the downtown Manhattan area, each with approximately ten to 12 members. It seemed wherever you turned, you would bump into a team.

One young man shared that he was a backslidden Christian, and he was walking around downtown when he saw the first Prayer Station. He was guilt-ridden over the life he was leading, so he decided he didn't want to approach a Prayer Station. He turned down an adjoining street, and there was another one. He made another turn, and again saw a

Prayer Station. At that point he decided he would simply try to walk past, but he ended up stopping and receiving prayer. Each day for a week he stopped and talked. Finally, he gave up, and rededicated his life to Christ.

During these days we experienced many miracles as we prayed for people's felt needs.

One gentleman who suffered from chronic high blood pressure received prayer. He returned to show us that his doctor had certified that his blood pressure was now normal.

Another man shared that his brother had just been taken to the ER and was not expected to survive. The team prayed for him, and a week later he returned to say that his brother was not only alive, but home! The man came to share the thanks of his whole family who were convinced that his brother was spared because of the prayers of the team at the Prayer Station.

A woman asked for prayer for a lifelong skin disease that was not considered curable. The Prayer Station team prayed for her and she also returned a week later, with the news that her dermatologist had pronounced her healed.

Angela reported, "A lady told me her nephew was in critical condition in the hospital. After receiving prayer, he was released in two days!"

Another team member reported, "I prayed for a police officer standing on the corner near us who said that his back was out. He told me later that the pain was gone immediately. I also heard him telling his partner about it."

During the months that we had a daily presence on the streets physical healings became a regular occurrence. Our teams were in awe as they heard story after story of miracles and changed lives.

One afternoon as I was talking with and praying for someone, I noticed a woman looking at the gifts on the Prayer Station table. When I was free, I approached her and asked if she knew what we were doing. She had no idea, so I began to explain what a Prayer Station was all about. I asked, ***"May I pray for you,"*** do you have a personal need, or can I pray for a family member?" When I said "family member" she immediately burst into sobs. She was so broken that it was a while before I understood. She was on her way to the hospital to see her mom, who was not expected to live. I prayed for both of them.

Another constant prayer request was for employment. This seemed to be our most requested prayer need. The wonderful thing was that many prayers for jobs were answered either the same day or the next. We began to joke that the Prayer Stations were probably the best employment agency in New York City!

On the first anniversary of 9/11 we had eight different Prayer Stations around the general area of Ground Zero. Rozanne and I were staffing one within a couple of blocks of the anniversary ceremony. An imam dressed in his traditional garb and carrying a large copy of the Koran, came up to one of our staff. He requested prayer for his wife who was looking for a job at that very hour. We prayed for her.

Meanwhile, Rozanne was standing on a very busy corner half a block away from the Prayer Station, handing out invitation fliers. I noticed that it was almost time for the bell to ring, signifying the exact moment the second plane had hit the South Tower. I managed to catch my wife's eye and signaled for her to join us for prayer. As Rozanne moved away from her position, there was an enormous crash! A huge pane of glass had fallen many stories from the building behind her, and shattered on the pavement at the exact spot where she had been standing just moments before! God had saved her from serious injury or worse, and miraculously not one person was hurt on that bustling corner.

The imam seemed reluctant to leave us. We invited him to join our circle while we all held hands for a moment of silent prayer as the bell tolled. Following the prayer, the imam left. A few hours later he returned with a smile on his face to report that his wife had found a job that morning. This gave us an open door to share the gospel with him.

Our relationship with the New York Police Department could not have been better. They were very happy to have us on the street and never hindered any of our activities. On occasion they merely suggested a different location if they felt we were in a narrow walkway or impeding the flow of pedestrian traffic.

Back in the mid-nineties, when our New Year's Prayer Station ministry began to grow from its humble beginnings, I visited one of the police precinct headquarters in Manhattan. I had prepared a professional-looking packet, as I wanted to leave no question in the mind of the NYPD as to our identity and purpose. I was directed to a lieutenant in charge of community affairs and who was delightful and very supportive. He said to me, "Thank you for coming to share with us about your ministry, but you need to know that you didn't have to, because this is your constitutional right." Then putting his finger in my chest, he continued, "And don't let anyone ever stop you!!"

One of our favorite locations was on Lower Broadway between Cortland Street and Liberty Street in front of the Nasdaq Building. Every time we began to set up our Prayer Station on Broadway, a group of two or three security people from Nasdaq would appear. They would tell us that we were not permitted to set up the Prayer Station in front of their building. Each time I would patiently ask why, and each time they would say that the sidewalk belonged to Nasdaq, and that they were in charge of both its maintenance and giving jurisdiction as to what happened there. As calmly as possible, I would let them know that I had already had this discussion with the NYPD who assured me that the sidewalk in front of any New York building was public property. I would always end the discussion by suggesting that they contact the NYPD. If the police instructed us to move, we would do so, but only at their direction. Each time the security officers would disappear into their building and not return, nor did any police officer ever come to move us on.

Prayer Stations helped many Christians who were timid about evangelism gain a whole new sense of boldness and passion for sharing the gospel. A middle-aged woman came to me at the end of her day of ministry and said, "You know I absolutely hate confrontational evangelism, but I can do this." It was wonderful to see this transformation take place in the hearts of so many of the volunteers, who came from a variety of denominations.

Paul reported at the end of a day with Prayer Stations, "I am so physically tired I can hardly move, but at the same time I'm so filled from what I saw and experienced. I want to hold onto this and remember it forever."

Heather said, "I loved this experience because God not only changed others' lives, but He changed mine as well."

The 9/11 outreach did continue week after week, month after month, for a solid year!

More than 2,000 volunteers came to us from churches, ministries and YWAM bases around the US as well as from a number of different countries. Prayer Stations were on the street six days a week. God gave us the opportunity to pray with more than 50,000 people during that one year, and well over 3,000 made the decision to follow Christ.

We had great partnerships with a number of ministries in the city. One ministry followed up on each person who came to Christ and connected them with churches throughout the metropolitan area. Anyone who completed a Contact Card and desired to receive ministry from a church in their neighborhood was contacted and received whatever assistance they needed. They were also welcomed into fellowship with a local church.

It would be fair to say that the year following 9/11 was both the most exciting and the most exhausting year of my life! Some weeks it was necessary to travel into the city from my home on Long Island very early in the morning. I would meet the teams that would be staffing Prayer Stations that day and give them a training session. From there I would take them to their different locations and set them up. When they were all situated, I would quickly return to the staging area and load up additional Gospels, tracts and Bibles, returning to each site to restock the teams. In the afternoon when they returned to our base, I would lead a debriefing session. After the teams left, each Prayer Station had to be inspected, if there had been rain that day banners and aprons had to be hung to dry. Two backpacks per team had to be refilled with giveaways and literature, and finally everything had to be laid out ready for the next day's ministry. I generally worked alone on this, often late into the night. Then drove almost 50 miles home for some sleep, waking early to do it all over again the next day. In the middle of that year,

Rozanne and I were able to take a two-week break at a friend's home in Florida. For most of the first week I did nothing but sleep!

I guess it could be said that this outreach put Prayer Stations on the map. During that year we received coverage from Christian media outlets such as: The 700 Club, *Decision* and *Charisma* magazines among many others, the Salvation Army, a host of Christian radio stations, evangelical newspapers, and online news services. We also had many secular media outlets contact us for coverage, including local TV stations, NPR Radio, and, as mentioned earlier, ABC *World News Tonight*.

Lisa, a Prayer Station volunteer, said, "I spoke with a photographer from *Time* magazine. He is an agnostic. We talked about the events of 9/11. He refused literature and prayer, but told me I was doing a good thing and to keep it up."

Dave shared, "I did get interviewed by a guy from the BBC. I hope he gets closer to God through this."

On one of the anniversaries of 9/11, we had eight teams out on the street. I stayed close to one that had come from a church in Lafayette, Louisiana that was pastored by a former YWAM leader and friend, Bob Ogle. He and I were observing his team praying for people near Ground Zero when a film crew approached them. They focused on one young woman in particular. Bob told me her name was Victoria, but they all called her Vickie, and she was Russian. After the filming, Vickie came over to us with tears in her eyes and shared that the crew represented the number one TV station in Russia. In fact, they broadcast in every one of the 15 nations that were once part of the Soviet Union!

Recently I received the following email from Vickie, sharing her experience. Her letter has not been edited and is included with her permission.

Remembering back to my time in New York City, I am amazed by how many opportunities I had to pray for people! I was a new English speaker—only a year into it, and I was concerned knowing I will most likely be struggling to understand people. But the Lord was so gracious! So many Russian people came up to me, asking for prayer! People were so willing to ask, I don't think we had many breaks between people. They just kept coming and coming telling their stories of loss, sharing their fears and feelings of despair. God truly opened windows for us to see into people's souls then. It was incredible! He moved mightily!

TV stations from all around the world were all along Broadway. So, somebody up the street knew I spoke Russian and directed the Russian TV crew to me. It was the 1st Channel, the TV station broadcast all through the former USSR. They asked who I was and what I was doing there? I decided I had nothing to lose, and was able to tell them plainly that we were there to pray for people who needed prayer, and why we were doing it, because we cared for their souls. They asked me what I believed, and I was able to share the gospel with them. I believe it was only about 10 minutes long or so, though it seemed much longer at the time.

We arrived back in Los Angeles and I called my parents. My father picked up the phone and asked if I was in New York City. I was surprised because I never told them I was going there. It was the purpose of my phone call to tell them about it. My father told me that he was sitting at home a few days prior, changing the channels on his TV when he heard a familiar voice…me sharing the gospel on TV.

My parents were concerned for me more since then, and it was through years of care and faithfulness of the wonderful people I was living with, that my parents saw the love of our Lord.

I believe God does not waste opportunities. I will never know how many people across the former USSR watched the program back then and gave their lives to the Lord. I am just humbled to be used by Him in that way and grateful for the opportunity. I believe He has planted seeds in both of my parent's hearts… I have noticed much softness toward God and the church in them in the past years.

Up until now Prayer Stations had only been a ministry of YWAM Metro New York. We had shared it with a number of local churches in the metropolitan area, but that was it. However, as a result of all the media coverage, our ministry became inundated with requests from around the world to help churches, ministries, and missionaries build Prayer Stations.

Rozanne and I had worked on a Prayer Station Training Manual, which basically gave how-to instructions, but now we were being asked to not only provide information and training, but to actually build and ship Prayer Stations to both US and international locations. We never planned on doing anything like this and began to pray and ask the Lord what we were to do.

A simple prayer evangelism strategy that God shared with me in 1992 to reach the hordes of people who came to New York City at New Year's, was beginning to catch on around the world.

Chapter 3

Long Ago and Far Away

Nick's Story

I was nine years old in 1955, the middle son of Sicilian immigrants living in Islip Terrace, Long Island, New York.

My mom and dad were not very religious. Raised Catholic, I fulfilled my duty to receive my first Communion, but apart from that our family never went to church, not even on Christmas or Easter. My maternal grandmother, however, was very religious and spent the later years of her life sitting in a chair by the window with her rosary beads, praying daily for her family. I really believe "Nonna" as we called her, knew the Lord and I also believe it was partly due to her intercession for me that I came to know Him too.

On this particular Saturday I was trying to think of something to do. The best I could come up with was to watch TV on our small black and white Motorola. I sat on the floor and did some 1955 channel surfing. There weren't many stations to choose from back then, even in the New York area.

As I turned the dial, I saw something that stirred my curiosity. A man was sitting in a metal folding chair on a platform with a microphone in front of him. On his left side there was a long line of people waiting to walk up a ramp and stand in front of him. When it was their turn, each person would share their physical problem with the man in the chair. There were some in wheelchairs, some on crutches, some who were deaf or blind, and on and on. There seemed to be all manner of physical diseases and disabilities. I watched, transfixed, as the man bowed his head and placed his hands on people, praying for them one by one. He scrunched up his face and prayed passionately, like no prayer I had ever heard before in my life. Coming from a traditional Catholic background, I was accustomed to recited, read, or memorized prayers. Nothing like this!

When I first turned on the program, the man was praying for a young boy who had a speech impediment, which instantly grabbed my total attention. The boy began to speak! I was completely stunned and immediately called for my mother, who was in the kitchen.

"Hey Mom, you need to come and see this! A man is praying for a little boy who can't talk, just like Junior."

My mother and two of her sisters had given birth to a total of seven sons who were mentally disabled. Two of my brothers were born this way: Angelo, who was six years my senior, and my younger brother Carmelo, whom we called Junior.

Mom came into the living room, and as she watched the program she began to weep. Many Catholics believe strongly in miracles, and her heart was deeply touched. She called my dad, who also became quite emotional watching what was unfolding. Before our eyes we saw people get out of their wheelchairs or drop their crutches and walk. The blind could see; the deaf could hear, it was so awesome! My brothers also began to watch. From that Saturday afternoon on, our family was glued to the TV set, watching Oral Roberts.

Back in the 1950s, Oral Roberts didn't have a university, just a large tent with which he traveled around North America, holding miracle services. One meeting from each crusade was broadcast on TV once a week. Each televised service began with worship, and then Oral Roberts presented a gospel message. Initially my family wasn't really interested in any of that. We would just try to sit patiently, longing for him to begin praying for the sick.

We had no real interest in spiritual things or any desire to develop an intimate relationship with Jesus. Only one thing was on our minds; our FELT NEED, healing for my two brothers. I have always marveled that our merciful and gentle God and Savior extends grace to us even when we come to Him selfishly desiring only a miracle, with no interest in repentance or asking Christ to come into our lives as Lord and Savior. God is so gracious toward us, patient and longsuffering, always ready to meet us where we are and then take us to where we need to be.

After weeks of watching the program and actually attending one of Oral Robert's crusades in Pittston, Pennsylvania, our family was drawn to Christ. He met us at the point of our FELT NEED and then revealed to us our REAL NEED of a Savior.

The Holy Spirit always orchestrates things in our lives in ways no one else could. The very day we watched Oral Roberts for the first time, my parents had rented an apartment in our home to an elderly woman who was partially disabled, Lillian Millen. Before the days of walkers, she would walk with a chair in front of her. She knocked on our door when the Oral Roberts program was on, and when she saw what we were watching, she said, "Oh, that's Oral Roberts, he believes the same as my church and I believe." She was part of a Pentecostal church just two blocks away from where we lived called The Full Gospel Assembly. A place I will forever be grateful for.

That summer, the Full Gospel Assembly sent some of their parishioners door to door, inviting children to a Vacation Bible School (VBS). When they came to our home, my mother, having seen all of me that she wanted that summer, found the thought of my going to a VBS very appealing. My dad was not sure if he really wanted his sons going to a Protestant church, but he went along with it. I will never forget walking into that church for the first time, hearing the children singing, and seeing their bright faces. Those two weeks in August were some of the happiest weeks of my childhood.

I was invited to Sunday School and was so excited. Initially my dad said "No way," but he later relented and allowed me to go. Soon I began attending other services. I will never forget the night, at nine years old, when I responded to an altar call and gave my life to Christ. That was it, I was spoiled for the ordinary!

The women of the church came to visit my mom on a regular basis, and each time they would share the Lord with her. They were precious ladies, very kind and loving. Mom was hospitable, and she would quickly put the coffee pot on and take out her famous homemade coffee cake. When the ladies got around to sharing about Jesus, Mom would become very nervous and often responded, "Look, anytime you want to come to my home to visit, you are welcome. We can have cake together and talk, but just understand that you have your religion and I have mine. Let's keep it at that."

Undeterred, the ladies came again and again, always sharing the love of Jesus with her. Eventually Mom began attending the little Pentecostal church and loving it. She gave her heart to Jesus and began to pray and read the Bible every morning at her sewing machine. Mom was a professional seamstress and worked from home, night and day. Being the youngest of five siblings, Mom's Protestant church attendance displeased her sisters. They would come by and tell Mom that she was hurting her mother's soul in purgatory. This upset her because she dearly loved her mom, who had passed away three years earlier. She began to have doubts. One night she cried out, "Oh God, am I doing the right thing? Am I hurting Mama's soul?"

That night she had a dream. In the dream she saw her mother sitting on the platform of our Pentecostal church with a great big smile on her face, singing the worship songs and clapping her hands. The next time my aunts came to visit, she told them about her dream. Catholics believe in prophetic dreams. They never tried to stop her from attending the church again. In fact, they would always bring their prayer requests for Mom to share with her church.

I grew up learning to love Jesus more every day. My church took their job of discipling me very seriously. Pastor Virginia Impellizzeri, who led me to Christ, watched over me like a mother hen, and God would always give her the "heartbeat" of my spiritual life. When something was wrong or I was getting sidetracked, I would always find Pastor Virginia's car at the door of my home. She would give me that look. "Nick, what's going on? God sent me to talk to you." The Holy Spirit, with a little help from my pastor, kept me on a short leash.

From the very beginning of my Christian life, I wanted to share the love of Jesus with others. Some Saturdays my two brothers would join me in our bedroom, where we would pray up a storm. We would then head down the road, knocking on people's doors and sharing Jesus with them. I couldn't have been more than 11 years old. I didn't know a lot about the Bible, nor did I really understand how to lead someone to Christ. All I knew was that I loved Jesus and wanted everyone to know Him too. How strange it must have been to answer the door and see three ragtag kids, two with developmental disabilities and one who didn't have his message straight. Actually, looking back, it was great fun. Many people must have had pity on us, because they invited us in for milk and cookies!

My idea of a great afternoon was to turn my father's open trailer into my platform and preach to my dog, pretending to be Billy Graham or Oral Roberts.

When I was 12 my pastor shared a message on the baptism of the Holy Spirit. I wanted that experience and went down to the altar to pray. I received the baptism and heard God speak very clearly to me that He was calling me into His service. I never forgot that night. Even now it is vivid in my memory.

Sunday lunch at the Savocas' was a coveted experience. In my humble opinion, my parents were some of the best Sicilian cooks in the world! I still miss their Sunday sauce.

One Sunday when I was about 13, following our morning worship service, my parents invited Sister Morano over to our home for lunch. Sister Morano, was like a spiritual mother, always encouraging me in the Lord.

I will never forget that particular Sunday, and not just because of the sauce! She walked through the back door into the kitchen, where the air was fragrant with Sicilian Sunday aromas. Sister Morano stood in front of me as I leaned on the refrigerator. Putting both hands on my shoulders and looking deep into my eyes, she asked me a question that took me totally by surprise, and one that I would never forget.

"Nick," she said. "Are you praying for your future helpmate? You know she might be somewhere around the other side of the world right now."

Honestly, I really wasn't that interested in girls at that point in my life, but I found her words intriguing, and the truth is I never forgot that day. It was as if God branded her words into my mind and heart. "What did she mean? Did God have an Asian woman picked out for me on the other side of the world?"

Rozanne's Story

I was born to Alan and Margaret Brett in Auckland, New Zealand, and yes, that would be the other side of the world! The younger of two children, I had an older brother David, whom I adored and always looked up to, even when I reached his height.

I was only about five or six years old when my dad, Alan Brett, was gloriously saved, so my memories of him before that are rather blurry. I do know that he smoked, was a heavy drinker like most of the men in his family, and drove a truck with a sign painted on the door, that read, "Gordon Brett and Sons." One of my earliest memories of my dad is climbing onto his lap, pulling his comb from his shirt pocket where he always kept it, and beginning to comb his hair. He would instantly relax and encourage me to never stop.

One night my dad came home excited, from a small Pentecostal prayer meeting he had been invited to. My mum, who was raised Presbyterian, couldn't understand what had happened to him. She had attended church her whole childhood and had never considered God anything to get worked up about.

Dad continued to attend the prayer meetings, which were held in someone's home. Soon he completely turned his life over to Christ. His salvation was real from day one. He stopped smoking cold turkey, gave up drinking and tried hard each week to convince Mum to attend the meeting with him.

Finally, after instructing God that He was not to embarrass her, my mum agreed to go.

Chairs filled the room and Dad and Mum took their seats. Mum had never been in a Pentecostal service before, and she was nervous, again reminding God of their deal.

By the end of the night, so I've been told, my classy, sophisticated, demure mum was lying under her chair, speaking in a heavenly language, and falling madly in love with Jesus!

I was sick with chronic asthma from the age of two, long before the days of inhalers and preventative medications. My dad learned how to give me hypodermic needles, and administered them to me up to seven times a day. I still remember him trying to find a spot that wasn't bruised. Mum took me to every doctor imaginable, even a hypnotist, but no one had any answers. School was always a struggle as I missed so much. When I was ten, my doctor would not allow me to attend classes for six months. There were no tutors, and I fell way behind in school and was never able to catch up.

The first time I was hospitalized for pneumonia, I was seven years old. One Saturday night a group of Presbyterians visited the children's ward and shared a Bible story. After the nurses got us back into our beds and shut off the lights, I was thinking about what they had shared. More than six decades later, I can still recall in detail what happened next.

"Why have you never given your heart to Me?" His voice was so clear. I knew it was Jesus.

Right there, in the dark, in a room filled with other children, I asked Jesus to forgive my sins and come into my heart. I prayed that prayer again at different times during my childhood, after all I had only been seven and I wanted to make sure I got it right!

That was the first time I heard God's voice, but I am so grateful that He has continued to speak words of comfort, love, direction, correction, affirmation, forgiveness, hope, and grace throughout my life.

On my fifeenth birthday, with less than an eight-grade education, I left school and started work in an office on Queen Street in Auckland. At the same time, I was also attending night school to improve my shorthand and typing.

At 16, with my parents' permission, I moved 400 miles south to Lower Hutt, almost at the bottom tip of the North Island of New Zealand. My brother David was living in a youth hostel there run by a large Assemblies of God church. He asked me to join him.

David was 17 when he was gloriously filled with the Holy Spirit, and he changed dramatically. My quiet, somewhat introverted brother became a flaming evangelist! We could be sitting with friends in a coffee shop and I would look around and realize he was no longer with us. I would find him in a booth with a group of young people sharing Jesus. It was his passion. His life verse was Paul's words to Timothy: "Do the work of an evangelist" (2 Timothy 4:5).

Back then we did not have a Bible school in New Zealand, so with God's calling burning in his heart, David left for Bible college in upstate New York. He didn't want to leave his family, his friends, or his beloved homeland, and as the ship pulled away from the dock in Auckland, and our streamers began to break, he put his head down on the railing and wept. Watching him from the dock, I wept too, but I knew the scripture God had given to him would be fulfilled: "He that goeth forth and weepeth, bearing precious seed, shall doubtless come again with rejoicing, bringing his sheaves with him" (Psalm 126:6 KJV).

Every Saturday and one night a week, I attended a part-time Bible course run by our church. One afternoon our pastor was very excited to share a vision with us. He said God had shown him that we were witnessing on the streets during the day or early evening, but that the lost and lonely often hit the streets in the late night and early morning. He went on to say that in a vision God had shown him an upper room where young people gathered for prayer, and then at midnight went into the streets. He said God had even given him a name: "Midnight Rescue Crusade" or MRC. Our pastor then challenged us to pray and ask God if we were to be a part of this outreach.

Lower Hutt is just a short drive from Wellington, New Zealand's capital city. Almost immediately we found a large upper room in Wellington that we could use every Saturday night at 11PM for an hour of prayer and intercession. We were still teenagers, and; we had no first-hand experience of what happened on the streets of the big city after midnight. We were about to find out.

Our pastor was right. When many Christians were climbing into bed on a Saturday night so that they would be ready for church the next morning, young people, searching for fun and excitement, were hitting the streets. We went into clubs and dives witnessing to anyone who would listen. We were surprised that those who looked the scariest were often the most receptive. There was a large motorcycle gang in the city and as the weeks passed, we befriended many of them. They would even invite us to their private parties that no outsiders were invited to attend. I remember getting my ankle cut at one of those parties when a beer bottle was thrown and smashed at my feet. Over time many of them showed up at our church for the large Sunday night evangelical service. Church folks got used to seeing their bikes lined up outside, and they learned to accept them and their unorthodox behavior in church. Many members came to know Jesus as their Lord and Savior. When one of them was killed in an accident, they came to the church for comfort and we cried together. Our youth group was totally revolutionized!

During this time, I was working as a keypunch operator at a paint company. One afternoon as I was punching out IBM cards, I clearly heard the Lord say, "I want you in New York City."

Now the Lord knew I never cared for overseas travel. I had been asked to go with girlfriends for a working holiday in Australia and declined. I had no desire to leave my beautiful homeland, family, friends, or my amazing church.

But I knew that Voice! It was the same one I had heard ten years earlier in a hospital ward, and many other times since.

Imagine being 17 years old and telling your parents that God is calling you to New York City in the 1960s! The decade of gangs, beatniks, acid, Vietnam War, protests, sit-ins, love-ins and assassinations!

They never hesitated. If God was calling their daughter halfway around the world, He had a plan and a purpose for her, and they supported me one hundred percent.

Meanwhile David's time in Bible college had ended, and he was now working with David Wilkerson at Teen Challenge in Brooklyn. We cabled him, and his response was quick and to the point, just four words: "Come immediately, job waiting." Within three weeks I was on my way!

So began the next chapter of my life, and up until that time, the very best chapter. I was so happy and healthy! I absolutely loved working at Teen Challenge (TC). It was a privilege to work with Dave and Don Wilkerson and their wonderful mother, whom we all called Mom Wilkerson. She was like a mom to all of us. I grew to love the dirty streets of Brooklyn and working with the "Little People," children of the women who entered the TC Women's program. My job was to find the children temporary foster care until their moms finished the program. I was still a teenager learning to drive an automatic for the first time, on the opposite side of the road, finding my way around Brooklyn, New York City, New Jersey, and Connecticut, without GPS assistance!

There were days when my work broke my heart. I still remember the day I had to pick up a child I had placed in a beautiful home in New Jersey, with loving Christian foster parents. I then drove to a tenement in Brooklyn, carried the child through hallways that reeked of urine, to a dirty little apartment where the only furniture was bare grey mattresses on the floor. The mother had left the TC program and I had no option but to leave her child with her that day; it was all I could do to walk away. I knew the mother received government support for each child she had. Money that I also knew would support her habit, not her babies. By the time I got back to Teen Challenge dinner was being served, but I couldn't touch a bite.

God was putting me through His intense training program. As hard as it was, I wouldn't have missed it for the world.

Every morning before our work day began, David and I would pray together. Throughout the day I would often retreat to the prayer room to seek direction or ask for wisdom as I endeavored to find the right home for a child. During this time, I also fasted and prayed every Friday. I was discovering the joy of sacrifice and learning to prioritize prayer in my life.

Friday nights we would go to The Lost Coin, a coffee shop that Mom Wilkerson ran in Greenwich Village. The Village was a hot spot in the mid-60s. We would sit around the small tables in the café with beatniks, acid heads and a variety of other lost and lonely souls, sharing Jesus. Some nights we would walk through The Village in pairs, talking with any who were halfway coherent, most were tripping on acid and conversation was difficult; they were often harder to reach than those on heroin.

My brother married David Wilkerson's secretary, Darlene. Our mum and dad sold everything they had to fly over for the wedding. They ended up staying in New York and working alongside us at the Teen Challenge Center. Eventually David and Darlene left Brooklyn to begin a similar ministry in Long Branch, New Jersey called Teen Outreach. It wasn't long before I followed. I had walked in David's shadow most of my life, and always I found it a safe, challenging, fun, and often life-changing place to be. This was to be no exception.

By now I was 20 years old. I had dated during my time in Brooklyn and a little since moving to New Jersey. Guys seemed to find my Kiwi accent fascinating. Inevitably when they would call for a second date I would say no as politely as possible. Casual dating was not my thing, and it wasn't long before I had had enough. I told the Lord that if He wanted me to serve Him single for the rest of my life, that was fine with me.

Approximately twelve months after I moved to New Jersey, rumors began to circulate concerning a new pastor who was coming to the Assemblies of God church just a quarter mile from Teen Outreach. Women from the church would often stop by our center to drop off food or clothing items for the men we were ministering to. They were always full of excitement about the new pastor. A few were already trying to match me up with him.

Pastor Nick, as we had all come to know him, eventually arrived in town.

One Saturday evening at a dinner we were attending, my brother made it his business to meet the new pastor, who apparently was also interested in meeting David. Ever the matchmaker, my brother grabbed me when dinner was over and said, "I have someone you have to meet."

From then on David was relentless in his quest to make Pastor Nick his brother-in-law! He would often visit him at the parsonage, and when it was time to leave, David would always have a scripture to share. "It's not good for man to dwell alone." or "He who finds a wife finds a good thing" were a couple of his favorites!

David also made a habit of inviting "the lonely pastor" over for dinner, which I would cook, but much to David's chagrin, would not stick around to eat.

Until the night I did.

Having once again invited Pastor Nick over for dinner, David realized he had a former engagement that night and left me to entertain his guest. The plan was that after dinner we would watch Billy Graham on TV with the guys who were in the Teen Outreach program. Neither of us can recall what Reverend Graham said that night. (Although we're pretty sure it was a salvation message!) When it was over Nick offered to drive me home, and I accepted. It was raining, so with a fast "thankyou" and "goodnight," I ran from the car to the house.

Upstairs in my bedroom, I looked in the mirror and said, "I'm going to marry that guy!"

Six weeks later we were engaged, and less than three months after that we were married. No surprise who officiated at our wedding!

Nick continues

By the time I reached my senior year in high school, many voices were speaking into my life and trying to give me guidance for my future. Teachers were recommending colleges and universities and asking me to apply. Many relatives had given me their suggestions as well. Even a new tenant who had moved into the apartment my parents owned, who was agnostic, encouraged me that I was intelligent enough to have a bright future and suggested I go on to university.

My parents had basically given me two choices for my future—doctor or lawyer. They constantly reminded me that I needed to become a professional, as one day I would be responsible for my special-needs brothers, who were both deemed unemployable.

Graduation was approaching, and I was becoming more and more confused and stressed. Having completed applications to three major universities, I anxiously awaited their response. My grades were decent in high school, so I figured my chances for acceptance into at least one of them were good. The problem, however, was that I had no peace.

I still vividly remembered God speaking to me when I was 12, calling me into ministry. What about that?

One Sunday evening a great man of God, Steven Gouluas, a missionary from Romania, spoke at our church. I don't remember what he said in his sermon that impacted me, but after the service I approached him and asked if we could talk. I explained that I was very confused about my future and could not determine what I should do with my life.

He saw my distress and smiled. "Nick," he said, "you are like most Christian young people your age. You are expecting God to write His will for your life in the sky. I want to make a suggestion to you. Go home, and before you go to bed tonight, kneel and just say this to the Lord with all of your heart. 'Lord, I promise I will do whatever it is that You want me to do, sight unseen. Just show me what that is and I will obey.'" That night I did exactly what he said, and I meant it with all my heart.

The following week I received letters from each of the universities saying that for one reason or another they were sorry, but they could not accept me as a student for the upcoming fall semester.

Talk about mixed emotions: surprise, disappointment, and a little intrigue.

"Now what, Lord?" I asked.

Immediately I knew I should apply to Zion Bible Institute in East Providence, Rhode Island. I had heard many good things about the college from different people at my church, some of whom had attended there. Unfortunately, when I shared my excitement with the alumni from my church, they told me that my chances were slim, as we were already into June.

Undaunted, I sent for an application, which arrived promptly. I completed it, sent it in, and waited. I remember going to the mailbox a few days later and seeing a letter from the Bible college. My immediate thought was that I had not completed the application correctly and they had sent it back, or I was too late and they were not accepting any further applications.

What joy when I opened the letter and read of my acceptance!

Then came the greatest hurdle of all....how would I share my great news with my parents?

I prayed, and a few days later, with some trepidation, I managed to convey my heart and my news. Although Mom and Dad loved the Lord and were happy about my spiritual life, they believed for purely financial reasons that I needed to become a professional. Afterall, when the time came, how in the world could I take care of my brothers on a minister's stipend?

The following Saturday morning I awoke and went down to the kitchen to fix myself some breakfast. I was standing by the stove in my pajamas and robe when my four Sicilian aunts walked in.

Something inside of me said, "Get out while you can!"

Too late. They all sat around the kitchen table with my mother and began to bombard me regarding my decision to go to Bible college. The kindest thing they said that morning was that I was selfish and did not care for my parents or my brothers. As I stood there receiving their blows, I wept.

Then that still, small voice spoke, "Nick, do not say anything until I give you the words to say."

My mother was silent while her sisters came to her defense. My dad, who was sitting in the living room listening, was getting emotional.

Suddenly one of my aunts turned on my mother. "We came here to defend you, and you sit there saying nothing!"

At that moment God gave me what to say. I opened my mouth and let God fill it.

"The reason my mother is not saying anything is because, although she is not happy about my decision, she knows God has His hand on my life and has called me to serve Him."

Soon after that, my aunts left. Within the next week my parents came to me and said that I had their blessing!

Oswald Chambers wrote in *My Utmost for His Highest*—"If we obey God it is going to cost other people more than it costs us, and that is where the sting comes in. If we are in love with our Lord, obedience does not cost us anything, it is a delight, but it costs those who do not love Him a good deal. If we obey God, it will mean that other people's plans are upset." He goes on to say, "Others are often pressed into the consequences of our obedience."

It is not our responsibility to try and stop that from happening, and that's the hard part.

God came through for my family. While I was in Bible college my older brother, Angelo, found a job working with the township in their highway department. He held that job for 25 years before having to retire due to an accident at work. At that point Angelo was still living with Mom and Dad, and he had enough income from his disability, retirement, and federal disability to support him for the remainder of his life. A few years after Angelo was employed, Carmelo (Junior) also found employment with the township as a custodian. He worked there for 39½ years before retiring with full benefits from his pension and Social Security.

As my parents released me to follow God's calling, my family went from poverty to middle class within a decade. They were pressed into the consequences of my obedience and God blessed and cared for them.

Rozanne and I have always found that no matter what it costs us or those we love, we must obey God. When we do, He always proves Himself.

Joy Dawson would often quote the verse found in Psalm 145:17 (NASB): "The Lord is righteous in all His ways and kind in all His deeds."

Chapter 4

The Pastor and the Missionary

With my Pentecostal background, I simply assumed that when God called me to Christian service, it meant that I would pastor a church. This was, after all, what I had spent four years preparing for.

At the conclusion of my senior year of Bible college, I was invited to be a candidate for a small church in West Long Branch, New Jersey. All was going according to plan, with one possible exception.

The New Jersey superintendent cautioned me that this church was not one for a rookie like myself. He shared that the congregation was "difficult," and that there was a long list of pastors that the church board had chewed up and spit out! He asked me not to consider this particular church. After much prayer though, I knew God was saying that this was where He wanted me. In August of 1968 I was installed as their pastor.

The superintendent did give me one promising suggestion. He said that if I went to the Monmouth County area, I should look up a young man by the name of Reverend David Brett. Rev. Brett, so I was told, had arrived about a year before me to begin a Christian drug rehabilitation ministry called Teen Outreach. I was told that this young man was from New Zealand and needed the support of the body of Christ for his challenging ministry.

Soon after my arrival in town, I learned that David Brett was going to be the speaker at a Full Gospel Businessmen's dinner in the nearby town of Atlantic Highlands. I thought this would be an excellent opportunity to meet him.

A couple of my buddies went with me, and we enjoyed the message from Rev. Brett. Afterward I joined a long line of those waiting to speak with him. Finally, I introduced myself. It appeared that David already knew who I was. He immediately said, "Wait here, I have someone I want you to meet." He returned in a few moments with his sister, Rozanne.

On the way home that night I remarked to my buddies, "Hey, I need to get over to Teen Outreach!"

I was 22 years old, and my new church had a number of single mothers and female divorcees. Some were doing their best to get acquainted with the new bachelor pastor. It quickly became apparent that it was not going to be easy to carry out my pastoral duties without some of them misconstruing my intentions.

I had actually been engaged in Bible school, but eventually did not feel this was the right young lady for me and I broke it off. Since then, no other suitable prospects had come along, and I felt alone. I was becoming mad at God for my singleness.

One morning I went into the bathroom to shave and clean up for the day ahead. I looked at myself in the mirror, my face covered in shaving cream, and I was embarrassed that as a spiritual leader I had such a terrible attitude toward God. At that very moment I bowed my head and repented.

"God if You want me to be a bachelor for the remainder of my life, I will continue to serve You without one complaint."

Rozanne and I had our first conversation that same day at the Teen Outreach Center. Just five months later, on January 25, 1969, we became husband and wife, and Sister Morano's prophecy came to pass. God gave me my helpmate from around the other side of the world—New Zealand!

Together we served the church until the end of August, 1969. It had taken me one year to finally realize that God had not called me to pastor a local church. God's plan in bringing me to this area was to meet Rozanne, who had always vowed she would never be a pastor's wife, so she was one hundred percent behind my decision! We had both been like fish out of water, but now what would I do? I had trained to be a pastor, and it was apparent I wasn't one.

After David married us, he and Darlene, who was three months pregnant with their first child, returned to New Zealand. Rozanne's parents had taken over the ministry of Teen Outreach, which eventually became Teen Challenge New Jersey. They invited us to come and serve with them. It started as a temporary position, but soon I was asked to be the assistant director of the ministry. For 3½ years God gave us the privilege of investing in the lives of many young men who came to us addicted to drugs and/or alcohol. Rozanne was thrilled to be back doing what she loved, and we just assumed we would be lifers with Teen Challenge.

We all lived together in the same house, ate, prayed, counseled, and studied God's Word together. The stories of the men in the program were all different, but there were common threads of hardship, homelessness, loneliness, rejection, and addiction. Some only stayed a few days, and our hearts would ache for them, but what a joy to see so many who fell in love with Jesus, and some who even committed their lives to Christian service.

Juan Ramirez was one such miracle story. Carmelo was a junior counselor at our Teen Challenge Center in Long Branch. He had come to us from the TC farm in Rehrersburg, Pennsylvania after completing his time in the program there. Carmelo told me about his cousin Juan, who lived in Manhattan and was hooked on heroin. He asked if I would be open to Juan coming to TC. Soon after, Juan arrived for an interview and we accepted him into the program. He had been born in Puerto Rico and then moved to Manhattan, where he had been in and out of trouble with the law for crimes connected with his drug addiction.

From the day Juan entered the program, he began to follow hard after God. He repented of his sins and received the Lord into his life. He was seeking the baptism of the Holy Spirit, and we were all very pleased with his progress. One day one of our counselors came to my door and asked if I would talk with Juan, as he had received a letter from a girl he had lived with in Manhattan. She told Juan that she was being threatened by the drug pushers he owed money to. If Juan didn't pay up, they would kill her. Juan felt it was his responsibility to deal with the situation, and he was planning to go back to Manhattan and talk to the drug dealers.

I endeavored to convince Juan that this was a trap and that if he left at this point, he would be headed back to his old life. We prayed together, and he assured me he wouldn't go to New York; he would pray for his friend instead. Later that day I was told Juan had left the center and returned to Manhattan. We were all very concerned, disappointed, and praying for his safety.

Our program was three months long, followed by nine months of training at the TC farm in Pennsylvania. We could accommodate only 13 men at a time and usually had as many as 20 young men on a waiting list. Our policy was that if someone left the program and then wanted to return, their name was placed on the bottom of our waiting list

After leaving for Manhattan, Juan called, begging me to let him come back. He said he realized he had made a huge mistake and was blinded by the enemy. He was already back on drugs and wanted to return and finish the program. I told him I would pray and ask the Lord for guidance, which I did. God spoke to me plainly. "Bring Juan back! Don't have him wait on the end of the waiting list, bring him back now." I shared this with the staff, and some were not pleased with my decision. They wanted me to stick to our protocol. But I obeyed the Lord, and Juan returned to us.

Juan left two more times in the weeks that followed. Both times he called, begging for mercy. Each time when I went to the Lord in prayer, the answer was the same: "Bring Juan back, and do it now!" The last time Juan left, he called me from the hospital in Manhattan, where he had almost died of an overdose. He said God had spoken to him, telling him this was his last chance. He needed to make a clear choice to leave his old life and give himself totally to the Lord.

That time Juan meant business. He began to grow like a weed spiritually. He was a great example to many who came into the program, challenging them to give their all to Jesus. In a few months Juan was ready to go to the farm, and we released him with tears. He had become family.

While at the farm, Juan continued to make great progress and felt like God was calling him to go to Bible college to prepare for the ministry. He was accepted at Elim Bible Institute in Lima, New York. A dear Christian friend and businessman paid his tuition, and Juan began his studies.

Juan wrote a letter letting us know that when he graduated, he believed God was calling him to go as a missionary to Mexico City. When the time came, he was accepted by a thriving church in the city and became their resident evangelist. Juan would go out to the streets of Mexico City and preach the gospel. He was powerfully anointed as an evangelist, and people came to the Lord and then into the church in large numbers.

In time Juan met a beautiful young woman, Velia. They were married, and soon after God blessed them with their first child. They had little of this world's goods, but that was not important to them. Juan and Velia began to pray and seek the Lord for His direction. God spoke to them to go to a town called Cuautitlán Izcalli, in the northern suburbs of Mexico City, about an hour's drive from the city center (on a good traffic day!).

This area had no evangelical witness except for a few people meeting in a home for prayer and Bible study. Juan and Velia obeyed the Lord, piled all they owned into their broken-down vehicle along with their new daughter, and left for Izcalli. Initially they lived in their car, as they had no home. Each day they would go out to the streets and preach the gospel. People began to come to Christ. Soon Juan, Velia and their daughter had a place to live, and their new church, "Grupo Nueva Vida" (Church of the New Life), was born.

Rozanne and I kept in touch with Juan and Velia. While we were in Concord, New Hampshire, Juan wrote inviting me to visit him and see what God was doing through their ministry. Finally, after a number of years had passed, I was able to visit.

I will never forget the first service I spoke at in Grupo Nueva Vida. Juan introduced me to his congregation by saying, "Tonight I want you to meet your grandfather!"

When I heard those words and looked out at around 800 people in the congregation, it was very hard to keep my composure. I had a picture of what heaven was going to be like. God had given me the privilege of being instrumental in leading this young man to Christ. Now he in turn had led hundreds of others to the Lord, my spiritual grandchildren!

Rozanne and I were now working with YWAM, and we began to send regular teams from our staff and students to Juan's church to help pioneer more churches in the surrounding region. Soon eight new churches had been birthed, along with a ministry called "Casa del Pan" (House of Bread) that fed disenfranchised children, and a Christian school with an enrollment that at times reached 500 children. Juan also had a thriving prison ministry. Those churches and ministries continue to flourish today.

All of this came from the seed of God's love and forgiveness planted into the heart of one young man, addicted to heroin, and headed for both physical and eternal destruction. Many thought Juan would never make it, but by God's grace and mercy he did.

Sadly, after a long battle with cancer, God called Juan home on March 1, 2014. He is survived by Velia, two daughters, and a son. Juan is dearly missed. He leaves behind a legacy that one day will be fully known.

In 1970, while we were still working at Teen Challenge in New Jersey, I met a dynamic young African American Pastor, John Braswell and his lovely wife, Audrey. They had a burden to reach out to the area of Monmouth County, New Jersey, where drugs were most prevalent. Their vision was to plant a church on the West Side of Asbury Park, where 30 percent of the population, some 17,000, were African American. They wanted to begin by establishing a coffee house ministry. In the center of this district was a street then called Springwood Avenue. They asked if Teen Challenge would partner with them in this effort.

Pastor Braswell and I prayer-walked up and down the avenue and spotted an empty storefront midway down the street. We made inquiries, and soon our Teen Challenge board voted unanimously to turn the storefront into "The Gaza." One of our summer interns, Vinny, had some carpentry skills, which was great, as my talent with a hammer and saw were very limited. We began work on the building early that summer and looked forward to a grand opening in July.

One morning Vinny and I drove to the lumber yard to pick up some needed materials, then headed down to Asbury Park and the future coffee house. Vinny was driving our newly purchased Teen Challenge van, and I rode shotgun. As we approached Springwood Avenue, we both saw a large plume of smoke at the far end of the street and wondered what was on fire. Not having a radio in the van, and being decades away from cell phones, we had no access to any news reports. As we began to drive up the avenue, it dawned on us that there was no other traffic in either direction. People were lined up on both sides of the street as if to watch a parade, except they seemed agitated and had their hands hidden behind their backs.

SMASH!!! The first bottle of whiskey hit our van! A barrage of whiskey, wine, and other liquor bottles followed. The local liquor store had been looted. Within a minute, every window of the van was broken and the windshield shattered, covering us in glass and liquor. I could tell that Vinny, who was still endeavoring to drive, was becoming overwhelmed by the attack. I tried to keep him calm as we both ducked the next bottle. Neither he or I could see ahead of us through the shattered windshield, but we both knew that if we stopped or hit anyone, we would be dragged from the van and probably killed.

I took a chance and poked my head out of the side window. There was a cross street coming up on our right. I gave Vinny the all clear to make a slow and careful right turn. Both of us were calling on the Lord for His help and protection. We made the turn and the road ahead was empty. I told him to floor it until we were out of the area. With Vinny's head stuck out of the side window and me praying desperate prayers, we cleared the neighborhood!

A safe distance away, we stopped the van and got out to assess the damage. Both of us were covered in broken glass. It was in our hair, in the pockets of our shirts, down our legs, and throughout the interior of the van. We had minor cuts on our faces and arms, and we reeked of alcohol. Every window of the beautiful new van that we had prayed and waited so long for, was broken and every panel dented. We climbed back into our sad-looking vehicle and slowly managed to drive the seven miles back to the Teen Challenge Center.

Upon our arrival no one could believe what they were seeing. Two hours earlier we had driven away in a pristine vehicle. Now it was badly damaged and Vinny and I were covered in glass, bleeding, and smelling like a brewery. My poor wife began taking glass from my hair and clothing, dressing my wounds, and thanking God for His protection.

The Asbury Park riots continued for about a week. Springwood Avenue sustained the worst of the property damage with broken windows, looting, and fires. After things calmed down, we went back to the coffee house and repaired what had been damaged. We opened The Gaza a couple of weeks later.

Racial tensions remained high, and many African American young people came into the coffee house angry and ready for a fight. Most of the time I was the only white face there.

Eventually, however, I became very comfortable with my new people group. Pastor John Braswell and I would walk Springwood Avenue late into the night, sharing Jesus with the African American youth, Black Muslims, and Black Panthers. He taught me that God had called me to be an ambassador for Christ to all peoples, and that meant all colors, races and creeds.

Many lives were saved through the coffee house ministry, some for eternity, and a church was established in the community. John and Audrey Braswell became lifelong friends and colleagues in the work of evangelism. Sadly, for us, they have since gone home to glory. They loved and embraced Rozanne and me so completely, and so did their church congregation. We were always overwhelmed by their loving hospitality whenever we joined in their church functions. Rozanne and I still miss them dearly.

Recently we have had the joy of reconnecting with their adult children and the church that was founded through the coffee house ministry. All of them have overwhelmed us with their love, and told us they consider us part of their family. What a privilege!

Chapter 5

No Title, No Salary, No Guarantees

In May of 1972 we became the parents of a beautiful baby girl, Anita Marie.

In November of the same year, we began to realize that God had something else new and life changing in store for us.

For two weeks we fasted and prayed through lunch. Slowly God began to make it clear that we were to attend a Youth With A Mission School of Evangelism (SOE). At that time YWAM had only four training schools in the world, one of which was just south of us in Hammonton, New Jersey. That sounded like a logical choice, at least to us, apparently not to God! Eventually He opened the way for us to attend the SOE in Hurlach, Germany, which was to begin in just four weeks.

We had no savings. The SOE housing and tuition, plus airfares, outreach fees, and baby supplies seemed an overwhelming hurdle. Then God raised the bar even higher.

"Share your direction, not your need" was His clear word to us.

We obeyed, sharing our excitement about this next step with family, friends, and my father-in-law's church. Two weeks went by, the deadline was looming, and we were no closer to our financial goal.

One evening I was invited to speak at a house meeting where I shared our upcoming adventure but not our need. As one gentleman was leaving, he slipped a fat envelope into my hand. Later Rozanne and I opened it and placed the $20 bills in neat $100 piles on the bed. There was enough to cover everything in our budget, pay tithes, and still have an additional $500! God's calculator is always better than ours, we knew He was the only One who saw all that lay ahead of us.

The three-month SOE course radically changed our lives! It wasn't easy, especially for Rozanne, as Anita suffered from severe colic. The leadership quickly relocated us to a remote part of the castle (yes, our school was in a castle), as our crying baby meant little sleep not just for us, but for all in close proximity.

We had both been raised in the church and already had some years of ministry experience under our belts. But we still learned things about God, His character, evangelism and missions, that ruined us for the ordinary. God gave our ministry a whole new perspective, and once again prayer and evangelism were underscored in our hearts. We were like baby birds with our mouths open, fed by great men and women who were not only teachers, but doers.

One of our favorites was Joy Dawson. She taught us, among many other things, how to hear the voice of God for effective intercessory prayer. One of our fellow students said to Joy in an open session of affirmation, "Joy, having you teach us intercessory prayer is like learning to play the trumpet from Gabriel."

Joy's teachings on prayer became a powerful foundation stone in our lives. It influenced everything we did from that point on. We had never understood the power of prayer as we did after our exposure to Joy's teaching. She has written a number of powerful books, including *Intercession, Thrilling and Fulfilling* which we highly recommend.

Outreach is always an important part of every YWAM training school. I will never forget the day Ron Pollard from YWAM England, came to our school to share. God had given Ron a vision to have Christians go to Moscow on May Day of 1973 and share the gospel in Red Square. He said he was recruiting a team to go with him. This team should be prepared to be arrested and to have everything confiscated. Immediately God spoke to me and let me know that He wanted me to be a part of that team. Really? But how would I tell my wife?

I didn't know that Rozanne had heard of this vision the day before, and God had already told her that I would be on the team! She was on board before I was. We were learning that God saw us as one. He would always be faithful to prepare both of our hearts for anything that lay ahead. It wouldn't be easy, but who said following Jesus was easy? Now we also both realized what the extra $500 was for!

Following the SOE, Rozanne traveled with Anita to spend some time with her brother David and his family, who were now missionaries in Scotland. David and Rozanne's maternal grandparents came from Scotland, and David had a deep love for the Scottish people. He had followed God's call to share the gospel in the land of his ancestors.

Meanwhile I joined the team leaving London for Moscow. This was an adventure unlike anything I had ever done before. It was the height of the Cold War during the Brezhnev era. We traveled in five vans across northern Europe and entered the Soviet Union through the Finnish border. We were watched constantly by our Intourist guides/ KGB. Finally, we were stopped at a roadblock in Novgorod, just a day's drive from Moscow.

A Soviet soldier pointed an AK47 through the van window, right at me. By God's grace none of us were harmed. Through this journey I learned a lot about the boldness the Holy Spirit can give in unfamiliar places and situations. We never did make it to Moscow, but we had divine opportunities to share the Lord and also encourage the underground church in the Soviet Union.

I wrote a book about our adventure, *Roadblock to Moscow*, with the foreword by the great Bible smuggler, Brother Andrew.

The full scope of all God did during that trip became even clearer about a year later. A Russian pastor had just been allowed to leave the Soviet Union and come to the US with his parishioners. He was speaking at a special all-day meeting in Manhattan, and I had the privilege of hearing him and giving him a copy of my book.

Through an interpreter, I explained what had happened the year before. A big smile crossed his face. "Yes, yes, I know all about what your team accomplished last year," he said. "I want you to know that it was the source of great encouragement and blessing to the underground church throughout the Soviet Union."

While attending our SOE in Hurlach, I remember the Lord speaking to me about my willingness to go wherever He might want to send us. My response was tentative. "Lord, You know about my responsibilities back home with my two special-needs brothers. My parents are now getting on in years. How can I possibly care for them if I am serving You as a foreign missionary?"

The Lord's answer was immediate and clear.

"Nick, you know My character and that I love your brothers far more than you do. Do you think that if I were to call you to serve in a distant land, I would not make loving provision for them?" "Yes Lord," was my humble and embarrassed reply.

It wasn't long before I received a message from the YWAM leader over the Americas, Leland Paris, asking if we would return to the States and begin a YWAM ministry in New York. Rozanne and I prayed about the invitation and received an immediate response: "Go!"

To say our first year of ministry with YWAM was challenging, difficult, turbulent, and at times just plain scary would be no exaggeration!

Like most evangelical mission agencies, YWAM missionaries are deputized fundraisers, which basically means that we need to raise our own support. Not only that, but back in those days in YWAM, we were encouraged to pattern our lives after George Müller, the great Christian evangelist and director of the Ashley Down Orphanage in Bristol, England, who never asked for anything except on his knees to the Lord. We had almost no support and obediently did not communicate our needs except in prayer.

It was 1973, the year of the oil embargo. Gas shortages and long, long lines at the pump had become the norm. (If you were fortunate enough to find a station that had gas.) We literally seemed to run our vehicle on the smell of an oily rag!

Not only that, but many people were out of work, nervous about the future, and holding tight to their wallets.

Our small team lived in Greene County, New York, just 30 miles south of Albany along the Hudson. One night we were invited to speak at a youth group in Coxsackie, a 42-mile round trip. We had no money, less than a quarter tank of gas, and our Plymouth station wagon had a hole in the gas tank. But God said, "Go!"

We had a great service. At the end of it we were disappointed but not surprised when there was no honorarium, no gas money, nothing but a handshake. Trusting in the God who had sent us, and with much prayer, we started home. When we were still a long way off, the gas gauge hit empty, but we prayed non-stop and the car kept going. By God's grace we made it home! The next day we were given a gift sufficient enough to fill the tank and to purchase some silicone to fix the leak, at least temporarily.

Food was always a challenge. One afternoon we gave one of our team members a dollar and sent her to the small grocery store near our home to buy dinner for the six of us. Back then you could get a pound of hot dogs for less than that, so off she went. In the store she met a friend from the small church we were all attending. The woman said, "I am so glad I bumped into you today. I have been wanting to give your team a gift." She handed our very excited team member a $10 bill, and we feasted on hamburgers that night!

We were asked to do a weekend of training and outreach with the youth group of a church in Elmira, New York. We had a wonderful kick-off service Friday night with not only the youth group, but the entire congregation. Saturday morning we were invited to have breakfast with the pastor and his wife at their home next to the church. During breakfast the pastor showed me a copy of the local newspaper. On the front page was the headline, "Satan Packs Them In." An article followed on how the movie *The Exorcist* had come to town and lines of people were waiting for tickets. I glanced at the headline and photo, but truthfully I was so focused on the teaching I was about to give the youth group, that it didn't fully register.

The morning began with worship and teaching. During the break I spoke briefly with the youth director and asked her what, if anything, she was planning for the outreach that afternoon. She replied, "I thought we might do some door-to-door evangelism." "That sounds fine," I responded. "That's the first thing I ever did in evangelism, but is it OK if we first pray and ask the Lord if that is His highest and best for our outreach today?" She heartily agreed. Following lunch, I gave a short teaching on how to hear the voice of God, and we then broke up into intercessory prayer groups.

As I prayed with my group, the front page of the Elmira newspaper came to mind. I wondered if we should be doing something regarding this movie? The groups gathered together for a time of reporting. Without anyone ever mentioning anything that morning about the newspaper article, we had all received the same thing in prayer. We then sought the Lord together for specifics as to what we were to do and how we were to do it. God was faithful, and the details began to come quickly:

- Go up to the people waiting in line for tickets. Remind them that they are about to see something that might be very disturbing.

- Assure them that God is greater than Satan, and that Jesus would help them if they called out to Him.

We also felt clearly that we were:

- Not to ask people to forgo seeing the movie, but simply to remind them of God's love and power.

- Create signs that would uplift the Name of Jesus, without speaking against the film.

- Be prepared to counsel anyone coming out of the movie who might be troubled.

- Contact the Elmira newspaper that had carried the article that morning and let them know what we were preparing to do.

God even gave me the exact words to say if anyone from the newspaper came to check us out.

Finally, I heard God say one more thing:

- "You need to end by 3 PM."

After receiving clearance and blessing from the church leadership, we left for the movie theater, which was located inside a shopping mall. We began to follow the directions God had given. People waiting in line were very appreciative of our words of comfort. A group of young teenagers came out of the theater very disturbed; some young ladies were crying. Our youth gathered around them and offered counsel, a witness, and prayer, and the teenagers went away comforted.

A woman identifying herself as a reporter for the Elmira newspaper came up and asked if I was the leader of the group. She asked what our purpose was in coming to the theater, and I shared exactly what God had given me to say.

While I was speaking to the reporter, I realized a New York State Trooper was standing on the other side of me, politely waiting and listening to every word. He asked if he could speak with me privately.

"I want to first say, off the record, that I am a Christian and I am totally sympathetic with what you all are doing here today. However, we have a problem: you are on private property and the owners of the mall are saying that your group is not welcome. They want you to leave." I assured the officer that I understood, that we did not want to cause any problems and that we would comply.

I looked at my watch, it was exactly 3 PM!

Folks waiting in line as well as the teenagers we had counseled let the officer know we did not tell them to not see the film, but only reminded them about God's love.

The next morning that same Elmira newspaper carried an article on page two with photos of our group at the theater. The reporter accurately wrote down everything God had given me to say to her. Through this experience, God reinforced a valuable lesson that He had taught me years earlier concerning prayer and evangelism. When we pray strategically before evangelism, God will give us divine guidance in detail. If we had gone door to door that day, I am sure there would have been some fruit for our efforts. However, because we prayed and obeyed God's specific guidance, a witness was given to the whole city through the newspaper article. Young people received prayer and comfort, and others who were troubled about the movie now knew that this particular church would be a place of refuge.

There is an amazing addendum to this story. Two young people from the Elmira church who were in the early stages of courtship took part in the outreach. The young man, Gary McKinney, had been praying and asking the Lord for direction for his life. When he saw how God gave us His divine guidance in putting together the outreach, he was impressed by the Holy Spirit's work and made a decision to serve the Lord in missions with YWAM. Later Gary and his girlfriend Deanna were engaged and married. Eventually Gary became the YWAM National Director for Spain. Gary and Deanna continue to serve in this capacity as well as mentoring YWAM leaders in the Ibero-America region where Spanish and Portuguese are the predominant languages.

Gary shared with me, "My participation in the outreach, and how I was challenged to hear the voice of God, was decisive in my decision to join YWAM and go to Spain."

God can take small acts of obedience and use them to produce fruit which can then multiply and impact thousands!

Rozanne continues

Nick has shared some highlights from our time in upstate New York, for which we are so grateful. We were learning the character and ways of God and putting into practice principles we had learned during our time in Germany. But as we all know, daily life is seldom lived on the mountaintop, after all you can't find water there. Generally, life carries on in the valley, and so it was with us.

I was a young mother in the mid-70s as well as a co-leader with Nick. Anita was around 18 months old, toddling all over the place and keeping me busy chasing after her. It was apparent we were raising a future leader, even at this early age. Intelligent, strong-willed, and always on the go, I was exhausted but totally in love with this challenging little human. Anita would often amuse herself by tormenting our beautiful Irish Setter until Kelly had had enough. At that point Kelly would gently knock Anita down and sit on her, smiling broadly, and obviously very pleased with himself. Anita would scream, pounding her little fists on the floor until I came and reluctantly rescued her, knowing full well that the whole scenario would play out on repeat.

Finances were a daily struggle. We were living in a nice house in the middle of a field, and our rent was just $250 a month. We were, however, still unable to cover it, and were going into debt. Eventually two of our three staff members moved on. Jerry, our last remaining staff member, moved with us into a smaller, more affordable house.

As a team, the three of us spent a lot of time in intercessory prayer. We prayed for finances, and then we prayed even harder. We confessed every sin we could think of, and even some we didn't think we had done just to be sure we didn't miss anything! But still the heavens were brass.

Eventually the pressure began to put a strain on our marriage. We were $1,000 in debt, with no relief in sight, a huge mountain that we had no idea how to move. So, we kept praying.

My parents were now living in New Ringgold, Pennsylvania. Dad was overseeing the construction of Blue Mountain Christian Retreat, and we were invited to come. Nick could help with clearing the mountain, and we would have free accommodation and earn a small income. We figured it would take about a year there to work off our ministry debt. Feeling like we had failed, we said goodbye to Jerry and made the move.

Nick dug up rocks with a tractor every day. A number of months passed, and the facility was far enough along to run the first retreat. I became chief cook and bottle washer, and continued to be so for a couple of years. I cooked most weekends, three meals a day for up to

200 people. I was also pregnant with our beautiful Rebecca, who arrived in the midst of a hot sticky summer on the mountain.

One night after we had been in Pennsylvania for about six months, Nick and I lay in bed talking and dreaming out loud. Nick shared his dream to train up young people in Christian discipleship and prepare them for missions. We laid the vision before the Lord and fell asleep.

The very next day Nick received a call from our YWAM area director, Leland Paris.

Leland shared a vision to begin Discipleship Training Schools. He explained that the original vision for Schools of Evangelism (SOE) had covered three main areas: the message, the method and the messenger. After a few years of running these schools, however, they had found there was a great need to cover the preparation of the messenger more thoroughly than the SOE had time to do. A Discipleship Training School (DTS) would put the emphasis on that aspect. Students would be encouraged to carry on their training at an SOE upon completing the DTS.

"Nick," Leland continued, "we would like you to pray about running one of our first Discipleship Training Schools."

We took time to pray, understanding that we could not rely upon YWAM for any financial support. This would be our challenge. We would need housing for both staff and students, somewhere to assemble for the lectures, a fully equipped kitchen, staff, and of course, students in a time when we couldn't recruit by website, email, social media, or cell phone. God's answer was simply, "Yes."

At the base of the mountain on the retreat property was an old unoccupied farmhouse that needed a great deal of work. The owner of the retreat told us that if we would do the work, the retreat would cover materials and we could use the building for our school!

The house was small and would require an extension off the kitchen to double as a dining room and classroom. Bud Adams, a dear friend with carpentry skills, was available to come and help with the project. He arrived at the same time as winter on Blue Mountain.

A foundation for the extension would have to be laid, but with cold weather setting in, the ground was too hard. We prayed. For two weeks the weather warmed up: long enough to dig and lay the foundation.

Other volunteers arrived, and the beautiful extension was finished. The entire kitchen was overhauled, equipped and fully stocked. The rest of the farmhouse, upstairs and down, was completely renovated and the outside restored!

I remember Nick saying to me one night, "I'm almost afraid to think anything, because as soon as I do, there it is!" He went on, "I don't even have time to pray about it."

It was then that we heard God speak so clearly, "You did pray. You prayed for a solid year, and now it's time!" It was as if our loving heavenly Father had stored all of our prayers up in a jar, and now He was pouring out the answers.

We still marvel as we look back on those days. We don't know how our staff found out about us, but two couples came, and so did twelve students. Every one of them was a treasure, a hand-picked gift from the Lord. Altogether we ran five Discipleship Training Schools there, and went on outreaches to Tennessee, Georgia, Florida, Boston, England, Scotland, and Mexico, where we worked with Juan Ramirez and his church.

Many of our dearest friends and coworkers came from those schools. Tammy Adams and her five-month-old son James were in our very first DTS. Tammy and her husband Dave served on staff with us until Dave passed away in 2001. Tammy is still on our Leadership Team, and we consider her family. Rob Purcell, who is on our Prayer Station Board today, was a student in our second DTS. Steve and Ann Martin served with us for a short time, returned to Northern Ireland, and then joined us once again in Jaffrey, New Hampshire. Dave and Ethel DeFebbo served with us at Blue Mountain and in New Hampshire, and they still serve in YWAM today. Other friendships were made during our three and a half years on that mountain. Relationships that have continued to enrich our lives for over 40 years.

God had answered every prayer far above and beyond our level of faith. He proved over and over that, "He is able to do immeasurably more than all we ask or imagine according to his power that is at work in us" (Ephesians 3:20).

Nick continues

In 1976, the US bicentennial year, we participated in a vision that God gave Leland Paris called "The Spirit in '76." A wagon train, led by our good friends, Woody and Dixie Woodward, crossed the country from California to Philadelphia, Pennsylvania. The journey took seven months, and they shared the Lord all along the trail.

As part of the celebration, our ministry embraced Boston, a city which had great significance in the early days of the US founding fathers. We worked with the local churches to put together a one-week outreach to the streets of the city. Each day concluded with an evening rally. A highlight was a speech by former Speaker of the US House of Representatives, the Honorable John McCormack, who spoke to us in Boston's historic Faneuil Hall.

Following the final evening service, where George Otis Sr. shared a powerful message, God directed us to take the entire group to an area of Boston called the "Combat Zone." In the 1960s and '70s this was the adult entertainment district in downtown Boston.

God's word to us was specific. We were to walk the streets of the Combat Zone worshiping, praying, and engaging in quiet spiritual warfare. We were not to confront anyone. If we were to strike up a conversation, we were simply to bless them and show the love of Jesus.

I don't believe any of us understood how strategic that night was until months later. One of the Boston-area pastors we worked with wrote me a letter sharing that the Combat Zone in Boston was on the wane. Eventually we heard it no longer existed!

We cannot and must not separate prayer from evangelism. Through prayer the battle is fought and won—before we do anything.

"The weapons we fight with are not the weapons of the world. On the contrary, they have divine power to demolish strongholds" (2 Corinthians 10:4).

The prayers we pray in obedience to the Holy Spirit's direction are powerful and mighty. As a result of the outreach in Boston, God laid New England heavily on our hearts.

Chapter 6

God's Frozen Chosen

In the midst of the bitter cold and snowy winter of 1978, we moved our entire ministry from the Blue Mountains of Pennsylvania, to the tiny town of Jaffrey, New Hampshire.

We had received an invitation from a minister, asking if we would be willing to come and occupy a large old Inn that had been built at the base of Mount Monadnock around the turn of the century. It was located in southern New Hampshire just about 42 miles southwest of Manchester.

Most of our staff were down in Mexico on outreach with our DTS students. Just a handful of us were left at Blue Mountain to hold down the fort and keep things from freezing.

During this time Rozanne and I took a road trip to check out the Inn. In hindsight, this is one journey I probably should have taken alone! My dear wife does not handle the cold well at all.

We were given a tour of a four-story, almost 80-year-old building that had not been occupied or heated in nine years! There was no insulation in the walls or insulated glass in the windows. It was January and the snow outside was many feet high. I knew this was not looking good. However, I am a visionary, and apparently an optimist.

That night we were housed in the annex building next to the Inn. I couldn't sleep with the excitement of all I envisioned we could do with this incredible facility. Meanwhile Rozanne was glued to my side, also unable to sleep. She was freezing and never wanted to come within a hundred miles of this place ever again!

After much prayer, and assurance from the Lord, five of us moved into the old Shattock Inn. The word of the Lord to us was that we were to make this a temporary base of operation until we found a permanent home for the ministry somewhere in the New England area.

The Inn was filthy, and the only utility that worked was the electricity. We had $1,000 in our pockets and in six weeks, our Discipleship Training School would arrive from their outreach in Mexico.

Rozanne and Tammy, both of whom had pneumonia, remained at Blue Mountain with the children until we could get water and heat running at the Inn.

God had told me that this would be my Goliath, but as I put my trust in Him, I would see the giants fall.

Two women from Lancaster County, Pennsylvania, were part of our team, and what a gift they were! In just six short weeks, they cleaned 30 rooms. Perhaps that doesn't sound astounding, but let me explain. First, they would plug in a small electric heater to get the room above freezing. If they didn't do this, the cleaning water would freeze the moment it touched any surface. They would then carry a 5-gallon Igloo water container to the annex building next door through many feet of snow. They would fill the Igloo with hot water and carry it back between them. They washed the ceiling, walls, floor, and windows of each room, then left the heater on until everything in the room was dry. They then had to move the heater, the only one we owned, to the next room. This process was repeated 30 times!

Locals seemed to almost relish informing us of the dire condition of our procurement.

They shared that the water had been turned off underground at the street. Others went on to say that the outside water feed was broken. I decided to check with the Jaffrey Water Works to ascertain the full extent of our woes. The workmen arrived to assess the situation and gave me their grim diagnosis. "We're sorry, but we will not be able to check out the break and fix it until the ground thaws, which will be sometime in the spring."

Considering current depth of the snow and the freezing temperatures, I figured spring would be sometime in late August! "Gentlemen, I'm sorry, but in six weeks I have about 20 people arriving. We will need water for drinking, cooking, bathing, and for heat."

They were adamant that this would be impossible, and they left the building.

Everything depended on the water running through our pipes. Without it we would not be able to use the bathrooms and kitchen, and we wouldn't have the steam boiler for heat. I called Rozanne and asked her to pray with us for a miracle.

I looked up to heaven, "Lord, You told us to come and take on this building now, and that as we did, we would see the giants fall. So, we trust You that You will give us water."

Shortly after, one of the men from the Jaffrey Water Works came back. He said he felt like he should come to the building and just try to turn the water on. It was a freezing New Hampshire winter's day, but he and Bud Adams went outside and dug through many feet of snow. They then began to use picks on the frozen ground until they found the valve that supplied water for the building. They took me down to the basement and had me stand in front of a large open pipe.

They said, "Okay, we are going to turn the water on. You yell out to us and let us know if water starts coming through that pipe." They left, and I stood there staring at that open pipe and praying like mad. Suddenly I heard something. A gush of water poured into the basement! I ran as fast as I could through the snow to let them know that water was flowing!

The workman scratched his head while looking at the plans he had brought for our building. He turned to Bud and me and said, "This should not be happening. My paperwork clearly shows a break in the line right here!" He came up with a number of scenarios, including that the frozen ground around the pipe was forming a temporary seal. He also predicted that when the ground thawed, we would have debris in all of our water. But that never happened!

The giants were beginning to fall!

Now that we had water, it was time to connect the water to the boiler. Again, we were given bad news. A few men who knew the history of the old building began to tell us how at one point the basement flooded. As a result, the boiler had been severely damaged, and the main pipes in the steam boiler were cracked. They told us we definitely would need a new boiler and gave me a contact for a dealer who sold them. He came down to check ours out and said a replacement would cost us $10,000! A huge amount of cash in 1978, and remember we had arrived with only $1,000 that had already been spent in one shot on a large fuel oil tank. We were broke!

Someone else gave us a contact for a man, Jim, who was a home fuel oil dealer, suggesting we should have him look at the boiler. When he went down to the basement and saw the size of the gun that would fire up the heat for the boiler, he said, "Sorry, this is commercial equipment and I wouldn't know the first thing about wiring up this gun to get it to fire."

We prayed and gave this next challenge to the Lord.

Later, lying in bed I thought to myself, "How crazy did we have to be to come to an ancient building like this, with a handful of people and almost no money, and think we would have it up and running in six weeks. Impossible! It can't be done. Cut your losses and run!"

But God had said, "Watch the giants fall!"

One evening following the bad news about the boiler, Bud and I were walking through the building when we heard noises coming from the basement. We went to investigate and found our local fuel oil guy, Jim, in the boiler room, fiddling with the boiler gun. He looked up at us as we entered, and then told us a story I will never forget.

"I was home watching TV with my family," he said. "All of a sudden I saw numbers, like a schematic, floating in front of my eyes. I reached for a pad and pencil and began to write down what I was seeing. When I was done, I knew it was the wiring schematic for the gun of a huge boiler—your boiler!" Jim was so excited he jumped into his car, drove straight over, and began to work on the wires. When Jim was done, he and Bud fired the gun.

It worked!

I could almost hear the THUD as another giant hit the basement floor!

The next step was to hook up water to the boiler and begin to fill it. They turned to me and said this would be the moment of truth. Once the boiler was full of water, they would fire the gun and begin to build up steam in the system.

"How will we know if the boiler is broken as we have been told it is?" I asked.

Jim smiled at me and just said, "You keep walking around the boiler and let us know if you see any water leaking out. If you do, then all the horror stories are true and you will need a new boiler."

I "prayer walked" the huge boiler, around and around, speaking in my heavenly language. Then I began to hear noises all over the basement. It was the sound of steam!

There was not one leak from the boiler!

Jim was stunned. He just kept saying over and over that he didn't understand how he had received the revelation about the wiring, since he had never worked on a boiler like this before in his life. Jim was not a Christian, and yet that night he received an amazing revelation right from God's throne.

I knew another giant had fallen, and even more importantly, a life had been impacted for eternity.

Miraculously, at the end of the six weeks we had running water, heat, beds, furniture in place, every room cleaned, the kitchen and dining room set up, and even a wood-burning stove in the lounge. By this time Rozanne, Tammy, and the children were with us and settled into our rooms on the second floor. We all looked around with deep gratitude at everything God had done. We even had 20 minutes left to sit with a cup of coffee before the bus with staff and students arrived from Mexico.

Many giants had fallen in just six weeks!

The Shattuck Inn at the foot of Mountt. Monadnock was our base for a year and a half. Our beautiful third daughter, Melissa, was born there during a very cold and icy February. We ran 3 DTSs, and once again God sent us amazing staff and students. Many remain lifelong friends.

One of those friends, Pastor Harold Hills, from Falls Creek, Pennsylvania, shared with me how he had never forgotten a local outreach I initiated when he was on staff with us.

There was a little town called Milford in southern New Hampshire, not far from Jaffrey. It was on the outskirts of Manchester, and apparently it was very much upon God's heart, for He laid it on mine. At His direction we went there once a week.

In the center of the village was a gazebo where we would gather to worship. That was all we planned: worship, prayer, and spiritual warfare for the town. We sensed it was God's strategy to do something in the heavenlies that would initiate a gospel witness. To our knowledge there was no evangelical church in Milford, but we did, on occasion, have the opportunity to strike up a conversation with passersby.

Harold remembered that he was not necessarily enthusiastic about the Milford idea, but in obedience to God's direction and out of respect for my leadership, he participated. The very first night, God gave him the privilege of speaking to someone who had just stopped by out of curiosity. Harold had such a powerful opportunity to share the Lord that he has never forgotten how it impacted his own life and ministry.

A number of years later, when I was leading the YWAM ministry in New York, I received an invitation to go back to Milford. I was to speak in an evangelical church and give training in evangelism. The pastor there told me God had done a powerful work in the town and that there were now three evangelical churches impacting their little community for Jesus!

Tracing the timeline back, we found that this had all started soon after our weeks of worship, prayer, and spiritual warfare in Milford back in 1978. God honors commitment and answers prayer.

Rozanne continues

We cannot leave the Shattuck Inn without mentioning dear Betsy.

Betsy came to us from Massachusetts to be a student in one of our DTSs. She celebrated her 70th birthday with us, and we all adored her. She had a beautiful spirit, never complained about anything, always had an encouraging word, and was a powerful intercessor. Betsy had also been in a wheelchair since she was 5 years old, afflicted with polio.

It was a normal occurrence to see Betsy rolling through the dining room or down a hallway with Anita, Rebecca, or one of the other staff children on her lap, all having a grand old time. The children loved her, as did we all.

Our housing in the 100-year-old Inn was all on the second floor. There were no ramps and no modern elevators. To get to her room, Betsy had to get her wheelchair into a small, ancient elevator and use a pulley mechanism to reach the second floor. Many times, we would hear her calling for help, stuck between floors. Still, Betsy never complained or lost her beautiful smile.

She had the heart of an intercessor and prayed for all of us.

When it was time to go to Scotland on outreach, we all just assumed Betsy would not want to go. Boy, were we wrong! There was no way she was going to miss out on an opportunity to preach the gospel and reach the lost.

When Betsy would sit in her wheelchair in some drafty old church in Scotland, sharing her testimony and speaking about spreading the gospel, everyone listening was left without excuse.

China was heavy on her heart, and Betsy interceded for that nation daily. Often, she would share her greatest desire with us—to go to China as a missionary. We would smile, and encourage her to continue to pray that the Lord of the harvest would send forth laborers into His harvest, and she did.

When Betsy graduated from the DTS, along with her mostly teenage fellow students, she went home and studied Mandarin for three years until she was fluent in the language.

We often received letters from her, continuing to share her desire to go to China. One day Nick felt the Lord urging him to tell Betsy to go. With more than a little trepidation he mailed the letter.

Turned out that was all the encouragement Betsy needed! After searching unsuccessfully for a traveling companion, Betsy went alone. She ministered in a small village for a year, teaching English and planting a church. Through all the difficulties and struggles, Betsy had only one complaint—her wheelchair was getting rusty and making it harder for her to get around!

She returned home grateful for God's grace and goodness. In her mid-seventies He had enabled her to live out her dream of being a missionary to China.

When we received the news in November of 1993 that Betsy had passed into the presence of her Lord and Savior, we rejoiced for her while our hearts ached. We had lost a precious friend and intercessor, one who had shown us by example, that all things are possible for those who love God and are obedient to His call.

Nick continues

In June of 1978 the World Cup soccer games were held in Argentina. At God's direction YWAM leadership planned a major global outreach to the games. I was at the YWAM staff conference in Arkansas when Loren Cunningham shared the vision. It all sounded very exciting, but for reasons I could not fully understand I had never had an interest in going to South America. I didn't know why. After all, I loved the world and wanted all of it to know Jesus. I even knew that the largest ethnic group there was from Italy, but even that did not move me.

During the conference I remember one of the leaders coming up to me, patting me on the back, and saying, "You're going to be part of this outreach, aren't you, Nick?" I smiled, but did not give an answer.

God began to work on my heart. I knew that obedience and vision begin in prayer, so I began to intercede for the outreach and for Argentina. Slowly, over weeks, God began to raise the tide of vision and desire in my heart. I have to admit, though, that the day I took the flight to Buenos Aires, I was still not totally on board for this particular mission's trip. It was never easy to leave my precious family behind, especially for a whole month in the days before email, texting, and easy, affordable communication. Nevertheless, I went in obedience to God's direction.

Upon my arrival in Buenos Aires, I learned that I would be going to the city of Rosario, the third-largest city in the nation. Within two weeks, I was bursting with excitement and vision! I could easily have sent a message home to Rozanne, "Meet me in Argentina! I sense God is calling us to spend the remainder of our lives here in ministry."

Long before this outreach, God had taught me important lessons on how to gain vision for lost people in the world:

- Seeking God for a revelation of His broken heart over the lost
- Interceding for unreached people groups
- Researching the world
- Giving to the work of missions

Now I was learning that going anywhere in the world with the gospel can change your heart regarding a people group or nation, even if you did not have any previous interest or desire to go. Argentina was a valuable lesson in my life that motivated and inspired me to be a World Christian!

After much searching in the New England area, God miraculously released to us the former campus of the Franklin Pierce Law School in Concord, New Hampshire.

At first the owners laughed me out of the room when I shared our proposal. Eventually however, they reconsidered. With much prayer and God's clear direction, we secured a lease/purchase agreement for the spacious campus. This location became a great multiplier for missions as we had the privilege of training and mobilizing hundreds of young people and sending them out to many nations.

In 1979 the world witnessed a great time of sorrow as we heard horrible stories of killing, torture and massacre in places like Vietnam, and

Cambodia. YWAM from around the world began to send workers to the refugee camps in Thailand and Hong Kong, set up by the United Nations. We sent teams to help and spent much time in intercessory prayer for the suffering people.

Rozanne continues

Anita was doing very well in an excellent Christian school in Concord. She could recite long passages of Scripture by the age of seven, which constantly blessed and amazed me. She even won the prestigious "Christian Character" award for the whole school when she was only in third grade.

We were having quite a baby boom among our staff. There were a few little ones under a year old, Melissa being one of them. However, we had enough three- and four-year-olds, Rebecca included, to begin our own preschool.

The preschool teacher incorporated some of the DTS curriculum for the children, at her students' level of course. As an example, they were not taught to pray simply, "God bless Mommy, God bless Daddy" prayers, but they learned to wait quietly and listen for God to speak. When He did, they were encouraged to pray His prayers. In DTS we call this intercession.

One afternoon when the children gathered for their regular prayer time, the teacher said, "Today we are going to pray for the refugee families in Hong Kong."

In terms that the children could grasp, she gave them some understanding of what a refugee camp looked like. The class then waited on God as they had been taught, listened, and prayed out loud whatever He directed them to say.

A few prayers were offered, and then Rebecca prayed, "Please Jesus, stop the babies from falling out of bed and bumping their heads."

This was quite a specific request, but the teacher did not have any understanding of what it meant—until a few days later.

Our overseas staff who were working in the refugee camps would send us updates on cassette tapes. That week, as the preschool teacher listened to their latest report, she was amazed to hear:

"One of our greatest prayer needs is this. The camps are so overcrowded that when a family arrives, they are assigned one bunk bed. These bunks are stacked 5 high. The whole family has to fit on one bunk. There is so little space that babies keep falling off the beds and suffering concussions."

Yes, four-year-olds can hear from God, probably more clearly than most adults. Their faith is simple; they don't make it complicated. They listen, and they expect their loving heavenly Daddy to speak to them. Jesus told us to come to Him as a little child. I believe He meant with the simple, trusting faith that children have before the influences of a fallen world silence His gentle whisper.

> The Lord said, "Go out and stand on the mountain in the presence of the Lord, for the Lord is about to pass by." Then a great and powerful wind tore the mountains apart and shattered the rocks before the Lord, but the Lord was not in the wind. After the wind there was an earthquake, but the Lord was not in the earthquake. After the earthquake came a fire, but the Lord was not in the fire. And after the fire came a gentle whisper (1 Kings 19:11-12).

Today Rebecca and her husband lead a nonprofit reaching middle- and high-school young people across America with an anti-bullying and anti-violence message. Their ministry is called: *Speak Life, End Bullying the Musical,* and so far they have reached over 365,000 students. As I write this, the ministry is preparing to go global through media.

Ministry finances were a daily struggle. We economized in every possible way, and as we did our part, God was always faithful.

One winter a payment of $10,000 was due on the purchase of our YWAM building in Concord, New Hampshire. We did not have the money. Nick was scheduled to lead the DTS students on outreach to Scotland. He was conflicted. How could he go with the payment due? Our leadership team prayed together, and we all felt God was still directing Nick to lead the outreach in Scotland. While Daddy was away, the girls and I were going to spend some time in Florida with my parents.

Soon after arriving in Florida, I was asked to speak at a women's meeting. I did not mention our need, but after the service one of the ladies put a check in my hand, saying she felt directed to give this gift to our ministry. The check was for $10,000!

Imagine Nick's relief when he called me later that day and I was able to share with him that God had provided the funding we needed. Had Nick not obeyed the Lord to lead the DTS in Scotland, I would not have spoken to a small women's meeting in Florida. As we simply trust and obey, we give God room for miracles.

Chapter 7

Where the People Are

During those years in Concord, God began to place a great burden on my heart for cities. Our family even prayed about beginning a YWAM city ministry in Boston. It became clear, however, that our role was to intercede and send in teams to "break up the fallow ground."

Back in 1977, when our ministry was based in New Ringgold, Pennsylvania, we ran a Summer School of Training. Janet, one of the participants from the Pittsburgh area, was a fireball for Jesus. Janet came from a youth group called "Power Group," and her youth pastors were Doug and Debbie Tunney. We did not know it at the time, but this was the couple God had chosen to pioneer YWAM Boston.

Doug invited me on several occasions to come and speak to his youth. As a result, you could say we emptied his youth group and poured them into YWAM. Over a period of a few years, most of them came to our DTSs and joined our staff. Today, many continue to serve in missions in different parts of the world.

Eventually Doug, Debbie, and their children decided they might as well come to a DTS with us in Concord, after all, that's where all their young people were! In 2006 God spoke to Doug and Debbie to move to Boston and begin a new YWAM center there. Today it is a powerful ministry with far-reaching influence, not only around the nation, but the world.

In 1981, while I was leading an SOE we took the students down to New York City for a week of urban outreach. It was a fantastic time of evangelism on the streets of Brooklyn, Manhattan, and the Bronx. We concluded the outreach with a Sunday morning service in a great church on Coney Island. I had come to know the pastor as a mighty man of God with a true passion for the people in his area. Everyone in the local neighborhoods knew him and loved him.

The church choir sang an old hymn that morning, one I had sung many times as a boy. "Coming home, coming home, nevermore to roam, Open wide Thine arms of love, Lord, I'm coming home." I knew it as a salvation hymn, but for some reason on this occasion I was moved emotionally. Sitting on the platform of the church, my head in my hands, I wept as the choir sang.

I couldn't understand what was happening to me. "Lord, why is this song affecting me so much?"

Suddenly I realized that the pastor was introducing me to speak. Quickly I brushed away the tears and managed to get out of my chair. As I took the few steps toward the pulpit God spoke to me so clearly and so profoundly that I actually thought I was hearing His audible voice.

"Nick, I am calling you back to the city of your birth."

I was stunned! I was born in New York City in Astoria, Queens. I looked at the congregation to see if anyone else showed signs of hearing what I had just heard, but no one else seemed to share my shock.

To this day I have no memory of what I preached on that particular Sunday morning.

Driving the YWAM van back home, I couldn't wait to share with Rozanne what had happened. Running into the big old white farmhouse we lived in on the YWAM property, I grabbed her, hugged her, and said, "We have to talk!" Sitting on our sad-looking orange couch, the one our cats had scratched so much that the stuffing protruded in odd places, I related my story to the one whose life was about to be turned upside down—again.

When I concluded, I waited. Rozanne smiled and said, "Great! When do we move?"

That day neither of us could possibly imagine the journey that lay ahead, or how many thousands of miles we would travel to get from New Hampshire to New York City.

About a year later in the fall of 1982, I was walking from the YWAM training center to the farmhouse, a distance of approximately 100 feet, when God spoke simply and clearly that our time of leading YWAM New Hampshire had come to a close.

Initially I was startled by the news, but soon anticipation began to rise in my heart as I contemplated finally moving, presumably to New York. Soon after, however, Rozanne and I received a personal letter from Loren Cunningham, the founder of YWAM, inviting us to attend their first Leadership Training School (LTS) in Kona, Hawaii, beginning in April of 1983.

In the ten years we had worked with YWAM, we had never taken a sabbatical. Was God saying now was the time? It would make sense for us to receive more training before making the move to New York, but we had no savings for five airfares, LTS fees, a correspondence course for the girls, or any other expenses.

After praying, we agreed very definitely that this was our next step!

Rozanne continues

Christmas was coming. Our leadership team released us to take a six-month sabbatical, which would include some time visiting both of our families and some friends on the East Coast, followed by the Leadership Training School in Hawaii.

Two weeks before we were due to leave, one of my dear friends in Jaffrey invited me over for a farewell lunch. I had met Carla soon after

Melissa was born, and she had been like an angel to me in a cold and difficult period of my life.

Carla knew how we lived, and she didn't pretend to understand it, but she respected us for it. After lunch she asked me the question others want to ask, but generally don't:

"How much money do you have towards your trip?"

"Not a dollar," I replied.

"But you leave in two weeks!" she responded incredulously.

"I know, and when we pull out of the driveway, we will need enough money to get to Long Island, where we will be with Nick's parents through Christmas. From there we will need enough to get to Florida by New Year's to be with my family. After that we will need our airfares to Hawaii, a correspondence course for the girls, and our LTS tuition and housing."

As soon as the words were out of my mouth, I heard the Voice.

"And that is exactly how I am going to do it."

To which I responded honestly: "But Lord, You know I don't like it when You do it that way!"

God had spoken, and I knew that this was going to be a daily faith journey. When we went to Germany on the Word of the Lord, God had provided down to the last penny before we took a single step.

Now our loving, heavenly Father had new lessons to teach us, new depths that He wanted us to fathom in the area of faith, greater trust that He desired to see developed in our characters as we learned more about His. Our great and loving Father desired us to embrace His plan. I knew doubt and fear could have no place in our hearts on this journey.

Two weeks later, having commissioned and prayed over members of our leadership team and installed Steve and Ann Martin as the interim base directors, we began our journey.

We had told everyone that we would be back in six months. I wonder what they would have thought as they waved goodbye that December morning, if they had known that we had just enough money in our pockets to cover gas and tolls to Long Island!

Christmas came and went, Nick's family bid us a sad good-bye, and we departed for Florida. We could not tell his family exactly when we would see them again, but we knew it would be at least six months. Christmas gifts had provided us with the necessary funds to make the journey to my parents, and we were always able to pay our way for the weeks we spent with them. Mum and Dad were in ministry, too, so we would never have presumed upon their generosity.

Three weeks before we needed to be on a plane for Hawaii, we attended a function at my niece's school. Before the program began, a good friend who knew of our plans asked me the dreaded question: "How much do you have toward your trip?"

I smiled and responded, "Not a dollar."

"WHAT! You leave in three weeks!"

"Yes, we do," I replied, "and God will provide in His way and in His time."

We had just taken our seats when another girlfriend knelt down next to me and placed an envelope in my lap. She explained, "My husband and I received some unexpected funds this week, and when we prayed about where to give our tithes, we knew some of it was to go to you and Nick."

When I opened the envelope there was a check large enough to cover all of our airfares and our LTS expenses! My other friend screamed when I told her!

How faithful our loving heavenly Father is. I knew that gift was not just for our benefit, but also for the building up of my friend's (1 Thesalonians 5:11).

Nick continues

The Leadership Training School was another life-changing experience for us. Most of the anointed speakers didn't just teach from theory, but came to us directly from the mission field. They were feeding us fresh bread, and our tired, weary bodies and spirits were being refreshed and renewed. Most of our fellow classmates were also missionaries, and some were dear friends. We were all in need of rest, spiritual nourishment, the beauty of Hawaii, and even some fishing! We relished every day.

On Sunday afternoons the YWAM campus encouraged family time. Our family used this time to intercede for New York City and our future ministry there. As we began to receive revelation, we took notes. We call this "prayer planning." God began to give all of us, even our young daughters, His heart for the city. Years later when we looked over the notes, we saw that so much of what God shared with us back then came to pass.

When the LTS was over, we were invited to stay on at YWAM Kona to help with a major project that Loren Cunningham was embracing. It was called The Year of the Bible, and the goal was to put a Bible in every home on each of the Hawaiian Islands. Meanwhile Anita was invited to join a King's Kids team ministering in Western Samoa for 35 days. Rozanne took Rebecca and Melissa back to her homeland, New Zealand—her first trip there in 13 years. Our six-month sabbatical turned into 18 months, and God graciously taught us many more lessons on faith and finances.

When we finally returned to Concord, we knew it would just be for a short season. The YWAM ministry there was now in the capable hands of our friends, Steve and Ann Martin and Dave and Tammy Adams.

Initially we assumed we would be preparing to begin our ministry in New York, but unexpectedly we were presented with a number of alternate opportunities:

- Return to Kona and head up The Year of the Bible project which was going to take far longer than 1 year.
- Assume the leadership of YWAM Washington DC.
- Consider the possibility of becoming the national leader for YWAM Italy.
- Accept Mercy Ships proposal to serve as the assistant director of the *MV Anastasis*.

We took a week to pray through these possibilities. It was clear that a couple of them could be eliminated right away. Soon we were down to New York, Kona, and the *Anastasis*.

During our time at the University in Kona, the *Anastasis* had come for a visit and was anchored off shore. One afternoon our family was very excited to go out on a small boat to visit the ship. To board, we had to climb a rope ladder up the side of the ship as the small boat we were in rocked back and forth with the swells.

I will ask Rozanne to share what happened next

I was a little nervous as I climbed the ladder, fully concentrating on each rope step while also watching to make sure our girls reached the top safely. With great relief I finally felt the hard metal deck beneath me, and in that moment, I heard the Lord speak. His exact words were, "You will spend a lot of time on this ship." I was stunned!

We spent a wonderful couple of hours exploring the incredible vessel that God had provided to YWAM. The highlight for me was being invited into the captain's quarters where Helen Applegate, a fellow New Zealander and one of the most gracious women I have ever met, served us tea. The Kiwi in me was having so much fun!

Nick continues

With such a clear word from the Lord many months earlier, things became very clear in a short time. God was calling us to serve with the Mercy Ship *M/V Anastasis*, which was currently in Honolulu, Hawaii for refitting. The director of the *Anastasis*, Don Stephens, was on trial in Athens, Greece for proselytizing a young Greek man, which was not permitted according to Greek law. As assistant director, I took on the leadership role in Don's absence. An incredible crew of 250 people was on board, including Captain Ben Applegate and John Brignall—Chief Engineer and Marine Superintendent. What a privilege it was to get to know all of them as we worked side by side.

Rozanne continues

One of the greatest joys of being in missions as a family has been watching God work not just in our lives, but also in the lives of our children.

Before we left for Kona, I had prayed very specifically that this new season in our lives would also be life-changing for our girls, and especially that Anita and Rebecca would receive the baptism of the Holy

Spirit. We believe that specific prayers get specific answers, so I asked God for exactly what I wanted to see happen.

Anita was invited to a friend's birthday party one weekend during our LTS. It was a sleepover, and the girls began to tell each other scary stories. Eventually they had frightened each other so badly that they decided to pray. They prayed fervently, the Holy Spirit fell on them, and Anita received the baptism of the Holy Spirit along with a couple of the other girls! When Anita walked into our room the next morning, I knew immediately that something amazing had happened: her countenance was different, she was changed.

Following the LTS, we were asked to stay on in Kona. We were now staff, and so our girls were able to attend classes in the YWAM Christian school. One week Rebecca's class was learning about the Third Person of the Trinity, the Holy Spirit. On the final day of that week, Rebecca was filled with the Holy Spirit while sitting at her desk!

Specific prayers do get specific answers. How God loves to give good gifts to His children!

Anita and Rebecca were involved in the King's Kids ministry. At the age of 11, as mentioned earlier, Anita went on a 35-day mission trip to Western Samoa without her parents. She learned so much at that time about trusting Jesus. She prayed for her own finances for the trip and God provided. What a privilege to learn about a whole new culture at such a young age while living and ministering among the islanders. They slept in *folies*, communal homes with thatched roofs and no walls. Anita showered outdoors, and I have fun photos of her and her young friends gathered around a bucket shaving their legs.

During the two years we served on the *Anastasis*, there were around 50 school-aged children on board. All of them loved Jesus and became each other's best friends. Anita, Rebecca, and Melissa were all a part of Ship's Kids and were involved in ministry both on and off the ship.

We spent one memorable weekend on an Indian reservation when the *Anastasis* was docked at Vancouver Island in Canada. Ship's Kids performed there a number of times, and the girls enjoyed forming friendships with the local children.

General William Booth, the founder of The Salvation Army, is quoted as saying, "Create and confirm in the hearts of your children the assurance that you yourself are what you want them to become." This quote so impacted me that I memorized it and have endeavored to live it before my girls. Whether we like it or not, that is what's happening. Every day, in all situations good or bad, they are watching, listening, learning and eventually becoming very like us! Every word that comes out of our mouths, the way we treat people, our devotional life, the principles we live by, the friends we hang out with, how we share our faith—through all of it, they're watching and learning. To this day Anita calls me "the voice in her head." I, however, am very happy that all three of our girls know God's Voice and are always listening for it, and are ready to obey.

Without trying, we model our values. Parents in particular demonstrate to their children what they consider important and valuable. Experience proves that children often follow the life patterns of their parents, repeating their successes and mistakes. Timothy is a prime example of someone who was influenced by godly relatives. His mother, Eunice, and grandmother Lois, were Jewish believers who helped shape his life and promote his spiritual growth (2 Timothy 1:5, 3:15).

My two main areas of ministry on board the *Anastasis* were counseling and personnel development. It was a privilege to meet with so many amazing volunteers who served every day without remuneration, raised their own support, and contributed financially each month to the ministry.

God was giving us more leadership training and preparing us for all that lay ahead in New York. We had the privilege of serving on the *M/V Anastasis* for two full years, and our children made great memories and lifelong friendships there. Then it became clear it was time to make our move to New York.

The journey had taken five years. From the day we drove away from YWAM New Hampshire our family had traveled over 88,000 miles, and God had provided for every mile of the journey!

Chapter 8

"Coming Home"

Nick continues

Looking back to that morning in Coney Island when God said to me, "come home," I can hardly believe the journey God designed for us to experience on the way there.

The people we met (some of whom were now going to join us in New York), the lessons God taught us, many very humbling and difficult, and most importantly the prayer base we built, would be vital for establishing YWAM Metro New York.

I believe it was Joy Dawson who taught us that when planting a new ministry, we should never move beyond our prayer base. Once again prayer became a vital part of our foundation.

In the Bible, especially the book of Acts, there is always a wonderful balance between prayer and action, but prayer always comes first! The point of intercession is to pray God's prayers, not ours. We must seek God's direction for what we are endeavoring to accomplish and continue to pray in specifics so our endeavors are led by Him and not by our best efforts.

During those five years of praying and waiting on God's timing, we made some very important and lifelong connections with people who would become a strategic part of our ministry team. David and Linda Cowie were two absolutely crucial leaders we met during our time with the University of the Nations in Hawaii. They were veteran YWAMers, having served in many strategic ministry locations in the early years of the mission. They helped pioneer YWAM ministries in Great Britain, Thailand, Mercy Ships and the YWAM University campus in Kona, and now they were joining us to help pioneer YWAM Metro New York.

Just weeks before the Cowies arrived, David, Linda, and their daughter Lisa, were almost killed in a boating accident in New Zealand. The three of them were out on Lake Tekapo in the South Island, when their small boat hit a submerged fence post that punctured the hull. The boat began to sink. They had barely enough time to take off their boots and make sure their life jackets were secure. A mile from shore, in glacier-fed, ice-cold water around 400 feet deep, they knew that it would take only about 30 minutes for hypothermia to set in, followed by unconsciousness and drowning. That day they had only seen one other boat on the lake.

Linda had bound the enemy as the boat was sinking. Now thoughts crossed her mind that Satan wanted to destroy them to keep them from going to New York City. Treading water, she began to intercede for New York. Suddenly a boat went speeding past them, apparently not noticing three heads bobbing in the water. Further down the lake, the driver of the speed boat, who had seen just the hull of a boat, decided to go back to investigate. He found the family just in the nick of time. God was up to something in New York and Satan was not going to be able to stop it!

David and Linda's stature and experience, especially in pioneering YWAM ministries, was invaluable. David became my associate director, and we had a blast serving the Lord together! Outside of the serious work we were doing, we enjoyed great fellowship, friendship, and lots of laughter that made the challenges and difficulties of pioneering so much more bearable.

God laid on Linda's heart a vision for a Prayer Target Week. This is how she describes it in her manual, *Reaching Your City With God:*

> In seeking God for a strategy for prayer in the city, He led me to 2 Chronicles 20 which is the account of Jehoshaphat proclaiming a fast and calling Judah to gather at the temple in Jerusalem to pray. A vast army was coming up against them and they desperately needed God's intervention. In those few days they were together, they saw a great victory. From this Biblical account came our plan to call selected YWAM leaders to New York City to pray.

Loren Cunningham had shared the concept that all of society is influenced by seven major areas or "mind molders:" church, family, government, education, arts and entertainment, business and commerce, and media.

We targeted each one of these during our special week of prayer. Linda was able to identify Christian leaders who represented each area of influence in New York City. We spent individual time with all of them, listening, learning, asking questions, and praying with them.

- In the area of Business and Commerce, we prayed with a businessman whose office was just off Wall Street. Later we prayer walked the full length of Wall Street ending with a time of prayer at Trinity Church.
- For Church we prayed at a large church in Manhattan
- For Government we prayed at City Hall
- For Media, Rockefeller Center
- For Arts and Entertainment, Lamb's Theatre, just off Broadway.

- For Education, Columbia University, the seat of secular humanism. During our walk around the university campus, we were struck by the engraving over the entrance to the library: "To the glory of God Almighty."

- For the Family, we prayed in one of the largest welfare hotels in the city, the Prince George.

- We also prayed in other significant locations including a prayer room in the Empire State Building, and in the foyer of the United Nations Building.

Through this week of prayer, strongholds in the city were revealed. As a prayer team we identified their locations and came against them in intercession and spiritual warfare. "In fact, no one can enter a strong man's house without first tying him up. Then he can plunder the strong man's house" (Mark 3:27).

Loren Cunningham once described our mission field this way: "New York City is not just a city; it is a nation." Our city, with all its complexities, history, and strongholds would require much prayer and spiritual warfare if we were to have any chance of winning it for God. This week of prayer, which had been prioritized before any major ministry took place, was essential and absolutely the right place to start.

The centennial for the Statue of Liberty was 1986. We fell in line with the celebration, calling our first outreach in the city "Operation Liberty."

Linda shared the following report concerning Operation Liberty in *Reaching Your City with God:*

"The Prayer Target Week took place in the spring of 1987 as a forerunner to Operation Liberty in the summer.

From the middle of July to the middle of August, 569 young people came from all over the US and fifteen other nations to be participants in this YWAM outreach to New York City. In addition to YWAM, seven other organizations conducted outreaches in the city that summer.

Teams worked with fifty churches throughout the city. Eleven teams using music and drama as an evangelistic tool gave 95 performances. Sixteen evangelism teams conducted countless meetings in churches, on the streets, in parks, in the subways, on empty lots, and anywhere there was a place to reach people with the gospel message. Whatever form the meetings took, the message was the same: "New York, Jesus loves you." Many were referred to churches in their area for follow-up and discipleship.

Children and young people filled with the Spirit of God touched the hearts of New Yorkers through YWAM's King's Kids International. Anita, Rebecca, and Melissa were all on one of the three teams that performed in many public centers such as airports, parks, and business plazas as well as churches. The young people's songs, joyful choreography, and personal testimonies overflowed with God's love and melted resistance to receiving God's truth. Young people can be powerful prayer warriors and evangelists.

God was laying the foundation for YWAM Metro New York. He was teaching us valuable lessons that would become an integral part of the fabric of our future strategy. We were learning in very practical ways that intercessory prayer and spiritual warfare were to lead and influence all we did moving forward. God was planting the seeds for what we would eventually call "Prayer Evangelism."

Halfway through Operation Liberty, God gave us a strategy we had not planned or anticipated in the days leading up to the outreach.

We called it "The Cross across Manhattan."

God's direction was that this was not to be an evangelism thrust but a prayer and worship walk across the length and breadth of Manhattan. God had given Linda Cowie a scripture earlier in the outreach from Genesis 13:17: "Go, walk through

the length and breadth of the land, for I am giving it to you."
This was the word God spoke to Abraham, But He gave Joshua
a similar word in Joshua 1:3: "I will give you every place where
you set your foot, as I promised Moses."

On July 22, 1987, 150 participants in Operation Liberty
walked North and South and East and West across Manhattan.
Starting in Battery Park at the southern tip of Manhattan, one
team walked north up Broadway. Another team began their
walk at the northernmost tip of Manhattan at 9th Avenue and
Broadway and went south. The other two teams began their
prayer/worship walks on both the east and west sides of 42nd
Street. All of the teams converged around noon at Duffy's
Square, a central pedestrian island in the middle of Times
Square.

The square was hot and teeming with lunchtime crowds that
day. We met together and began to worship and sing songs of
spiritual warfare like "Summon Your Power O God." God's
presence was so real that in spite of the noisy traffic and the
fumes, there was a strong sense of God's supremacy over what
was happening. That afternoon, all we had known to be true
concerning Times Square, seemed to bow and acknowledge
that Jesus Christ is Lord!

The young people turned to all four corners of Manhattan,
praying and engaging in spiritual warfare. I had never in
my lifetime been involved in anything of this magnitude,
and I trembled at what God was doing. Everyone on their
lunch breaks were staring at us, seemingly transfixed by what
was happening in Duffy Square. People began to cross both
Broadway and 7th Avenue and come to us as if they were
drawn by some invisible force. No appeal or altar call was
given; they just came. Alan Williams, one of YWAM's great
evangelists, was in charge, leading us in each act of worship
and prayer.

A young Hispanic man, a backslidden Christian, suddenly broke through the crowd! He was shaking, obviously convicted by the Holy Spirit to make his peace with God. A young black mother came forward to receive Christ. She prayed the Sinner's Prayer as sunlight reflected off the tears streaming down her face. Others began to come, all without coercion or invitation. They were falling on their knees and calling out to God.

I had never seen an altar call happen without an altar call before! People were being embraced by God's Spirit and finding Him irresistible. There was nothing they could do but surrender to His presence.

The following year Pastor David Wilkerson pioneered Times Square Church just four city blocks from Duffy Square.

Chapter 9

And Then There Were Four

It was our expectation that at the conclusion of such a dynamic outreach, God would release a permanent YWAM Metro New York facility, a place that would enable us to establish a training and mobilization headquarters for ministry throughout the city.

With the help of realtors, we searched long and hard, following up on every possible lead. However, we were not successful, and our small group of staff was beginning to dwindle. It was time for the Cowies to follow God's direction to establish a new ship ministry within YWAM International, which they did with our blessing and prayers. Others were feeling it was time for them to move on as well.

We had planned to begin our first YWAM DTS in New York that fall, but not only did we not have a building or enough staff—we were not even able to recruit enough students to make the school viable, which seemed especially strange after such a large outreach.

Rozanne and I were becoming discouraged. With just four of us left on staff, we faced an unpredictable future.

In September of 1987, Rozanne and I met with our two remaining staff members. I had my head bowed in discouragement. "Well, team," I began, "we have worked very hard this past year to pioneer this ministry. All I can say is that if we are in no better position by this time next year than we are today, we can say to God and our friends that we tried our best, and move on."

I looked up and was staring straight into my wife's eyes. Rozanne was obviously not happy with what I had shared. She began to speak in her prophetic voice, "Nick Savoca, if that is how you really feel, then we may as well quit right now. Did God speak to us and say that we were to come to New York and establish this ministry or not? If He did, and we both know He did, then there is no giving up, no matter how things look at present or a year from now. We need to continue to do what He has called us to do until He tells us something different."

I knew everything Rozanne said was true. It echoed with every principle God had ever taught us. I was embarrassed that I had said what I did to the team, and asked for their forgiveness. We clasped our hands together in a circle and I led in prayer, renewing our commitment that no matter what, we would obey the voice of the Lord and expect Him to lead us and make our crooked places straight.

God specifically spoke to me through Exodus 14:13 (NKJV): "And Moses said to the people, 'Do not be afraid. Stand still, and see the salvation of the Lord, which He will accomplish for you today....'" I wanted so badly to do something, anything, that I found it hard to hear those words. I have always been a man of action, and waiting quietly and patiently has never been one of my strengths, I asked the Lord to confirm His word to me through a disinterested third party.

A day or so later, I received a personal letter from a man who had heard me speak in Pittsburgh. I didn't know this person, but he said that God had given him a word for me and my ministry. He first checked the word with his pastor, who was a dear friend and old Bible college buddy of mine. The pastor gave him the all clear to share it. I remember he began by saying, "Brother Nick, if you feel this word is not right for you, then I repent right now. But God asked me to say to you, 'Be still and know that I am God.'"

Two weeks later someone handed me a brochure regarding a large hotel in Elizabeth, New Jersey, that a church had endeavored to transform into an urban retreat center. It happened that we knew the pastor of the church quite well. I was told that the church was not able to make the retreat center happen and they were about to lose the building in foreclosure. I called and made an appointment to meet with the pastor.

Very quickly we worked out a lease/purchase agreement with the church, and as a result the bank did not foreclose on their mortgage.

The building was strategically located: just half a block from the center of Elizabeth, twenty minutes from midtown Manhattan via the New Jersey Transit trains, only two stops from Penn Station, and seven minutes from Newark International Airport. The hotel had 75,000 square feet of floor space on eleven levels. There were 105 hotel units, each with a private bath, eight meeting rooms, a 500-seat auditorium, reception areas, new full kitchen facilities, a dining room seating more than 100, a gift shop, a floor of offices, and an attractive two-story lobby. The facility was ideal for our vision! The church continued to hold services in the building, run the gift shop, and use the office space.

With a total of four of us on staff at the time, we prayed earnestly for God's direction. We would need to raise the lease payment of $14,000 a month immediately! In addition, the hotel had been built in 1928, and the 105 units were currently uninhabitable. We had been in similar situations before, but now the zeros made it so much larger than any challenge we had ever embraced.

"Why do four staff need 75,000 square feet of space?" asked one of my YWAM friends. Many others, I'm sure, were thinking the same thing.

After consultation with our board and other trusted confidants, we asked the Lord for His word and He gave us the story of Jonathan's armor bearer in 1 Samuel 14:7.

Jonathan was about to do something seemingly crazy and impossible. "Do all that you have in mind," his armor-bearer said. "Go ahead; I am with you heart and soul." So, we did.

For the next four years God brought tremendous fruitfulness to our ministry. We recruited over 400 volunteer mission builders, many of them professionals, who renovated four of the five floors of hotel units, making them habitable. Our staff grew from four to 65. We ran 12 training schools, all registered with YWAM's University of the Nations and supervised four Mission Bridge Schools (miniature versions of the YWAM DTSs but operated in local churches) with 296 students. We hosted 5,000 short-term missionaries evangelizing in the Greater New York area, and also helped to plant 10 new churches. Forty short-term mission teams were sent out to 30 nations. We conducted seven conferences with over 900 participants. Dave Adams led a King's Kids team to Ukraine, with our 17-year-old daughter Rebecca as the team choreographer. Our eldest daughter Anita married Ron Setran in the beautiful auditorium on September 5, 1992.

We never dreamed any of this could be possible when we said yes to God's direction. There had been no money, no guarantors: just a handful of staff who believed God meant it when He said, "Do all that you have in mind;, I am with you heart and soul!"

If Rozanne and I ever looked at our wallet to determine whether we should accept the next challenge God had for us, the answer would always be, "NO WAY!" Hearing God's voice, believing what He says, and taking the necessary steps of obedience while trusting in His character, was and is, all we know to do.

Joshua 3:13 says, "And as soon as the priests who carry the ark of the Lord—the Lord of all the earth—set foot in the Jordan, its waters flowing downstream will be cut off and stand up in a heap."

The Jordan never rolls back until you put your foot in it!

In 1991, Rozanne and I, along with Bill and Karen Blatz, ran two Mission Bridge Schools in churches on Long Island, both culminating with a two-week foreign outreach.

We shared with the students important lessons concerning God's character and how to receive clear direction from God by hearing His voice. Two very important foundational principles. "My sheep hear my voice and I know them…" John 14:21.

One student asked me, "Where are we going to do our outreach?" I will never forget the startled look on her face when I answered, "I don't know; we all need to pray." "You mean those of you leading this school don't even know where we are going to go for our outreach?" She seemed incredulous!

After sharing some teaching on intercessory prayer and hearing the voice of God, we gathered in small groups to pray and listen for God's direction. Each group chose a scribe to take notes. When it came time to report, one woman asked, "Is there such a country as Ukrania?" I responded, "Well, there is a country called Ukraine." Another student shared that she had received a picture of a woman with a scarf around her head and went on to describe a *babushka* (an older woman in Russia or Ukraine). Various other pieces of the puzzle were shared, and it became more and more clear that God had chosen Ukraine for our outreach.

This was during the period when the Iron Curtain was falling, as was the Soviet Union, of which Ukraine had been a part. No one knew if it was even possible for us to go there on outreach at this point. We began to do some research. Back in 1980, one of our teams had gone to Ukraine during the time of the Olympics in Moscow. The team was small and had to stay very clandestine. Back then Ukraine was firmly in the grip of the Soviet Union, and there was no freedom to share their faith.

Through God's direction we made contact with the pastor of a Ukrainian church in Union, New Jersey. He had been trained in a YWAM School of Evangelism and loved the mission. The pastor was happy to help us connect with the body of Christ in Ukraine. Well-known in the Christian community there, he proved to be a treasure chest of vital information. Through his contacts we were able to connect with two groups, one in Kiev and the other in Ternopil. These were not only our contacts for ministry, but also for housing, food, and a source through whom we ordered 20,000 Bibles which were printed in Ukraine in the Russian language!

The outreach was a huge success. We were given complete freedom to have outdoor meetings where hundreds of people gathered. We preached the gospel in the open with sound systems, had altar calls, and distributed free Bibles to the people at the end of each meeting. Bible distribution required a really good strategy as people would rush forward, almost crushing us, eager to obtain a copy of the Bible. Up until this time, the Bible had been outlawed.

Hundreds of people came to Christ and were followed up by the local churches we partnered with. The two-week outreach ended with a banquet such as I have never witnessed in my life! The food just kept coming, course after course, as the precious Christians there kept thanking us profusely for our labors among them.

My youngest daughter Melissa, who had just turned 13, was with me on this outreach. What a blessing she was to the team. I asked her recently what she remembers from that trip, and she said, "It was the joy of people finding freedom in Christ for the very first time and how they rushed us for Bibles!"

Short-term YWAM teams continued to visit Ukraine regularly after that, coordinated by Bill Blatz who partnered with the churches in Ukraine.

Kelly Hoodikoff, who served with us at the hotel in Elizabeth, met with our leadership one afternoon. Kelly shared that he felt God was speaking to him to take a team to Kiev and plant a permanent YWAM ministry in that city. As our short-term outreach leader, Kelly had led many teams to different nations of the world and had done an outstanding job. We commissioned him to direct the next DTS and recruit as many of the students as he could to help pioneer this new ministry.

The following is a report Kelly sent to us regarding the ministry in Kiev, originally pioneered by YWAM Metro New York:

> A team of five staff from YWAM New York (Kelly Hoodikoff, Vicki Messina, Jerry Perkins, Noemi Catinchi and Laura Slager) worked together to lead a YWAM New York DTS of 24 students on outreach to Ukraine in January 1993.
>
> We arrived in Kiev, Ukraine on January 6, 1993. That year, we hit the ground running with the DTS outreach and pioneering the YWAM base in Kiev. Eight students stayed on staff with

us which made our team a total of 13 people. Our vision was to reach Ukraine as a way to reach the nations and from day one engaged in the YWAM three-fold calling of evangelism, training and mercy ministry.

The Soviet Union had collapsed a few years prior and created a spiritual vacuum. Many people were coming to know Jesus. For the first five years, we hosted about 20 teams per year for a total of 100. These teams worked with over 60 churches in 30 cities throughout Ukraine. Each team came back with reports and powerful testimonies. A conservative estimate was that about 30,000 people came to know Jesus in those first five years. The harvest was ripe as many more tens of thousands came to faith as reported by other ministries and churches across the country.

Training was also a big part of the vision and in September of 1993, we pioneered the first DTS with 46 students and 14 staff. Many people said it would be impossible but this was a Word of the Lord to us and God was faithful every step of the way. Our vision was for the nations and believed that God not only wanted to bless Ukraine but that Ukraine would bless the nations by sending missionaries. So, our first outreach from Ukraine went to Russia and Kyrgyzstan. In later years, we sent teams to India, Kenya, Israel, Kazakhstan, Poland, Hungary, Romania, Bulgaria, Georgia, Armenia and Turkey.

The vision for training expanded to a holistic view of the nations with a message of the Kingdom of God. God began to lead us to develop a University of the Nations campus in Kyiv that would serve Eastern Europe. This was a huge vision but we already saw God answer prayer. So we began starting various schools within the University of the Nations (U of N) and by 2008, we ran 11 different training schools within 4 colleges of the U of N. During this time, we rented various facilities and in 2004 God answered our prayer and provided a

2.2-million-dollar gift to build a training campus in Kiev. It was truly a miracle and the staff were very excited.

There were many challenges along the way as we saw the enemy wanting to destroy this ministry. At one point, our neighbor tried to steal our property and made all sorts of threats. After a number of years in court, the land was deemed rightfully the ownership of YWAM. No one said that missions in the former Soviet Union was going to be easy.

Today, YWAM Kiev has a beautiful property on the outskirts of Kiev along the Dniper river. The land used to be an old summer camp during the Soviet days but we are now developing it into a campus to train and mobilize hundreds of students per year to take the Gospel into all the world and into every sphere of society.

Mercy ministry has also been a big part of the mission over the years. It began with serving street children in the mid-1990s and expanded to include crisis pregnancy, counseling, orphans, humanitarian aid, business training, HIV/AIDS seminars, hospital visits, refugees and launching a mobile dental clinic. Tens of thousands of people have been served, loved and heard the Gospel over the years.

Within the first 15 years, our staff grew to over 70 people from 14 nations. Many new ministries were launched that included King's Kids, Family Ministry, Sports Ministry, Church Planting, Boating Ministry, Anti-Human Trafficking Campaigns, Prayer Stations and Preschools to name a few. It would take a book to write about all their stories of adventure as they followed the Word of the Lord in faith and obedience.

The YWAM Kiev U of N campus has served to train many staff throughout Eastern Europe and has hosted multiple U of N International events and workshops. From Kiev, new YWAM bases were pioneered in Russia, Turkey and various cities throughout Ukraine. Many students have been trained and are serving throughout Ukraine and around the world. It would be difficult to now know the impact of this mission as God continues to see the fruit multiply globally.

In the fall of 2018, YWAM Kiev celebrated their 25-year anniversary. A few hundred people, including former staff, local leaders and friends came to thank God for all that He has done through this ministry over the years. A huge thank you to all the staff, volunteers, YWAM leaders abroad, families back home, local friends and supporters over the years who helped make this mission possible. May God get the glory!

Throughout the decades that we have been in ministry I have heard people complain about short-term missions. Some say it isn't worth the financial investment to send a team of people out to do something short term, claiming it is just giving them a free vacation. (Obviously they have never been on a short-term mission trip!) The money, they say, should be invested in career missionaries. However, we went to a nation with absolutely no assurance of being permitted to do any type of open evangelism. Not only did we see God do mighty things and bring many to Himself, but it opened the door for a permanent team to pioneer a new ministry in what was thought to be a closed country. That short-term outreach has now grown and multiplied itself to many other nations. Truly, little is much when God is in it!

In 1994, after working hard to raise the funds to purchase the hotel in Elizabeth, we realized we were running out of time to make it happen. Unfounded rumors were at work to undermine our credibility with the church that owned the building, and we were faced with an unthinkable reality: we needed to vacate.

The day we finished cleaning and left the hotel for the last time was one of the saddest days of my life. I had so many questions and absolutely no answers. I felt like I could never ever trust myself again to hear from God!

How would I face my YWAM colleagues the next time I met with them? What would I say when they asked, "Nick, what happened with the Elizabeth hotel?" I wanted to be able to give them a quick list of reasons why it didn't work out, but I didn't even have one that I felt was legitimate.

Rozanne and I were in the dining room, taking a break from cleaning the building that had been the launching pad for some of the most fruitful years of ministry we had ever experienced. While we sat silently sipping our glasses of water, Rozanne turned to me, took my hand, and asked a simple question, "Honey, where do we go from here?"

In the pit of my discouragement and disappointment, I snapped back at the love of my life and the co-founder of our ministry, "Please don't ask me any questions, I have no answers!" I saw the tears in her eyes as Rozanne quietly left the room. I was feeling sorry for myself and embarrassed that all that had been accomplished in the last four years now seemed to have blown up in my face.

"God, please tell me why all of this happened. Everything was going so well. I don't understand!" It was at that moment, as I paced the dining room alone, that God reminded me of Philippians 4:4-7: "Rejoice in the Lord always. I will say it again: Rejoice! Let your gentleness be evident to all. The Lord is nearby. Do not be anxious about anything, but in every situation, by prayer and petition, with thanksgiving, present your requests to God. *And the peace of God, which transcends all understanding, will guard your hearts and your minds in Christ Jesus* (italic added)."

God showed me that my wanting understanding now was for selfish reasons. I felt like I couldn't have His peace in my mind and heart without it. But His still small voice spoke: "Nick, I can give you peace without understanding if you will receive it from Me." I raised my hands toward heaven and replied, "Yes, Lord. Even though I don't understand, I do receive Your peace." Later I shared with Rozanne what God had done in my heart. I asked for, and received, her forgiveness.

I realized for the first time that, out of the death of our vision to raise 2.2 million dollars to purchase the hotel in Elizabeth, God brought resurrection! Our staff in Kiev were given that exact amount to build their ministry and training campus in Ukraine. The funds we prayed for were provided in God's way and in God's place. How great is our God!

Through many years afterwards, I lived in the abundance of God's peace. People would contact me with their questions: "How are you doing, what are you doing?" I would respond that even although I did not understand, I was at peace.

Still the rumor mill was grinding out all types of stories about me, the ministry, my integrity, and even about our marriage. God's peace remained abundant through it all!

Not long after we moved out of the building, I learned a judgment had been levied against our YWAM corporation. I was not overly surprised as two years earlier the Lord had impressed upon me the words from Psalm 69:4: "I am forced to restore what I did not steal."

Rozanne continues

Two years earlier, when Nick shared Psalm 69:4 with me, and said he felt God was impressing this scripture upon his heart, I remember commenting, "I don't think I like that scripture." At the time we both smiled.

Now that it was actually happening, that same scripture brought me comfort. All that really mattered was that we were innocent in God's eyes. We had not stolen, but given. Once again, we were so grateful for God's amazing love for us, and we knew that in His time and in His way, He would fulfill Romans 8:28: "And we know that in all things God works for the good of those who love Him, who have been called according to His purpose."

Those were extremely hard days as we both endeavored to make sense out of it all. One Friday afternoon I was driving to a women's retreat where I was the weekend speaker. While driving I was listening to a message I had been given called "What To Do When Your Dreams Don't Come True" by David Shibley, President of Global Advance and a much-respected missionary statesman.

It was a long drive from Long Island, across the Throgs Neck Bridge, onto the Cross Bronx Expressway, and eventually north on the NY Thruway. I listened patiently all the way as Reverend Shibley listed ten possible reasons why we had not seen our dreams come true. Not one applied to our situation. He paused, then added, "There is one other possible reason why our dreams suddenly do not come true." I perked up again, somehow sensing that I needed to pay close attention.

> "There was a missionary, a noted leader of the Baptist House in Jerusalem," Brother Shibley explained. "One day the missionary saw a young Arab boy playing alone in a field. The missionary knew it was a minefield. Without any thought for his own safety, he ran into the field, picked up the young boy and threw him clear of the danger. In the process the missionary lost his leg. To the villagers he was a hero, but not to the little boy. The little boy did not realize the magnitude of what had just happened to him. He felt hurt, intruded upon, forcibly shoved out of the way. He cried angrily because of the 'mean man' who had thrown him out of the way into the dirt as he was happily playing. As the boy grew, however, his gratitude and admiration grew for Dr. Lindsey. In retrospect he realized that he owed his life to this gallant Christian pastor."

David Shibley went on to explain that sometimes, on occasion, we can be working for God and having a wonderful time, and all of a sudden it is as if God just picks us up and throws us out. We are left, as it were, sitting on the sidewalk with our head spinning, and wondering what in the world just happened.

"That's it! That's exactly what happened," I thought. "But why?"

> "God sees things we can't see, He knows things we have no way of knowing, in His great love for us, He protects us and removes us from danger," David Shibley explained. "It may be years before you have answers, or you may never know. But you can trust the God who loves you and desires only the very best for you, your family, and your future."

For the first time in weeks, I was at peace. I couldn't wait to get home and tell Nick what I had heard.[2]

---

2. Twelve years later, by God's grace we were released from the judgement levied against the ministry and completely exonerated.

Nick continues

I was asked to provide leadership for March for Jesus in New York City. How wonderful it was to see the body of Christ from the Greater New York area come together each summer and march up Madison Avenue to a rally at a prayer gathering near the United Nations complex. My staff and I, along with many pastors and spiritual leaders in the city, were privileged to help organize the March for Jesus for three years. It was a blessed time of unity, witness, and spiritual warfare.

In that capacity, I had an appointment to meet with the assistant pastor of Times Square Church. Pastor David Wilkerson was the senior pastor of the church at that time. I told my friend who was with me that under no circumstances did I want to talk with Pastor Wilkerson, as he had given his endorsement to our fundraising campaign to buy the Elizabeth hotel. I knew there was a prophetic side to Pastor Dave, and I was afraid of what he might say to me about our failure to raise the funds and purchase the hotel.

Upon arriving at the church office, we were asked to wait in the lobby. The assistant pastor came over and apologized that he was not able to meet with us at the exact time of our appointment. He explained that he was providing counseling regarding a serious situation in the life of one of his parishioners and needed a little more time. We told him we could wait. He came back one more time and apologized again. Finally, he acknowledged that he was going to need much more time and had asked Pastor Wilkerson to meet with us instead. Suddenly I had a pit in my stomach.

Within a few minutes we were ushered into Pastor Dave's office. I made a quick decision that instead of waiting for Pastor Dave to ask me what happened, I would be forthright and say that I wanted him to know we had been unable to purchase the hotel and had already vacated the building.

Before I could say any more than that, Pastor Dave responded, "I want to know how you are doing."

Really? I was struck by the tenderness in his voice, and that he was much more concerned about me than about our project. I was able to tell him all God had spoken to me, and how He had given me the peace that transcends all understanding. He was pleased and prayed for me.

Chapter 10

Old Roots with New Shoots

In the late 80s, I was introduced to a wonderful Christian businessman with a heart as big as all outdoors. I will never forget that first meeting.

He was sitting at his desk and as I was about to shake his hand, he raised both his arms and simply said, "I don't know what you need, but I just want you to know I don't have anything to give you right now." (His business was suffering from a downturn in the market at the time.)

Smiling, I said that I hadn't come with my hand out looking for a donation, but only because our mutual friend thought it would be good if we met, and shared with him what our ministry was all about. "Fine," he said, and we had a very cordial first visit.

Just a few weeks later, on a Sunday morning, I was sitting in church prior to the start of the service and calling on the Lord for His help. Next week I needed $15,000 for a lease payment on the hotel and I had no idea where this money was going to come from. As I sat pondering all of this, someone tapped me on the shoulder. It was the Christian businessman I had met a few weeks before.

"Nick, I wanted you to know that I just wrote a check to the church, and I have asked them to give your ministry $15,000 from the amount I gave them." I sat stunned and almost speechless at both the goodness of our God and the generosity and love of this dear man. I had not said a word to anyone about needing the $15,000, but God heard my plea, and He laid it on the heart of my new friend!

After we lost the hotel, we moved the center of our operations to our home in Islip Terrace, Long Island: the property where I was raised. More specifically, we relocated to the garage where my dad had his ornamental iron business back in the '50s and early '60s. We built two offices and a half bath in there, and that became my retreat in the months that followed.

As a staff we were decentralized, living in four different parts of Long Island. Some members were assisting teams coming to work in the city, while others directed our DTSs from a 4-H club facility out on the east end of Long Island.

During those days my businessman friend would call me faithfully every couple of weeks. In his conversation he would always say something to the effect of, "Nick, how are you doing? You know God has a property for you and I'm going to help you." My response was always, "Thank you dear brother, I appreciate your encouragement. I am doing great and God's grace and peace are abundant." Truthfully, at that point in time, property was a dirty word. I had no interest in looking for, or trying to purchase, a facility for the ministry.

Five years passed since leaving the hotel. One day I received a phone call from a close friend and supporter, alerting me that a church property in Smithtown, Long Island, had just been put on the market. It was the original site of the church our family was currently attending.

I called my businessman friend and told him about it, and he lit up!

"Nick, I know the property well. My family attended church there for years, and it would be perfect for YWAM."

Months of negotiations ensued. With much help and a large investment from my friend, we were able to purchase the property on December 17, 1998. It became our YWAM ministry location for the next 18 years. There we ran Classic and Performing Arts Discipleship Training Schools, taught English to international students, and ran Mission Bridge Schools and large seminars as well as Mission Adventure and performing arts camps for teenagers. We hosted over 70,000 participants in our short-term City Outreach teams, while our Global Outreach teams reached 54 nations.

Rozanne continues

In addition to all the activities, no matter how busy the schedule became, we reserved one day every October to celebrate God's goodness and provision—**A Day of Celebration.**

One afternoon back in 2005 as I was reading I Chronicles 29 I was struck by the fact that although the temple had not yet been built, David was rejoicing and celebrating all of God's provision. He also kept careful and detailed records of all that God had given, reveling in the knowledge that all of it had come from the Lord. "Everything comes from you, and we have given you only what comes from your hand" (1 Chronicles 29:14).

I felt like a light bulb was going on in my mind! Whereas a celebration usually takes place when the building is complete and the project is finished, David was celebrating the process in detail as it unfolded and as the Lord provided. In fact, David would never build the temple: that privilege would go to his son, Solomon.

As I prayed over this chapter, it became clear that God wanted us to keep detailed records of every provision: financial and material, but especially people and the various ministries of the Base.

From that time on I began to write *The History of YWAM Metro New York* each year. Every single volunteer, intern, and Mission Builder, their names, where they were from, and their involvement. Every new staff member and student was welcomed, and celebrated. When a staff member completed five years of service, we would honor them as part of our Day of Celebration and present them with a commemorative gift. Every material and special financial provision, every school and outreach, every milestone, every Prayer Station sent out, all of it became a part of our history each year. Most of all, it was a day of praise and worship to the Lord for His amazing faithfulness. We took communion together and brought our Love Gifts to the altar. The day would end with a Love Feast as we gathered around the table and shared a special meal together. These days became precious to all of us. We looked forward to them and even dressed up for them (not a common occurrence in YWAM), and we rejoiced in God's love and faithfulness to His ministry.

One of our staff from Canton, Ohio, Cindy Mandrell, planned a unique and powerful outreach each year. On the first Saturday of June, teams from local churches converged on a chosen neighborhood for one day of community service. They would paint, pour concrete driveways, clean up yards, and install windows, doors, and porches, among other things. All supplies were donated, and the work was done by volunteers. They would also offer prayer and spiritual help to the people of the community. To date, 400 churches have been involved, 772 homes have been renovated, and 3,850 volunteers have participated. This ministry will now be replicated in other cities.

Nick continues

2001 is a year that lives in infamy for most of us. For our family and ministry however, it remains memorable for more than the events of 9/11.

It all began in February of that year, when we received news that Tammy Adams' mother had passed away after a long battle with cancer. Rozanne and I attended the funeral in South Jersey, and afterwards we encouraged Dave and Tammy to take some time off, as they had cared for Tammy's mom before her passing. A few weeks later we received the news that Tammy was being admitted to the hospital for emergency surgery. Dave called often, giving us updates on her condition.

One evening he shared that Tammy was not doing well and asked us to pray. He lingered on the phone, asking about our family and the ministry. He seemed reluctant to say goodbye. We had worked side by side for 21 years.

A week later I arrived home from the base, looking forward to a quiet evening with Rozanne. We had just settled on the couch after dinner when the phone rang. A mutual friend of ours and the Adams, was calling from South Jersey.

"Nick, are you sitting down?" he asked. I tried to brace myself for the worst possible news concerning Tammy. "Dave Adams passed away today of a massive heart attack just as he was preparing to go see his wife at the hospital."

"What? No!" My mind refused to wrap itself around this unexpected and seemingly impossible news, even as I relayed it to Rozanne. We were both in shock.

The following morning, we left for South Jersey to help the family cope with their dad's funeral arrangements while their mother was still not out of the woods in the hospital.

Over 600 people attended Dave's funeral. Tammy was granted a few hours of release from the hospital in a wheelchair with a nurse at her side. It was many weeks before Tammy was well enough to return home, and a year before we welcomed her back to our ministry.

In May, following that difficult time, we planned a trip to Sicily to visit my father's family. Our daughter Anita, her husband Ron, and our grandchildren, 4-year-old Caleb and 18-month-old Karissa, were going with us. It was a family trip we had planned for months, and we were all so excited.

That spring was especially financially stressful for our ministry. We had fallen behind with our accounts payable, and creditors were calling and threatening to cut off our utilities. YWAM Metro New York needed $43,000 immediately! The day before we were to board our flight to Rome, there was still no sign of any financial breakthrough. Meanwhile I was wrestling with leaving our staff in the lurch for two weeks. If something didn't happen immediately, within the next 24 hours, I knew I would have to cancel our plans.

I fasted and prayed that day and put up a sign on my office door that I was not to be disturbed. I cried out to the Lord for His help.

Back home, Rozanne was also praying desperate prayers for provision, and asking the Lord how we could possibly leave the next day.

Isaiah 55:12 popped into her head: "You will go out with joy and be led forth in peace, the mountains and hills will burst into song before you, and all the trees of the field will clap their hands." She knew God was about to make a way through the wilderness.

As I agonized in prayer, the Lord gave me a word from Galatians 6:9: "Let us not become weary in doing good, for at the proper time we will reap a harvest if we do not give up."

I remembered a poem that my pastor, Virginia Impellizzeri, had given me some years earlier. I had framed it and hung it on the wall of my office. It was entitled "Don't Quit" by John Greenleaf Whittier:

When things go wrong, as they sometimes will,
When the road you're trudging seems all uphill,
When funds are low and the debts are high,
And you want to smile but you have to sigh,
When care is pressing you down a bit,
Rest if you must, but don't you quit.

Often the struggler has given up
When he might have captured the victor's cup,
And he learned too late, when the night slipped down,
How close he was to the golden crown.

Success is failure turned inside out—
The silver tint of the clouds of doubt,
And you never can tell how close you are—
It may be near when it seems afar;
So, stick to the fight when you're hardest hit—
It's when things seem the worst that you mustn't quit.

I began to weep as the presence of the Lord swept over me. "Lord, I won't quit. I will be faithful."

It was then that I heard my daughter Anita's voice. Her office was in a separate house on the YWAM property, and she had run to find me. She burst through the door, waving a check in her hand. It was for $10,000 and was from a couple that I had reached out to some months earlier. Anita looked at me with a tentative smile. "Dad, please tell me this is for our general fund?" I smiled through some tears. "Yes, honey, that is general fund money. You can use it to pay bills." We both rejoiced and praised God!

Within an hour I received a phone call from the financial officer of one of our supporting churches, alerting me that he had a check for our ministry for $5,000. Could someone come over to his office to pick it up? Neither of these donors knew anything of our urgent need.

We now had the necessary finances to satisfy our most urgent creditors, releasing us to travel. God however, was not yet done....

That evening Rozanne and I were happily finishing up our packing when the phone rang. One of our board members was calling to share that while he was working. the Lord had told him to give our ministry $40,000! Our God is truly awesome!

The next morning, we did indeed "go out with joy, and were led forth with peace"! We enjoyed a wonderful two weeks, first in Rome as tourists, then visiting YWAM friends in Perugia, and finally to Sicily to visit family.

Upon our return we were able to satisfy every ministry account and a few more bills that had arrived during our absence. YWAM Metro New York was once again in the black. God's ways are indeed perfect and His timing impeccable.

Rozanne continues

My mum was ill with bladder cancer. Soon after we returned from Italy, my dad let me know that Mum's doctors were giving her about six months to live. For some reason I was not comfortable with their timeline. I felt God impressing me to book my flight immediately. My brother was in the States traveling and speaking, and I let him know I was leaving for New Zealand.

Upon my arrival, a friend met me. We drove out of the more populated area of Auckland and into the lush countryside, so beautiful that it always takes my breath away. I never get used to it: the lush green hills dotted with white sheep, the gorge with steep cliffs falling away into crystal streams below. I drank it all in like a thirsty soul in the desert. Somehow, I knew I needed to hold on to these precious moments, as the road ahead would be rocky.

Almost three hours later we arrived at the hospital, and I saw my mum for the first time in over a year. She treated me as if I had been with her an hour earlier. There was no recognition that I had just traveled more than 30 hours from New York.

I spoke privately with one of Mum's doctors. He told me we could take her home, as there was nothing else they could do. A hospice nurse would come daily to administer the medications that had already changed her personality, stolen some of her memory, and would take her even farther from me in the days ahead.

"How long does she have, doctor? My brother is in the States and I need to let him know."

"Approximately two weeks."

I cared for Mum at home along with a hospice nurse who stopped in each day. My dear friend Linda Cowie came daily to care for me as I cared for my mum. Linda was an angel: she prepared meals, greeted visitors, kept the tea kettle hot, massaged my feet, prayed for us all and ministered with such gentleness. David arrived three days before our precious mum went Home. I had been with her for 12 difficult and emotional days.

Just two months later it was 9/11/01!

Five years passed and Nick's brother, Angelo, developed kidney cancer, and my dad was diagnosed with Alzheimer's in New Zealand.

Nick and I cared for Angelo at home as he grew progressively worse.

One day I felt the Lord urging me to go be with my dad. His new wife, Annette, who had married my dad about 3 years earlier, had not indicated that there was any urgent need.

"Perhaps the Lord wants me to see Dad while he still recognizes me." I shared this thought with Nick, but how could I leave now when Angelo was so sick? I had no answer for that question, but I knew I had to go, and Nick was 100 percent supportive of my decision.

Dad was in a nursing home. He looked good the day I walked in—he knew me and was so happy to see me. The following Sunday, we brought him home for a family dinner. We asked him to say grace, and his prayer was perfect and beautiful. Dad thanked the Lord that we could all be together, and he was completely in the moment in all that he prayed. I shared with David later, "If we could just keep Dad praying, he would always be with us."

One week later he had a massive stroke in the nursing home. Annette and I took shifts each day sitting with him. David came as often as he could, but he was ill with non-Hodgkin's lymphoma, and I worried about him making the long trip back and forth from Tauranga.

Within a week our irreplaceable dad entered the presence of Jesus. Angelo was there to welcome his favorite friend, having entered eternity 33 hours earlier. Our family was in mourning on both sides of the world.

Meanwhile, David's illness progressed, but he continued his itinerate ministry as long as he could. When he would travel to the States, he always came to stay with us. We had a bedroom known as "David's room" with a closet full of his belongings. I will never forget the day he packed his bags full and told me to do what I wanted with the rest. We both knew he would not be coming back.

I desperately wanted to be with him every day, but I certainly longed to be there when the end was near. There was just one problem: David called me "the angel of death" because I knew when it was time to return home to New Zealand for both of our parents. He told me not to come.

In November of 2005 I prayed, "When should I go, Lord?"

"March, next year," was the clear reply.

"How will I tell David?"

Crickets.

In January an invitation came to my niece's wedding. It was for March 12 in New Zealand! Thank You, Jesus. How could my brother be surprised or concerned that I wanted to attend his daughter's wedding?

David was doing very well when I arrived. The following day was postcard perfect, and he took me for a ride to one of our favorite places,

Mount Maunganui. We sat in a cafe eating lunch and looking out over the water. I pumped him to tell me more of his amazing stories of missionary adventures. David had made over 90 trips into China smuggling Bibles and other Christian literature. He had also taken the gospel to many other places around the globe. His stories always blessed and challenged me.

The following morning, he had a doctor's appointment. I had planned to go with him, but due to jet lag I overslept. I heard him calling me when he arrived home, his wife Darlene was out running errands. We sat on the couch, and I knew he did not have good news.

His blood platelets were dangerously low, his cell transplant had not helped, there was nothing else they could do.

In that moment my heart broke. I put my arms around my brother. There were no words.

On March 12th I watched David slowly walk his lovely daughter through a garden to marry her best friend, but he was not well enough to stay for the reception. Cars and driving had always been one of David's passions, I didn't argue when he insisted on driving us away from the venue before the reception. However, I switched places with him a few miles down the road.

A month later as the sun was rising, Darlene, their children, one of their grandchildren, and I, were gathered at David's bedside as he entered the presence of his Lord and Savior, whom he loved and had served so faithfully. I was sitting by his head and I put mine down next to his on the pillow and cried inconsolably.

After a final goodbye to family and dear friends, I said *Kia ora* to my beloved homeland.

Nick continues

It was from our Long Island location that the Prayer Station ministry grew by leaps and bounds and eventually became global. Between 1992 and 2017, more than 1,000 Prayer Stations were built and shipped throughout the world in 11 different languages. In addition, approximately 200 churches from the Metro New York area were equipped with their own Prayer Stations.

Pastor Harry and Stephanie Berger from Harrisburg, Pennsylvania, asked if they could participate with us in one of the many Prayer Station outreaches we were leading in New York City. Harry and Stephanie were the parents of one of our staff members, and had ordered a Prayer Station for their ministry. They wanted some hands-on experience before using it in Harrisburg. We mobilized a team to 14th Street in Manhattan, not far from Union Square. I led the team, and we prayed specifically, asking for divine encounters.

Soon after, I noticed an Asian young man walking down the street toward me, and I asked, "May I pray for you?". He looked somewhat surprised and unsure at first, so I probed a little deeper. He told me his name was Guihan, and that he was from China. Eventually he relaxed and even shared a rather personal prayer request, asking for wisdom regarding a young woman he had a relationship with in China. "I am thinking of proposing to her and just want to know if she is the right girl." I prayed for him and his girlfriend asking God to give him under-standing as to whether she was to be his wife.

We prayed and then talked some more. He was very friendly and told me he had come to the US to do his graduate work. He had his mas-ter's degree and was now in a doctorate program. We spoke regarding his life and his experiences in the United States. He was an agnostic, but not at all hostile to the gospel. He was actually very receptive, though guarded. After talking for close to two hours, I asked if he was ready to commit his life to Jesus.

"No, I am not there yet, but I will think about everything you said."

I gave him a copy of the Gospel of John, and we exchanged contact information. Guihan glanced at my business card and asked where I lived. I told him Islip Terrace, Long Island. Guihan had spent the past summer doing an internship in East Islip, just three miles from my home! He told me he might be going back for another summer internship in June. "That would be wonderful," I replied. "If you do please let me know, and we can meet again and have lunch together." He smiled, and we parted.

The moment I left Guihan, I heard the Lord clearly speak to me: "I want you to pray for Guihan's salvation every day." I obeyed the Lord and included him in my daily intercessions.

In June of 2007 I was at LaGuardia Airport in Queens waiting to go through security when my cell phone rang.

"Hello Nick, this is Guihan. Do you remember me?"

"Do I remember you? I have been praying for you every day since we met back in March!"

There was a pause, "You have?" Guihan shared that he was back on Long Island in East Islip for the summer, continuing his internship. Then he added, "Nick, do you remember you prayed for me about the girl I was interested in?"

"Yes," I said.

"Well, I went back to China and we're married. Her name is Lily and she is with me now."

I was about to go through security, so I told Guihan I would be back home on Sunday. I asked him to call again on Monday and we would set a time for us to have lunch together. He called, and Rozanne and I had the joy of meeting sweet Lily and sharing together.

Guihan, Lily, Rozanne, and I met often after that. At the end of each meeting, we would have prayer together. On one occasion Guihan and Lily invited us to their apartment, as they wanted to cook us an authentic Chinese meal. At the conclusion of the evening we prayed for them. Lily lifted her face, tears running down her cheeks, and said, "I feel so warm all over."

Guihan and Lily came frequently to the YWAM Center for meals and special occasions. They loved it, and the YWAMer's loved them.

The summer ended and Guihan was working with a company in our area. We continued to fellowship together, and prayed often for their salvation.

In the fall I received an email. Guihan and Lily had found a Chinese church on Long Island and were beginning to attend. Such fantastic news!

Just a few weeks later they shared, "Nick, you and Rozanne will be happy to know that yesterday at church we went forward and received Christ as our Savior." Heaven rejoiced, and so did we! *Five Little Words* had changed two lives.

When Lily gave birth to their first child, David, our godson, Guihan's mother came to visit them from China. She began to attend church with them and also gave her heart to the Lord. We were invited to the service where Guihan, Lily, and Guihan's mother were all baptized as a family. Not many weeks later, Guihan's father arrived for a long visit. He also became a Christian and was baptized. Upon their return to China, Guihan's parents started to attend a church in their home town.

Not only had God answered our prayer on that day in March 2007 for a divine appointment at the Prayer Station, but in His time a whole family came to Christ. *Five Little Words* can change a family and a community.

Chapter 11

"Follow"

When God first spoke to us to go to New York, it was not a hard sell. We both loved the city and were enthusiastic at the thought of spending the rest of our lives there. Surely this was what everything else had been about: all the struggles, the tests, the training were preparation to impact the Big Apple. Or so we thought.

For 29 years we lived on Long Island. All but the first two years we were in the home my parents bought in 1949 when I was just three years old. I was raised there and loved it. Every square inch of the house and ¾-acre property, was chock-full of memories.

It had begun as a little duplex bungalow that my dad kept adding on too. Eventually it became a two-story home with a three-bedroom, two-bath apartment on each level and a large workshop out back.

The upper apartment of the house was where my two brothers Angelo, Carmelo and my cousin, Sonny, lived. Rozanne and I and our three girls moved into the main floor of the family home. This place would become as dear to our three daughters growing up, as it was to me. Here they finished their education, brought home various hopeful young men to meet mum and dad, and from there they married and departed one by one.

Rozanne continues

Anita met Ron Setran at Smithtown Gospel Tabernacle Youth Group, and they were married in September 1992 at the Elizabeth hotel. Shortly after their marriage they attended a DTS in Lakeside, Montana, together. They have three children. Caleb (who is married to his lovely wife, Diana), Karissa, and our special treasure Kiersten. Kiersten was born with Down Syndrome and a very large hole in her walnut-sized heart requiring surgery. At nine weeks old she had the operation at Columbia Presbyterian Children's Hospital in Manhattan. Anita and I spent nine days there with her, Anita never leaving her bedside. The surgery was successful, and today our treasure has a perfect heart. Kiersten graduated high school in 2021.

In sixth grade Rebecca heard the Lord speak to her and say, "Your husband is in this class." Rebecca looked around and said, "Oh please Lord, NO!" A few years later when she was in high school, one of her sixth grade classmates became her best friend. He would go to the mall with her when she needed help picking the right dress for a special date. He was the first one she would call if she had something to share, or when her heart was broken over some other guy. He was patient, persistent, and not willing to give up hope that one day Rebecca would know what he had known for a long time. Rebecca graduated and went off to DTS in Quebec. He joined the Continental Singers and traveled across the US and parts of Europe. They communicated regularly through letters. Eventually, in God's perfect timing, Rebecca married her very best friend, Dan Burd, in March of 1996 at Smithtown Gospel Tabernacle on Long Island. They now have three sons, Tyler, Toby, and Malakai. I am happy to report that Dan and Rebecca are still best friends.

Melissa was our quiet one. With two older, extroverted sisters, it wasn't easy for her to get a word in edgewise at the dinner table. We would joke that we didn't really know Melissa could talk until her big sisters left home. Still waters run deep, and that proved true with our beautiful, intelligent, and well-read youngest. I loved being alone in the car with her when she was a teenager. I could ask any question about anything, and she would give me a well-thought-out response that would leave me in awe. Melissa remains a fountain of wisdom and knowledge for anyone smart enough to let her do the talking. After her sisters were married, I told Melissa I needed a break from weddings! "No worries Mum, I intend to travel. I have no plans to marry for many years after I graduate." Famous last words! While in high school, Melissa started working nights to help raise money to attend DTS in my homeland. The very night she started her new job, so did a tall, handsome young man, Erik Schindler. They were married at our YWAM Center in May, 1999, and they have given us three more beautiful grandchildren, Diana, Aidan, and Liam.

All three of our children's families have experienced major health issues over the past two decades, and have seen remarkable divine intervention through faith, much prayer and perseverance.

After being misdiagnosed for 17 years, during which time Rebecca was desperately ill and eventually bedridden, our precious daughter was finally correctly diagnosed with Late-Stage Neurological Lyme Disease. Although just having a "name" after so many years was a relief, finding the correct protocol was yet another journey that I will leave for Rebecca and Dan to tell one day when they are ready. It took 13 years from diagnosis to Rebecca, once again, being able to fully embrace their ministry to teenagers, "Speak Life—End Bullying the Musical."

In 2009 Melissa's husband Erik, was diagnosed with pulmonary hypertension, also having been misdiagnosed for many years. His health steadily declined and on June 6, 2018 Erik was airlifted to Tampa General Hospital. Melissa and I drove over the following day, and so began seven agonizing weeks as the Schindler and Savoca families prayed and waited for new lungs for Erik. With very little time left, Erik received new lungs the night of July 24th. Our hotel room, where family had gathered, erupted in praise, worship and dancing after receiving the news! It has been a long journey, but today Erik is amazing us all, including his doctors.

Ron and Anita were diagnosed with COVID-19 in September of 2021. Anita, was told by her doctor to call an ambulance and go immediately to the ER as she was continuing to decline. With much prayer and the help of family, she was able to recover at home. However, Ron quickly progressed to COVID pneumonia and was rushed by ambulance to a local hospital. Two days later he was moved into the Covid ICU, where he continued to decline. Friends from the body of Christ around the world prayed fervently for his healing. To the amazement of his medical team Ron literally improved overnight. After eight days, as the nurse transported Ron out of the ICU, Ron asked, "How often do you get to do this?" "Not very often at all, most patients in the ICU never get to see their families again," his nurse replied.

Nick continues

For 23 years we cared for my brothers and my cousin. Following their passing, we housed a few staff in our home, providing them with an affordable place to live while working with YWAM Metro New York. We had no plans to move and no desire to go anywhere else.

Eventually Rozanne began to have more and more health issues, especially during the hard New York winters. A native New Zealander with chronic asthma, she had lived in the northeastern US and southwestern Canada, practically all of her adult life. The cold winters were now beginning to take a toll on her. She began to suffer from pneumonia, the flu, and/or chronic bronchitis more regularly. Twice she was so sick she passed out, requiring an ambulance to take her to the hospital. Our daughters and I were becoming concerned. Rozanne's doctors told me a warm, humid climate would help her condition enormously.

In 2014 our youngest daughter, Melissa and family, decided to make a move to Jupiter, Florida after Erik was diagnosed with pulmonary hypertension. His doctors had also recommended a warmer climate.

Rozanne continues

In the fall of 2014, I flew down to Jupiter for the first time, to visit Melissa and the family. As the wheels touched the runway at Palm Beach

International Airport, I was gazing out of the small window at sunshine and palm trees. At that very moment I heard myself think, "I'm home." "Home?" I responded, knowing Who just dropped that thought into my head. "But Lord, we live in New York. New York has been our home for the past 29 years."

Nothing else was communicated, but like Mary, I pondered those two words in my heart during the time I spent with Melissa. We even looked at a couple of homes under construction, and of course I shared the experience with Nick.

Nick continues

The summer before, I had led a team to downtown Brooklyn, joining with some of our friends who had a regular Prayer Station ministry near Borough Hall. That evening we took the team to Brooklyn Tabernacle for the midweek prayer meeting.

Pastor Cymbala spoke from Genesis 12:1 (NKJV): "Now the Lord had said to Abram: 'Get out of your country, from your family and from your father's house, to a land that I will show you.'"

It was another emotional moment for me as the words of that verse leapt off the page and brought tears to my eyes. I did not fully understand all God was saying, but I knew it was a *kairos* (opportune) moment. I was living in my father's house. Was God saying we were to make a move? If so, where?

In January of 2015 Rozanne and I flew to Florida together to visit Melissa, Erik and our grandchildren. Never in my wildest dreams did I ever expect to live in Florida, but while visiting I heard the Lord speak to me again.

"Rozanne has followed you to every place I have led you both to go for over 46 years, without ever complaining. Now it is time for you to follow her." God's Word to me was as clear as I have ever heard Him speak. We began to do some serious house searching.

The previous year, without any inkling that change was coming, we had put into motion a process to get our Long Island home up to code. Among other things, I knew that our home did not have a legal

Certificate of Occupancy, (C of O) due to my dad adding rooms to the house without obtaining the legal permits and inspections. God orchestrated miracles for us! We were able to obtain not only a C of O on the two apartments in our home, but also on the back building. We ended up owning the only home within many miles of our neighborhood to have a legal two-family house Certificate of Occupancy!

Our home went on the market, and within three weeks we had a buyer. The Savoca family had lived at 780 Greenlawn Avenue since 1949, and we had the biggest yard sale imaginable, giving away much more than we sold. The leftovers filled a box truck!

We closed on July 1, 2015. It was a difficult day in many ways, but also a day full of promise and excitement as we anticipated a new beginning. That same day Rozanne and I loaded our Honda Accord and headed down to Florida, visiting friends and supporters along the way.

We had seen a newly built home we liked very much in May of that year, but because we had not yet closed on our Long Island home, they wouldn't allow us to enter into a contract to buy. The contractor held out no hope that the house would still be available in three months, which was when we were due to close. Every evening Rozanne would house hunt on her computer, and each night the last home she would go to was the new build. Her heart was set on that home, and she was praying it would not sell until we could get back to Florida with cash in hand.

On July 30, 2015, we closed on that home, the house the Lord had saved for us, at a much lower price than we would have paid three months earlier. We moved in immediately, sleeping on the floor until our furniture arrived. We were just one mile from Erik and Melissa.

Our initial plan was to eventually move the Prayer Station ministry down to Jupiter. Our oldest daughter Anita was the director of YWAM Smithtown, New York. I began to travel back and forth from Jupiter to Long Island at least twice a month to assist her, and continue our work with Prayer Stations.

Rozanne continues

Anita's heart had always been to serve with her dad. She began doing that when she was still in high school, working as bookkeeper for the ministry when she was just 16. Although she was fully capable, directing a YWAM Center without her father was not her passion.

Unexpectedly, her husband Ron was laid off from the job he had held for 15 years. He was given a severance package of six months with full pay. Was God up to something? It wasn't long before Ron and Anita shared with us their desire to assist in establishing the Prayer Station ministry in Florida.

Not knowing how all of this would work, we prayed earnestly that God would give us wisdom. "In his heart a man plans his course, but the Lord determines his steps" (Proverbs 16:9).

Nick continues

One morning as I rose for my devotional time with the Lord, I heard God speak to me. "Move the whole ministry down to Jupiter and focus all your efforts on Prayer Stations."

This was such a revolutionary idea that I was not sure it would sit well with our board and YWAM leadership, but at the next annual meeting of our board I made the proposal. They were unanimously in agreement that we should sell the Smithtown campus and invest the assets into Prayer Stations.

My heart leapt! After 25 years of trying to fit the Prayer Station ministry into the larger vision of running schools, outreaches, housing staff and students, and all that running a large YWAM Center involves, finally God's gracious vision that He had shared with us would be put front and center!

We shared the great news with our staff in New York. In the beginning many were excited and ready to make the move with us. Later, however, one by one they shared that God had given them new directions. We released each one with our blessings, hugs, prayers, and some tears.

The Smithtown campus went on the market, and we prayed that God would help us keep it in His kingdom. Many religious groups came to look at it. Finally a new church plant from the largest church in New York City contacted us, and we closed with them on September 8, 2017.

After much prayer and searching, God helped us find the perfect property in the town of Jupiter Farms, Florida: one that provided not only living and office space, but additional acreage to build a workshop. Within a year construction was complete, and for the first time in 27 years Prayer Stations had a beautiful, fully-equipped home!

One morning I read the well-known story of Jesus turning water into wine at the wedding celebration in Cana. As I read John chapter two, verse 10 seemed to pop off the page: "Everyone brings out the choice wine first and then the cheaper wine after the guests have had too much to drink; but you have saved the best till now."

The last few words of that verse penetrated my heart, and I heard the Lord speak: "Nick, I have saved the best till last."

Rozanne and I had been in ministry for a combined 100 years! Apparently our awesome and faithful God, Who had walked and talked with us all these years, still had a hope and a future for us.

Since 1992 I had longed to put the ministry of Prayer Stations front and center. Reaching the lost and the hurting, praying for desperate individuals, and bringing hope, salvation, faith, and a future through this simple tool had been my dream. At last, it was happening!

The mission of Prayer Stations is to provide a proven, effective, and fruitful evangelism strategy. It began in New York City and is now a global force in every continent of the world except Antarctica. It is a simple tool for the body of Christ to use to reach out to the lost with God's grace, favor, and power through prayer.

In 2020, during the COVID-19 pandemic, a sister ministry of ours in New York City, The New York School of Urban Ministry (NYSUM) took up the same mantle God gave YWAM during the 9/11 tragedy. With our assistance they are using 20 Prayer Stations to mobilize the churches in the city and reach out to people who have been devastated by the COVID-19 virus.

Today our challenge is to raise up an army of Prayer Station First Responders, teams that are ready to mobilize within 48 hours of a disaster. "EQUIP" training seminars prepare Christians to work alongside other first responders through the Prayer Station ministry.

Chapter 12

The Great Commission

Following the resurrection, the Bible tells us in Acts 1:3 that Jesus appeared to His disciples on five different occasions over a period of 40 days. It is interesting that in some of these appearances the disciples did not recognize Him (John 20:14; John 21:4; Luke 24:15-16). There is an important message here. Jesus does not always present Himself to us as we think He should. We need to be careful not to miss Him just because of preconceived ideas of Who we think He is.

Jesus wanted to make sure there was no question, especially in the hearts and minds of His disciples and followers, that He was indeed risen from the dead.

He wanted to bring them comfort, challenge their commitment to Him, and reinforce the teachings He had shared with them during the three and a half years they spent together.

Finally, in His last hours on earth, He wanted to emphasize the most important message of all.

Imagine their anticipation, the hush that must have fallen over them, the weight of that moment.

Final Words

Anyone who has an opportunity to share some final words with those they love, will prepare very carefully, prioritizing their thoughts so as to speak only of the most important things on their heart.

We can only imagine how it must have felt to be one of the 500 present at Christ's ascension. Jesus, whom they had walked with, shared bread with, who had fed multitudes, healed the sick, cast out demons, raised the dead, and who ultimately conquered death, was about to share His most important message. Scarcely daring to breathe, not wanting to miss a single word, they waited.

Would He underscore the importance of loving one another, meeting together regularly, studying and meditating on the Scriptures, taking care of the poor and the widows, praying for the sick and casting out demons? Or would He remind them to never overlook the children, to play with them as He loved to do, to remind them that their Heavenly Father loves them? Would He reiterate one of hundreds of other things He had taught over the years they had been together?

Before His death and resurrection Jesus had spent 40 days of communion alone with His Father.

Time to think, talk and pray about what His final words to His followers should be. His words would have been chosen only after hearing the heart of the Father. Mark 16:15 and Matthew 28:19 record those most important final words.

Jesus said, "Go into all the world and preach the gospel to all creation" (Mark 16:15).

Christians refer to this scripture as "The Great Commission" or "The Last Commandment." These words were marching orders. Jesus did not say "Grow" but "GO"! It was a call to action! Heaven's top priority, the most important agenda.

The great missionary to China, Hudson Taylor, said it best, "The Great Commission is not an option to be considered; it is a command to be obeyed."

Were they already so perfect that they were no longer in need of more in-depth discipleship? Not at all. In fact, when we realize how much His followers didn't understand, it is amazing that Jesus would want them to represent Him to a lost world at all!

Most of the time as we read through the four Gospels, we find that the disciples and Jesus were frequently not on the same page. They had little understanding regarding what He desired to teach them, no understanding of the Cross, no knowledge of why He came to the earth and God's plan of salvation for mankind.

The Dirty Dozen

I once heard a story about a certain pastor who wanted to do a series of sermons on the lives of the disciples. He began to consider what the title should be. After careful study of their lives, he decided on "The Dirty Dozen"! For most of the three and a half years they spent together, the disciples who had come from a variety of different backgrounds, were remarkably clueless and not in sync with who Jesus was and what He had come to accomplish on the earth.

Jesus was totally aware of their deficiencies. They had been given all the pieces of the puzzle, but somehow didn't understand how to fit them all together. For this reason, He gave them detailed instructions.

Before they began their ministry they must first wait for the power of the Holy Spirit in Jerusalem.

"I am going to send you what my Father has promised; but stay in the city until you have been clothed with power from on high" (Luke 24:49).

Jesus made Himself very clear when He gave the 500 His "Last Commandment." He looked directly at them and said, "YOU, GO."

He laid down one of the most important principles for all of His disciples to follow. They were the ones who were to take the initiative and GO to where the people are.

Go Means a Change of Location

Loren Cunningham, co-founder of YWAM stated it this way, "Go means a change of location." You can't go and stay where you are, and neither should we expect the people of this world to come to us.

Many criticize Christians because they GO to people all over the world to "proselytize" them. Often in my lifetime, while sharing my faith, I have been asked by some who are unsympathetic to the gospel, "Why do you Christians insist on trying to make everyone else accept your gospel message?"

My response is simple, "For starters, this is not our idea. It was Christ's idea and He asked us to share it all over the world to all of His creation."

Charles Spurgeon, an English Baptist preacher, known as the "Prince of Preachers," was asked by a student, "'Will the heathen who have not heard the gospel be saved?"

His answer, "It is more a question with me whether we, who have the gospel and fail to give it to those who have not, can be saved."

Evangelism Is a Privilege

Over the years I have shared what I believe to be the Biblical view of evangelism.

The apostle Paul put it this way, "I thank Christ Jesus our Lord, who has given me strength to do his work. He considered me trustworthy and appointed me to serve him" (1 Timothy 1:12 NLT).

Paul counted it a privilege that God called him into His service. He wasn't complaining even though his Christian life was filled with suffering.

"What is more, I consider everything a loss because of the surpassing worth of knowing Christ Jesus my Lord, for whose sake I have lost all things. I consider them garbage, that I may gain Christ" (Philippians 3:8).

Paul knew, as few other Christians have known, what suffering for the sake of the Gospel really means. In 2 Corinthians 11:23-28. Paul wrote,

Are they servants of Christ? (I am out of my mind to talk like this.) I am more. I have worked much harder, been in prison more frequently, been flogged more severely, and been exposed to death again and again.

Five times I received from the Jews the forty lashes minus one.

Three times I was beaten with rods, once I was pelted with stones, three times I was shipwrecked, I spent a night and a day in the open sea,

I have been constantly on the move. I have been in danger from rivers, in danger from bandits, in danger from my fellow Jews, in danger from Gentiles; in danger in the city, in danger in the country, in danger at sea; and in danger from false believers.

I have labored and toiled and have often gone without sleep; I have known hunger and thirst and have often gone without food; I have been cold and naked. Besides everything else, I face daily the pressure of my concern for all the churches."

In spite of all this suffering he had no regrets and even added that he was privileged to be counted trustworthy for Christ's service.

When I was receiving my training in Bible college, I remember one of my teachers sharing this simple quote with me from Jordan Grooms. I have never forgotten it. "If God calls you to be a missionary, don't stoop to be a king."

In Isaiah 52:7 the Scripture says, "How beautiful on the mountains are the feet of those who bring good news, who proclaim peace, who bring good tidings, who proclaim salvation, who say to Zion, 'Your God reigns!'"

I pondered the question, why did Jesus give the church the Great Commission to take the gospel to the world and to every creature. Did God have any other options? With my knowledge of God and the scriptures, I could think of at least two others. One was to do world evangelization all on His own without the assistance of any other being in the universe. After all, He is omnipresent, meaning He can be everywhere all at the same time. He could have chosen this option.

Just think with me for a moment. He knows every moral being on earth (after all He created them). He knows their ethnicity, race, language, background, their thoughts and questions, their history... everything! He could appear to each one individually, and with total sensitivity share with them their need of a Savior. Think of it, no need to learn a language, study a culture, travel, literature, housing and feeding of workers, etc. Not only that, no problem with the purity of the message, MEGA ANOINTING! Bang! In no time the world is evangelized and every being has the opportunity to make a choice.

Then there is also the option of Jesus asking the angelic host of heaven to do the job. God could have looked down on our pathetic performance and turned to His archangels, Gabriel and Michael and said in effect, "Hey guys, meet me in My office, I have a mission for you to do for Me." How many angels are there? The Bible says "myriads." No one really knows how many that is, but I guarantee there would be no problem with them appearing to every person individually. Angels have a much better track record with obedience than humans do and they would have many of the benefits I attributed to God regarding sensitivity, language, presentation of the gospel, etc. Closure to the Great Commission in no more than one day!

So why did God give this commission to the church? We have not done a very good job of it in more than 2000 years. We have majored in the minors and minored in the majors! We have certainly not prioritized His last commandment. Today it is estimated that there are 7.9 billion people in the world. 2.3 billion are Christian (748 million are Evangelical Christian)[3]. Joshua Project; Barrett and Johnson 2001, 20

I have come to the conclusion that God asked His church to bring closure to the challenge of world evangelization because it is simply our privilege to partner with Him! Not to make our lives difficult, or to put us in peril, but because He knew it would be our greatest joy.

I remember the day I received Christ into my life as a nine-year-old boy. It was such a happy day, a day I will never forget. I have to say though, that I have actually experienced greater joy and blessing leading others to

---

3. Joshua Project; Barrett and Johnson 2001, 20

Christ. What a privilege! The well-known missionary to Africa, David Livingstone, said, "People talk of the sacrifice I have made in spending so much of my life in Africa. It is emphatically no sacrifice. Say rather it is a privilege."

In my first year in YWAM I will never forget how God brought home to me this wonderful understanding regarding the privilege it was to serve Him. It was through a very homely experience I had while Rozanne, Anita and I were living in upstate New York.

One morning Rozanne took Anita, who was barely two years old, to pick up some groceries. I, meanwhile, was working on my typewriter at the dining room table which doubled as my office. When I heard our car pulling onto the gravel driveway, I grabbed my coat and went out to help bring in the bags of groceries, placing them on the other end of the table. As I went back to my work, I observed that Anita had decided to help unpack the bags of groceries. She climbed up on one of the dining room chairs, reached into a bag, picked out a can and climbed back down. She then carried it with both hands to the cabinet under the kitchen counter where we kept our canned food and placed it inside. I watched this with great concern, for fear that Anita would fall, drop the can on her foot, or some other catastrophic event would happen. She returned to the table and began the whole routine over again. I grimaced with each can she reached for and was about to "rescue her," when Rozanne caught my eye. I knew that look, and so I tried to return to my typing, but clandestinely I continued to watch all of this unfold.

I wondered why Rozanne took the risk of allowing Anita to "help" when obviously she was slowing down the process. Normally Rozanne is very efficient and well organized. I have often said that she can get more done in an hour than I can in a whole day, and all without making a list! Why then was she willing to take the risk of having a two-year-old help her when she could do it so much more efficiently on her own?

The answer was all over Anita's face when the job was done, she was smiling from ear to ear—she had helped Mummy! Her joy in being "Mummy's little helper" as a toddler was building her self-assurance and her self-esteem, teaching her the joy of serving others. (Something she has continued to do all through her life.)

In that moment the Holy Spirit spoke to me, "That's why I have you working with Me to reach the world with the gospel."

What a privilege and joy to be His "helper."

To be a soul winner is the happiest thing in this world. And with every soul you bring to Jesus Christ, you seem to get a new heaven here upon earth.—*Charles Spurgeon*

It is the greatest pleasure of living to win souls to Christ.—*Dwight L. Moody*

Evangelism Is a Responsibility

Somewhere I learned that in the Kingdom of God there is an equation that goes PRIVILEGE = RESPONSIBILITY. For every privilege we enjoy there is a corresponding responsibility.

Jesus said it this way, "When someone has been given much, much will be required in return; and when someone has been entrusted with much, even more will be required" (Luke 12:48 NLT).

God has entrusted us with Truth. He has also given us a mandate to share that Truth with the whole world, everyone! Our privilege is not just to know the truth of the gospel, but also to share it.

Ezra 7:10 says, "For Ezra had devoted himself to the study and observance of the Law of the Lord, and to teaching its decrees and laws in Israel." This gives us a wonderful understanding of what we are to do when it comes to the Truth of God. Ezra, the high priest, first devoted himself to **study** God's Word. The next progression was to **observe or obey** what he read and studied, and finally to **teach** it in Israel. So, it should be with every Christian. When God entrusts us with His Truth our first application should be to study it, then to live it, and ultimately to put it into practice and share it.

Someone once used the geography of the Holy Land to illustrate how this ought to work.

The Jordan River flows southward from its sources in the mountainous area where Israel, Syria and Lebanon meet. It then passes through the Sea of Galilee continuing its flow south until it reaches the Dead Sea. The lesson is that the Jordan flows into the Sea of Galilee from the north and exits from the south. Because the Sea of Galilee receives the Jordan and then gives it out, it is full of life. The Gospels are replete with stories of the disciples fishing and harvesting a great catch from that beautiful body of water.

The difference between the Sea of Galilee and the Dead Sea is that the Dead Sea does not have an exit point. What comes into it stagnates and dies. You could have the best bait in the world and the best fishing equipment, but never catch a thing in the Dead Sea. God has called us to be Sea of Galilee Christians, not Dead Sea Christians! If all we do is receive truth and never share it, then like the Dead Sea that truth will die. Truth must always have an inlet and an outlet.

Dawson Trotman, founder of The Navigators shared a forty-seven-minute message with his staff in 1955 entitled "Born to Reproduce." This was a message that burned deeply in his soul. It was transcribed and published as a booklet that has been read by thousands over the past 65 years. He made the case that every Christian was born to reproduce him or herself in others. It is consistent with the commission Jesus gave the church. It is not a commandment given to just pastors, ministers and missionaries, but the whole church. There were not just the 11 disciples on the Mount when Jesus gave us this order. All of His followers were present and so we also have been given the same commandment.

These days you can buy seedless grapes, watermelons, citrus or tomatoes, but there is no such thing as a seedless Christian! God has placed within us the seeds to reproduce in others the life He has given to us. Children are the natural outcome of the loving union between a husband and wife. If a couple cannot have their own children, it indicates a problem in their reproductive organs. I have always believed that the primary reason God keeps us on planet earth after we come to know Him, is because we have a mission, to bring more children to Himself.

R.A. Torrey, the great American, evangelist, pastor and educator said, "To win men to acceptance of Jesus Christ as Savior and Lord is the only reason Christians are left in this world."

Today statistics say that only 8 percent of regular church attenders believe that sharing their faith is "very important." 74 percent of Christians seldom have a "spiritual conversation" with anyone. Here is a shocker, 51 percent of U.S. churchgoers say they've never heard of the term "The Great Commission"!

David Jeremiah, the evangelical Christian author, founder of Turning Point Radio and Television Ministries and senior pastor of Shadow Mountain Community Church, put it this way, "It's a sad fact that the vast majority of people who sit in the pews on Sunday never tell anybody about Christ on Monday."

I believe God is serious about this whole business of evangelism being our responsibility.

God said to Ezekiel, "When I say to the wicked, 'You will certainly die,' and you do not warn him—you do not speak out to warn the wicked to turn from his wicked lifestyle so that he may live—that wicked person will die for his iniquity, but I will hold you accountable for his death" (Ezekiel 3:18 NET BIBLE).

I am not making the case that we need to involve ourselves in evangelism because if we don't, "God is going to get us." This should never be the motivation for our service to the Lord as I will discuss more fully in the next chapter.

Evangelism Is a Necessity

Paul the apostle shared with us some very profound logic in Romans 10:13-15. "For everyone who calls on the name of the Lord will be saved. But how can they call on him to save them unless they believe in him? And how can they believe in him if they have never heard about him? And how can they hear about him unless someone tells them? And how will anyone go and tell them without being sent? That is why the Scriptures say, how beautiful on the mountains are the feet of those who bring good news, who proclaim peace, who bring good tidings, who proclaim salvation."

This begins by giving us the wonderful proclamation, "Everyone who calls on the name of the Lord will be saved." To which the Church says a hearty AMEN! He then follows the logic that you cannot call on the Savior unless you believe in Him and goes further, you cannot believe unless you have heard about Him, and then, you cannot hear unless someone tells you about Him, and finally you cannot have someone tell you about Him unless he or she is sent.

I will never forget something I heard from the late Floyd McClung, one of the founding fathers of YWAM, when he spoke in our School of Evangelism in 1973. He simply said, "God's program is PEOPLE." The Great Commission basically tells us that God's methodology is people reaching people. That will never change! No matter what new innovation we use to share the Good News of the gospel, it always comes down to people reaching people.

I heard a pastor speculate that when Jesus ascended into heaven the angels turned to Him and asked, "What have You done with this wonderful plan of salvation?" Supposedly Jesus replied, "I entrusted it to 11 men." The angels replied, "What if they fail?" Jesus is reported to have answered, "I have no other plan."

We are IT! We are God's plan and program, and it is a necessity that we, the Church of Jesus Christ, share this good news with our world!

There is a greater interest today in the second coming of the Lord Jesus than has been true in recent decades in the Church. When Christians see some of what is happening in our world, they realize that we truly may be living in the "Last Days." We need to remember however, that Jesus shared with His followers one of the most important things that must take place before His return.

In Matthew 24:14 Jesus makes it clear that the "end" will come when the gospel is preached to all nations. More precisely, as is written in the Greek τοῖς ἔθνεσιν or "ethnos" which means, "a number of people living together," "company," "body of men," "tribe," "a people." It is therefore even more accurate to say that Jesus was not talking so much of political nations, but "people groups."

The Joshua Project which gathers statistics of World Missions explains it this way: "People groups are what Bible scholars believe are referred to in many mission-oriented verses, such as Matthew 28:19, 24:14, and Revelation 7:9. According to one database, there are 16,562 people groups in the world. Of these people groups, 9,715 have been reached with the Gospel message, leaving 6,847 people groups still unreached. To be unreached means less than 2% Evangelical Christian, the sizable proportion thought to be needed to reach their own people."

We can preach about the second coming, sing about it and write about it, but the most important marker that must be accomplished before Jesus returns, is that we bring closure to the last commandment He gave His church. We have not yet accomplished that. If we are eager about the second coming, we must prioritize the proclamation of the gospel to every people group and then, and only then, will it be possible for Jesus to return for His church.

To understand what Jesus intended regarding the Great Commission we must track how the early church responded to His command, and what their obedience looked like. I believe they had a much better understanding regarding Christ's words than our 21st century Church does today.

To ensure that the message was clear and powerful Jesus put an addendum on the commandment He gave on the mount. Luke 24:49 (NLT), "And now I will send the Holy Spirit, just as my Father promised. But stay here in the city until the Holy Spirit comes and fills you with power from heaven." Jesus gave the commission on the Mount, and the power to perform it, on the Day of Pentecost.

When I read the book of Acts, I am amazed at the change that took place between the thoughts and the actions of the disciples. They went from being clueless and totally out of sync with the whole plan of salvation, to being not only theologically correct, but empowered just like Jesus. They had begun to think like Him, act like Him.

It was said about them by the Jewish Council in Acts 4:13, "When they saw the courage of Peter and John and realized that they were unschooled, ordinary men, they were astonished and they took note that these men had been with Jesus."

The Difference!

What made the difference? They didn't take a crash seminary course after the accession. They weren't given ministerial credentials, or a title. Something very powerful and dynamic happened that made everything

Jesus had said and done in the 3½ years they were with Him, fall into place. Suddenly they were given complete understanding regarding who Jesus was, what He taught, and what He wanted them to do.

Jesus sent them the Holy Spirit in the upper room on the Day of Pentecost and on that powerful day the Church of Jesus Christ was born! He was the factor that changed everything for the 120 that had obeyed the instruction Jesus had given them, "First spend time in Jerusalem and wait for the empowering of the Holy Spirit."

The 11 had gone through a process to fill the vacant post left by Judas. Basically, they drew straws to choose Matthias. It is interesting that we never read another word about him, not in the book of Acts, the Epistles, or in any other accounts of church history. Apparently, Matthias was not terribly noteworthy. Perhaps if they had waited, it would have become clear in time that God's choice for that position was actually Paul.

After what seems to have been a futile exercise they finally got down to the business at hand, the reason Jesus had them gather for those 10 days. To PRAY and WAIT for the endowment of power from on high.

When you are filled with the power of the Holy Spirit, you cannot contain the blessing! The first thing you want to do is to tell others about Jesus.

When I received the baptism of the Holy Spirit at age 12, my Christian life was revolutionized! I didn't know a whole lot about the Bible or the principles of evangelism, but I knew I wanted everyone to know Jesus like I did. I wanted to tell the world!

In Acts 2:4 we are told that the 120 were filled with the Holy Spirit.

Thousands of people had come to Jerusalem from many different locations for the feast of Pentecost. The upper room was not large. How 120, shut in together for 10 days, survived, I'm sure was only by the grace and mercy of God!

Ed Silvoso, a respected Christian leader, who is the founder and president of Harvest Evangelism and leader of the Transform Our World Network, describes what happened in the upper room as being the birthplace of the Church "in seed." The church was truly born however, when the 120 went down from the upper room into the marketplace.

He says that the stairway from the upper room to the street actually became the "birth canal" of the Church.

I believe God was impressing something on His newly-born Church. We are not only the Church when we meet inside four walls, but we are equally the Church no matter where we find ourselves. The message is clear—"The Church is not a building, but a Body."

From day one, the Church of Jesus Christ was on outreach!

Newly empowered, they circulated among the thousands that had gathered for the feast of Pentecost in the marketplace and began to share their faith. Peter, full of the Holy Spirit, preached an anointed message and 3,000 came to faith in Christ. The Church was born that day in the marketplace where the people live, work, and play. God's plan has always been that the Church would be where the people are. This was consistent with how Jesus lived and ministered. He loved people and continually gave of Himself to them, usually seeking and finding the neediest of all.

Jesus said to them, "It is not the healthy who need a doctor, but the sick. I have not come to call the righteous, but sinners" (Mark 2:17).

General William Booth, co-founder of The Salvation Army said "Go for souls. Go straight for souls, and go for the worst."

The book of Acts is full of stories of the new Church always out where the people were, ministering to their needs just like Jesus. They understood the commission clearly, "YOU, GO!" It was the marketplace where all the action was, where evangelism happened!

The message hasn't changed. YOU, ME (Christians) are to go to where the people are.

When the Church met together it was for basically four reasons.

1. Discipleship

2. Nurturement or pastoral care

3. Fellowship

4. The equipping of the saints to prepare them to go out to the marketplace and share their faith

If evangelism happened during the meeting together of the believers it was more by accident than on purpose. People were coming to Christ in the marketplace and then invited to the meeting of the believers for the reasons listed above.

The Master Plan

This was the Master's Plan of Evangelism!

It is interesting when you study church history, that for the first 335 years of Christianity there was not one structure to be found for the specific purpose of Christians meeting together. For the most part they met in homes. Yet within that same number of years, they not only evangelized the then known world, but Christianized it as well! All of this without the assistance of one structure! Amazing! The only way to account for this is that early century Christians clearly understood Jesus' last command. YOU, GO!

I spoke in a church in Brooklyn, that was on fire for evangelism. They had quite a number of Prayer Stations and sent their people out to the streets of downtown Brooklyn every Saturday. The pastor shared with me, "Nick, people don't come to the Lord in my church building anymore, they come to Christ on the streets at the Prayer Stations." I replied, "There is nothing more New Testament than that, Pastor."

I firmly believe that the Church of the 21st century suffers from what I call spiritual dyslexia. (Dyslexia means to see things backwards.) Jesus said to His followers on the mount "YOU, GO" and the early church understood that and therefore they were constantly among the people. By virtue of what we do today we have to conclude that the 21st century church reads that verse backwards. We say to the world YOU, COME! Instead of us moving out of our comfort zone, we expect them to move out of theirs. What's wrong with this picture?

Come to our church and hear our pastor preach, or, come hear our choir sing the Christmas or Easter cantata, come listen to the traveling evangelist, come to our special program. My experience has been that if most churches give any training to their people at all, it is to train them to invite people to church, not how to invite them to Christ!

Why is this true? We love to be with people who are like us. People who share the same values, who are nice, kind and behave themselves properly. People who understand the language we speak. I don't mean English, Spanish, etc. but "Christianese." Yes, we even have our own language, and people who are not Christians often don't get it.

Let's Get Uncomfortable

Being "out in the world" can be uncomfortable. They use awful and offensive language, talk about subjects we have no interest in.

It is uncomfortable, and yes, it's often inconvenient, but Jesus commanded us to share His love and forgiveness with those He died for.

In the entire universe what would be the comfort zone of all comfort zones? Would it not be heaven itself? Certainly, no place could be as beautiful and enjoyable as that.

Jesus is, as it were, the "main man" of heaven, everything revolves around Him. One day, the Father sent His Son to this sin-cursed earth to live. He came not as a man, but as a helpless infant. Before He was born, they were already plotting to kill Him. For 33 years He was misunderstood, reviled, falsely accused, beaten mercilessly, and finally murdered, dying a cruel death.

Talk about being out of His comfort zone!

Why did Jesus do it? So that everyone of His creation might, through His death and resurrection, have the gift of eternal life.

When Jesus was preparing His disciples for His departure, He said to them in John 20:21, "Peace be with you! As the Father has sent me, I am sending you." We have the same commission they had, to leave all that is pleasant and familiar and go wherever He leads, in order that the people of this world receive the message of redemption and salvation.

One of the first verses of Scripture to challenge my life for Christian service as a teenager was Matthew 9:38, "Ask the Lord of the harvest, therefore, to send out workers into his harvest field." When doing a word study on "send out," I discovered that in the original language the words "send out" and "cast out," as in casting out a demon, were the very same words. My conclusion? That in the Church of Jesus Christ in our world today we need a "holy exorcism" to exorcise Christians out of their pew and into their world!

Years ago, I read a book on evangelism written by an African American evangelist in New Jersey. In his book he said that if the Church of Jesus Christ was a football team, we would be constantly penalized for spending too much time in the huddle. In the NFL, a team playing offense is allowed 40 seconds from the time a play is whistled dead, until the snap of the ball for the next play. If the team on offense takes longer, they are penalized five yards for spending too much time in the huddle. I'm sure you feel as I do when watching the Super Bowl, I'm not interested in watching 11 men in a huddle. I want to see running, passing, tackling, and kicking. That's what makes the game exciting. Huddles are not what football is all about, and the same is true for the Church!

Churches have huddles almost every day of the week for one age or gender group or another. Most however give little or no time to being outside of the church building where the people are. Please don't misunderstand me, I love the meeting of the believers and being with God's people. Scripture teaches us that meeting together is an important part of Christianity. Hebrews 10:25 (AMP), "Not forsaking our meeting together [as believers for worship and instruction], as is the habit of some, but encouraging one another; and all the more [faithfully] as you see the day [of Christ's return] approaching."

When a Christian uses the term "worship" they are speaking of music and singing, which I enjoy. One of my former pastors used to say that we have a "singing religion," so true. I enjoy the many anointed hymns and worship songs of the church. I sing them all the time, at times even in my sleep. This, however, should not be the total sum of our worship. Some of my most precious worship times have been spent at a Prayer Station sharing prayer and words of life with someone in need! That, to me, is as much worship as any great song of the Church!

Billy Graham said, **"The greatest form of praise is the sound of consecrated feet seeking out the lost and helpless."**

The Church in Action

My favorite book in the Bible is the book of Acts. Now that statement won't be a surprise to anyone who knows me well. I love action! I love to see the Church in action! As I read and re-read the New Testament, especially the book of Acts, but not exclusively, I see Jesus, the apostles, and the church in action proclaiming the message of the gospel, and being active in signs, wonders, miracles and healings.

Mark 16:19-20 (NLT) says, "When the Lord Jesus had finished talking with them, he was taken up into heaven and sat down in the place of honor at God's right hand. And the disciples went everywhere and preached, and the Lord worked through them, confirming what they said by many miraculous signs."

We serve a miracle-working God! Scripture, both Old Testament and New, is full of the divine supernatural. The ministry of Jesus through the Gospels is one of signs, wonders, miracles and healing. In part this gave credence to Him as the Messiah. Jesus' reply to John the Baptist's disciples in Matthew 11:5 was, "The blind receive sight, the lame walk, those who have leprosy are cleansed, the deaf hear, the dead are raised, and the good news is proclaimed to the poor."

Growing up and being discipled by Pentecostals and Charismatics, the supernatural was not new to me. After all, miracles were what first drew me to the Lord, watching Oral Roberts healing ministry on TV. There was a time, however, during the '70s when some embarrassing excesses that I heard of, and even witnessed, especially in the growing charismatic movement, made me want to distance myself from some of it. I remember saying to the Lord in prayer one day, "Lord, You know about how my calling is that of an evangelist, so I think I would rather not be very involved with the gifts of the Spirit, especially that of miracles, healing, signs and wonders." After all, I thought, my work is that of the evangelist and I think I will leave the operation of the gifts of the

Spirit to others. "Nick," He responded, "Go back to Mark 16:15 and read on to the end of that chapter."

I began to read,

> He said to them, "Go into all the world and preach the gospel to all creation. Whoever believes and is baptized will be saved, but whoever does not believe will be condemned. And these signs will accompany those who believe: In my name they will drive out demons; they will speak in new tongues; they will pick up snakes with their hands; and when they drink deadly poison, it will not hurt them at all; they will place their hands on sick people, and they will get well." After the Lord Jesus had spoken to them, he was taken up into heaven and he sat at the right hand of God. Then the disciples went out and preached everywhere, and the Lord worked with them and confirmed his word by the signs that accompanied it.

Even though I had read those scriptures dozens of times before, I understood with new clarity that the supernatural was actually part of my commission as an evangelist.

In the early '80s I had another awakening. We had invited an evangelist to come and speak to our YWAM staff and students in Concord, New Hampshire. He shared on evangelism and asked all of us a simple question, "Where in the book of Acts did all the signs, wonders, miracles and healings take place?"

The answer was obvious…on the street, in the marketplace! In my Pentecostal tradition the operation of the gifts were often relegated to church buildings, tents, or other gatherings. The New Testament venue was clearly on the street with an audience of non-believers. Some call this "Power Evangelism." Scripture calls it normal living for the believer.

Power Evangelism

I began to read the New Testament with renewed interest and excitement focusing on the story of the crippled beggar in Acts 3:1-10.

One day Peter and John were going up to the temple at the time of prayer—at three in the afternoon. Now a man who was lame from birth was being carried to the temple gate called Beautiful, where he was put every day to beg from those going into the temple courts. When he saw Peter and John about to enter, he asked them for money. Peter looked straight at him, as did John. Then Peter said, "Look at us!" So the man gave them his attention, expecting to get something from them. Then Peter said, "Silver or gold I do not have, but what I do have I give you. In the name of Jesus Christ of Nazareth, walk." Taking him by the right hand, he helped him up, and instantly the man's feet and ankles became strong. He jumped to his feet and began to walk. Then he went with them into the temple courts, walking and jumping, and praising God. When all the people saw him walking and praising God, they recognized him as the same man who used to sit begging at the temple gate called Beautiful, and they were filled with wonder and amazement at what had happened to him.

Peter and John were on their way to the Temple where they passed through the gate Beautiful. A man was camped out at the gate who was crippled, probably since birth. He must have tried to look as pathetic as possible with his hands cupped reaching out, hoping to engender compassion from passersby. There was no welfare, no government programs to assist him, begging was his only option.

With the beggar's full attention, Peter spoke, "Silver or gold I do not have, but what I do have I give you. In the name of Jesus Christ of Nazareth, WALK!"

Peter had a life-giving message and he didn't hesitate! He met the beggar at his point of need, and revealed to him the compassion and the power of almighty God!

In years of Mercy Ministry, we have worked with the homeless, alcoholics, drug addicts, and many others with life-controlling problems. Most were faced with what appeared to them to be impossible odds that left them homeless and hopeless.

All of us have basic physical needs for food, clothing and housing. The challenge, as Christians, is knowing how best to meet these critical needs when confronted with them. The obvious answer is always do the possible! As I once heard a missionary say, "Empty bellies have no ears."

You would not need to be a mathematician to list Peter's monetary assets, but Peter had an asset worth much more than silver or gold. He had the same asset available to every born-again Christian—ACCESS WITH GOD! If you are a believer then you have this too! No matter who we are, when we come to know the Lord we have access to the King of Kings and Lord of Lords. We are welcomed into His throne room. He knows us by name.

There are no barriers or restrictions. Not gender, age, Christian maturity, clergy or layman, known or unknown in the Body of Christ. As a born-again believer we all have the same access!

Power of Prayer

In 1983 when Rozanne and I attended the Leadership Training School in Kona, Hawaii, all of the staff and students gathered at 7:14 AM for prayer. This was in keeping with 2 Chronicles 7:14. One particular morning I was sitting with our oldest daughter, Anita, who was 11 years old. The YWAM founder, Loren Cunningham, was leading the prayer meeting. Each day we interceded for different needs, requests and prayer targets. Loren shared that he felt we should break up into small groups and pray for one another. Anita and I were sitting near the front and we ended up in the same group as Loren. Each person in our group shared a prayer need, Loren was the last to share. He was candid and said he was suffering with back pain and needed healing as he had a very busy day ahead.

Anita was sitting next to Loren and without being asked or prompted, she reached her hand behind Loren, put it on his back. and began to pray the most amazing prayer for his healing. I admit I couldn't resist peeping. My eyes were fixed on Loren. I saw him bow in prayer and then suddenly open his eyes, smile and turn to Anita, "Honey, the pain is gone, thank you for praying for me." Our daughter who loved

Jesus prayed for a veteran man of God and her prayer was answered! Anita had access with God!

God has given us access to His throne room not just for ourselves and our own needs, but so we may give it away to others, even complete strangers. My experience in Prayer Evangelism is that everyone needs prayer for one thing or another, and most of them welcome God's help. I have prayed with people of all religions at Prayer Stations, as well as atheists and agnostics. Most people seem to feel, "Hey, I need all the help I can get!" Prayer can be so disarming. People who need help are generally not opposed to where it comes from. Many believe God can help them, but the problem is, THEY DON'T KNOW HOW TO APPROACH GOD FOR HIS HELP!

It may be because of the guilt of sin, or just because they simply do not have any kind of relationship with God. They don't know the first thing about asking for His help. We have the privilege and joy to go to God on their behalf because we do have ACCESS. We can pray for them with absolute assurance that God will hear our prayer!

Healing is provided for us all! Jesus spent a lot of time in His earthly ministry healing the sick. I have heard it said that healing is cosmetic for the Christian because one day God will give us all a glorified body. No diseases, ailments, disabilities, or limitations of any kind for all eternity! For the person who does not know the Lord however, healing can mean the difference between eternal life and eternal death. So many have come to Christ because either they reached out to God for help themselves, or a Christian prayed on their behalf and God healed them. As a result of that healing or miracle, a life was surrendered to Christ and came into the kingdom of God.

Rozanne's doctor, who is a Christian, asked us if we knew a particular Christian cardiologist in our area. We didn't, so he told us the following story: "The cardiologist had to pronounce someone dead. He had tried his best to revive him but all signs indicated that he was gone. As the doctor sadly walked away from the body, God spoke to him and said, 'Go back and try again.' He obeyed and asked his staff to once again use the defibrillator on the patient. They looked at the doctor in disbelief and said, 'Why? He's dead.' The cardiologist insisted they do what he asked, and so they shocked the patient one more time. His lifeless body awakened!" Rozanne's doctor then casually said, "You know the patient became a Christian after that!"

As mentioned earlier each of us has both a FELT NEED and a REAL NEED. Felt needs can be very diverse, healing, marriage difficulties, children, employment, housing, emotional instability or a thousand other possibilities.

In chapter 3 I told the story of how our family stumbled onto the Oral Roberts TV program and became obsessed with watching each Saturday. It wasn't because we were seeking a relationship with Jesus, but rather that we sought healing for my brothers.

I have often heard preachers say something like, "Everyone walks around with a Jesus-size hole in their heart and they are all searching for a relationship with God." In over 60 years of sharing my faith with others, that has not been my experience. The majority of people I have encountered have zero spiritual interest, but that doesn't mean they don't want God to help them with something in their life, everyone is up for that!

God is so gracious and merciful that He meets us where we are, and then takes us to where we ought to be. No matter how selfish and skewed our motivation might be, we take one step toward Him and He runs to us with open arms drawing us to Himself.

"Come now, and let us reason together," says the Lord. "Though your sins are like scarlet, they shall be as white as snow; Though they are red like crimson, they shall be like wool" (Isaiah 1:18 AMP).

Often it is the troubles of life that make us vulnerable and even sensitive to spiritual things. God often uses these challenges we face to get our attention on what really matters, an eternal framework. Everyone's REAL NEED is a relationship with God through Jesus Christ His Son. Helping people come to that revelation should be our objective with all those we meet.

Eternity Stamped on our Eyeballs

As my YWAM colleague, Danny Lehmann, has said, "We need eternity stamped on our eyeballs."

I am all for helping people with their temporal needs through mercy ministry, as long as our endgame is to lead them to Christ. This is what the ultimate in Christian compassion ought to be. If all we are doing is feeding the hungry, providing clothing and shelter for the poor and homeless, providing medical assistance to the sick or meeting any other temporal need, and we don't seek to bring these same people into a relationship with God that will change their eternal destiny, we do them the greatest disservice!

I see no tension between mercy ministry and evangelism. They are partners in demonstrating God's love for the world. My difficulty is with Christian ministries whose total focus is meeting the physical and temporal needs of people while showing no regard for their eternal destiny! One sad statistic I came across was that Christians worldwide only give a very small percentage of their income toward ministries whose focus is on the eternal (evangelism, salvation) and the vast majority toward ministries whose primary focus is to meet only temporal needs.

One of the major negative megatrends in missions today is that of prioritizing the body over the spirit!

It is not difficult for anyone in the world with any humanity to have their hearts touched at the sight of thousands of people being forced from their homes, some killed, others separated from family, starving, homeless and sick. You don't have to be a Christian to have such compassion. But how many of us have our hearts broken by the fact that there are multiple millions of people in the world today who are eternally lost and thousands going to a Christless eternity each day? A study showed that 25 percent (one in four) pastors say that meeting a person's physical needs takes priority over telling them about Jesus[4]

I shudder to think how many who call themselves born again Christians actually believe that there is a heaven to win and a hell to

---

4. *Barna, Translating the Great Commission, 2018.*

shun? One statistic shares that 69 percent of churchgoers believe that everyone will go to heaven. 65 percent of all Christians believe there are multiple paths to heaven[5]. If all this is true it is no wonder that evangelism has such a low priority in today's church agenda. David Jeremiah said, "If we understand what lies ahead for those who do not know Christ, there will be a sense of urgency in our witness."

Occasionally some churches or ministries complain about the price of a Prayer Station, and for some it truly can be a challenge. Whenever we can, we endeavor to assist those who value evangelism but are in more impoverished areas. I admit, however, to being saddened when the complaint comes from those who think nothing of spending more than the price of a Prayer Station on a microphone. A Prayer Station is a tool that can, if used properly and regularly, bring many to Christ, and into the congregation. We need to keep our perspective always in line with the worth of a soul.

My family and I have spent our lives working both with mercy ministries and purely evangelism and missions-oriented ministries. From experience I know the easiest projects to raise money for are those that are focused on mercy and temporal needs. Sadly, it is always much harder to raise money in the body of Christ for projects that focus on the eternal.

You Lose Them Both

C.S. Lewis said, "If you live for the next world, you get this one in the deal, but if you live only for this world, you lose them both."

Prayer Stations are not only about praying for people, as wonderful as that is, it is Prayer Evangelism, meaning, that yes, we address the felt need and pray the prayer of faith, believing that God will help with their special request. The ultimate goal however, is always to share the Good News of the gospel. What a privilege to give them the joy of answered prayer for their temporal need, and then, most importantly, to pray for their greatest need, receiving life's greatest treasure, a personal relationship with Jesus and the promise of eternity with Him.

---

5. U.S. Religious Landscape Study, Pew Research Center, 2014

When a church team came to do a Prayer Station outreach with our YWAM New York ministry some years ago, I asked the leader if they had ever done Prayer Stations before? "Yes," he said with very little enthusiasm in his voice. Later, after we had experienced a great day of Prayer Evangelism on the streets of the Bronx, he turned to me with a smile. "The Prayer Station ministry we did in New York today was very different from our first experience in a city on the West Coast." There the ministry that took them out to the streets instructed them to just pray for people and not share a witness. I was horrified! What a remarkable difference it made for them to not only pray for people's felt needs, but also address their real need of a Savior.

It is not just prayer; it is Prayer Evangelism!

When we pray for someone, it is not a gimmick for the gospel, not a hook to proselytize them, but an earnest intercession on their behalf that God will grant their request whatever it may be. We express the Father's heart of love for them and their needs, we pray, and then take it one step further because we desire that they might come to know Jesus and receive eternal life. There is nothing selfish about that!

Because of my personal experience, I love to tell people I meet that I have been able to live my life with few regrets, I want that for them too. When you find something that is so life changing and available to all, you naturally want to share it.

That is what evangelism is all about.

Critics of the faith often try to attach sinister motives to Evangelical Christians. They may assume we have a selfish motivation, as if we were trying to recruit people into some pyramid scheme that would bring great personal benefit to us. Yes, I have heard Christians talk about the jewels they will have in their crown when they get to heaven. Crowns and jewels however, will have no value compared to the joy of being in the presence of Jesus forever. In fact, Scripture gives us insight as to what we will do with our crowns when we stand before His throne.

Revelation 4:10-11 says, "The twenty-four elders fall down before him who sits on the throne and worship him who lives for ever and ever. They lay their crowns before the throne and say: 'You are worthy, our

Lord and God, to receive glory and honor and power, for you created all things, and by your will they were created and have their being.'"

No Apologies

I make no apologies for sharing my faith with others. If you were standing at the only exit of a burning building where many were trapped by the fire and smoke, would it be selfish for you to cry out to as many as you could that you know where the only exit is for them to save their lives?! Should I feel embarrassed to lift my voice and proclaim to everyone the words of Jesus, "I am the [only] Way [to God] and the [real] Truth and the [real] Life; no one comes to the Father but through Me" (John 14:6 AMP).

Kirk Cameron said, "If you had the cure for cancer wouldn't you share it?…You have the cure to death…get out there and share it."

Today I think most evangelicals don't appreciate what the name *evangelical* means. It comes from the root word *evangel* which is simply defined as "Good News." So, an evangelical is someone who shares the Good News, who evangelizes, not just someone who believes what the Bible says.

G. Campbell Morgan, who was a British evangelist, preacher, a leading Bible teacher, and a prolific author, said, "To call a man evangelical who is not evangelistic is an utter contradiction."

When I was a child, the people who sometimes complained about those knocking at their door to talk about religion weren't referring to Jehovah's Witnesses or the Mormons, but evangelicals! If only that was true today!

Unfortunately, in today's world of Christianity, evangelism is sometimes thought to be a dirty word. For 15 years I served as the North American Director for Cities in YWAM. Biannually we held conferences for YWAM missionaries serving in cities in the US and Canada. We wrote a manifesto at one of these conferences. I suggested we include our commitment to evangelism as one of the tenets. One leader objected to the use of the word evangelism, reasoning that Christian young people of this generation do not relate to that word.

Perhaps if the Church of Jesus Christ had as much passion for leading people to Christ as they do social justice and global warming, we might have brought closure to the Great Commission by now!

The greatest injustice done by all of mankind is that we provided the need for the pure and sinless Son of God to die on a cruel cross in order to provide salvation and redemption. Our first and greatest aim in life must be to persuade people to come to a place of repentance and ask God to forgive them for their sins and receive the gift of God in Christ Jesus.

"How shall we escape if we ignore so great a salvation?" (Hebrews 2:3).

"The man who mobilizes the Christian church to pray will make the greatest contribution to world evangelization in history."

—Andrew Murray

Chapter 13

Motivation for Evangelism

God is more concerned about why we do what we do, than by what we actually do!

Obligation?

Some who serve the Lord do so out of obligation. We recognize these Christians by their lack of joy. There is never any excitement or enthusiasm in anyone who serves the Lord only because they feel they have too. They may be very grateful for all He has done to bless their life, or simply appreciate what Jesus did on the cross, but nevertheless, they serve because they feel they must, often with what we might call, a "martyr's spirit." Their service might be diligent and conscientious, but never effervescent or contagious. They are not fun to work with or a joy to be around, in fact, they are often downright depressing!

Fear?

Some serve out of fear! They sense that if they don't serve, God will punish them. Here again, joy does not reside and it is usually quite obvious that their heart is not really invested in what they are doing.

Pride

There are others who appear to be serving the Lord, but are in reality serving themselves. "It is all about them." Their greatest concern is what other people will think of their service. Their motivation could be to impress others through their newsletters or promotional materials, as they expound on how much they have accomplished for the kingdom.

God takes no delight when we serve Him out of obligation or fear. Neither does He appreciate those who are more interested in promoting themselves than in giving God all the glory!

Love Relationship?

The only Biblical motivation for serving the Lord and doing anything for Him is that of a LOVE RELATIONSHIP WITH JESUS.

Paul the apostle said it best in 2 Corinthians 5:14, "For Christ's love compels us." By "love compelled" is the only way! I remember a dear Hispanic friend of mine once interpreted this scripture by saying, "The love of Jesus squeezes everything out of me." That says it all. We serve the Lord and do the will of God only because we love Him and desire to please Him.

I am not fond of putting out the garbage twice a week at our home, but because I love my wife, I do it to bless her. What a difference it makes in our service when love is the motivation for doing what we do.

In the Gospel of Mark there is a miracle story that helps us understand something about motivation.

"Then He came to Bethsaida; and they brought a blind man to Him, and begged Him to touch him. So, He took the blind man by the hand and led him out of the town. And when He had spit on his eyes and put His hands on him, He asked him if he saw anything. And he looked up and said, 'I see men like trees, walking.' Then He put His hands on his eyes again and made him look up. And he was restored and saw everyone clearly" (Mark 8:22-25 NKJV).

After Jesus prayed for the blind man the first time, He asked him for a testimony. The man announced that he was no longer totally blind. He was able to see light and see figures, but his vision was severely blurred so that he could not differentiate between people or trees walking. Today he would probably have been diagnosed as being legally blind. Perhaps some may have encouraged him to be happy with this partial miracle, after all, he was not in total darkness anymore, but Jesus was not satisfied and He prayed for the man again. He gave him what I like to refer to as the SECOND TOUCH. The man was asked to testify again. This time he could see "everyone clearly."

Over the years, I have seen those who have received the gospel, and, in so doing, have been transformed from the kingdom of darkness into the kingdom of light. I have also observed that some received only a partial transformation; they appeared to have a similar issue as the blind man who Jesus touched. Their vision after conversion seemed somewhat blurred. They had problems telling the difference between things and people. Someone said, "God gave us things to use and people to love, but the problem is that some people often end up loving things and using people."

As Christians we must be careful not to confuse these two. We may say the right thing, but the evidence is in the way we live our lives and what we value most. If we sense that the Holy Spirit is saying this is true in our lives, then we need to ask Jesus to give us the second touch so that we can see:

People for who they really are.

People for who God created them to be.

People as God sees them—through His eyes!

Everything?

There is a story told regarding John D. Rockefeller, who was the world's first billionaire. On the day Mr. Rockefeller passed away, May

23, 1937, his family and staff held a news conference to announce his death. After the official announcement they opened the floor for questions from the news media. One newspaper man asked, "When Mr. Rockefeller died today, how much did he leave?" One of Mr. Rockefeller's staff stepped up to the microphone, "Today when Mr. Rockefeller passed away, he left EVERYTHING!"

So, it will be for all of us! No matter how many things we collect in our lifetime, we can't take any of it with us when we pass from this life. Someone jokingly said, "I have never seen a funeral hearse pulling a U Haul trailer."

We need to see mankind through the grid of eternity! We need an eternal perspective! I have been so obsessed with eternity in recent years that I now sign every letter I write, "For His eternal purpose."

To truly embrace God's perspective of our fellowman, we must first understand what His original intentions were in creating us.

The Bible says in Revelation 4:11 (KJV) that "Thou art worthy, O Lord, to receive glory and honor and power: for thou hast created all things, and for thy pleasure they are and were created."

Now that almost sounds selfish, when the Bible says we were created, "for Thy pleasure." It begs the question, "What is the pleasure of the Lord?"

I submit that God's greatest pleasure is His desire to bless us. He did not create us as His robots to simply do His bidding. No matter how important we think we are to the work of the kingdom of God, the truth is that God doesn't really need us. We, however, desperately need Him!

He created us "in His image," so like God who is infinite, we in a finite way have been created with His personality:

Intellect
Free will
Emotions

Intellect

Our intellect is beyond that of the plant or animal world. Like no other creature on earth, we have a finite intellect like our infinite God. He also has given us the same power of self-determination as He has.

Choice is a gift from God that allows us the possibility to pattern our life after His, or, to go our own way.

Some Christians believe that everything that is part of the character of God is fixed. That it is true about God simply because that is the way God is. The Bible clearly says, "God is love." Do we believe that is true simply because He is love, or has He *chosen* to live in Love toward all of His creation?

Free Will

My life was revolutionized more than 48 years ago when I began to hear a Bible teacher speak on the character of God and posed this essential truth regarding God's free will. When I understood that God's character, like our character, is what it is because of the choices made, I had a new understanding about God that I never appreciated before.

God loves me, not because that is fixed in His being, but because He has chosen to love me. Without choice there can be no virtue, so when I understand that He loves me because of His choice it blesses me beyond measure.

If my wife, Rozanne, was a robot that I myself created, so that when I pushed the right buttons on my remote, she said, "Nick, I love you," what virtue would there be in her love? I created her to say and do that. What reason would I have to experience a "warm fuzzy" in my heart? It is because Rozanne has chosen to love me over every other man in this world, that I revel in her love and feel what I feel in my own heart toward her.

Emotions

So, when I consider that God is a God of emotions, and that the only reason I, and every other moral being in this world, have emotions is because God created us in His image, that also blesses me. I have to admit that for most of my early years as a Christian I saw God sitting on His throne with a serious look on His face. When sinners did evil things, in my mind's eye I would not see God responding to their actions or even changing the countenance on His face. It would simply be the same expression, as if to say, "Well, boys will be boys," or

"Nothing is new under the sun." In the same manner I thought there was no real response to the righteous who would be doing their best to please the Lord. He would respond as if to say, "Well, that's just their reasonable service."

Scriptures like Zephaniah 3:17 (AMP) became very real to me, "The Lord your God is in your midst, a Warrior who saves. He will rejoice over you with joy; He will be quiet in His love [making no mention of your past sins], He will rejoice over you with shouts of joy."

The Full Reward

In 1973 I was reading a book about how we need to make Jesus the focus for all we are and do. It was very much the same message that was shared by the two Moravian missionaries who responded to the plight of 3,000 African slaves. The slaves had been brought to an island in the West Indies by an atheist British owner that would not allow any missionaries to go among the slaves and convert them to Christ. The only way the two Moravians would be allowed to go was to sell themselves into slavery. They were willing to do so for the sake of the slaves that they might be able to bring to Christ. As the ship began to clear the dock they linked arms, raised their hands and shouted to their friends, "May the Lamb that was slain receive the reward of His suffering." This then became the call for all Moravian missionaries.

I was deeply moved by all this and by the words from Scripture in Nehemiah 8:10 "…the joy of the Lord is your strength." I began to see that scripture in a new light. Not thinking about our joy, but rather "the joy of the Lord." This gave me a vision for a special celebration, a "Joy for Jesus Celebration," subtitled, "Making Happy the Heart of God"! I worked with some Christians in the Greenville area of New York and we were given the use of a farmer's field. I began to share with local pastors the vision of gathering together on a special Saturday to bring joy to the Lord!

I was part of a group of pastors that met regularly in Catskill, New York. I shared with them my vision and gave out some very basic fliers for them to share with their congregants. One of the pastors that I knew from my days with Teen Challenge in Long Branch, New Jersey shared that he thought I had a typo in the flier. I apologized and asked him to show me where we had made the mistake. He then pointed at the name of the gathering and said, "You have here, a 'Joy *for* Jesus' celebration, shouldn't it be a 'Joy *in* Jesus' celebration?" I replied that he had missed the point of why we were doing this. It was not for our joy, but to bring joy to Jesus! He looked at me like I was some kind of heretic and blurted out, "I never heard such a concept."

The reality is that we have the opportunity each day to bring joy to the heart of God! This actually should be the mantra for every Christian. I often begin my day by praying and asking God how I can bring joy to His heart by both my thoughts and actions through that day.

Dog and Cat Theology

Some years ago, Rozanne and I attended a mission's conference at one of our supporting churches. Upon arrival we were handed a bulletin and then joined the procession of missionaries walking to their seats. Once seated I scanned the information inside my bulletin. The special speaker that morning had entitled his message, "Dog and Cat Theology." I turned to Rozanne and screwing up my face, I commented, "What in the world is Dog and Cat Theology, and what possible relevance does this have to missions?"

The speaker began his message by asking the congregation how many had dogs as pets. A large number raised their hands. "You know," he said, "you love a dog, feed a dog, care for a dog and the dog looks up at you as if to say, 'You must be God!'" He then asked how many cat owners there were, and a number raised their hands. He went on, "You love a cat, feed a cat, care for a cat and the cat looks up at you as if to say, 'I must be God!'"

It has been said that dogs have masters and cats have staff! When a person has a dog theology it's all about God, when a person has a cat theology, it's all about them.

The Bible presents only one theology, that is that our lives should be lived to bring happiness and joy to the heart of God. I know nothing that brings more joy and blessing to God's heart than for one of His creation to come into a place of reconciliation, and receive the blessing of eternal life.

Each Christmas I am challenged, and I endeavor to challenge others, that we are celebrating Christ's birthday, and the greatest gift we could give to Jesus would be a new son or daughter in His kingdom!

I received revelation of this while reading the story of Paul and Silas. They had travelled to Philippi to preach the gospel, and in Acts 16:16-40 we read how they experienced a beating much like Jesus did at the Praetorium before His crucifixion. Those who saw the movie, *The Passion of the Christ* will remember those horrific scenes.

Paul in Prison

"The crowd joined in the attack against Paul and Silas, and the magistrates *ordered them to be stripped and beaten with rods. After they had been severely flogged, they were thrown into prison,* and the jailer was commanded to guard them carefully. When he received these orders, he put them in the inner cell and fastened their feet in the stocks" (Acts 16:22-24).

When I read this passage, I began to see it from God's perspective.

I could see God looking down at what was happening in a locked, damp, dark, cold cell in Philippi. He saw His two sons, Paul and Silas with their backs ripped open, bleeding, shivering from cold and blood loss, singing hymns and glorifying the Name of Jesus.

In their situation, I thought of how tempted I would have been to complain or ask the big question, "WHY, GOD?"

I could imagine God calling all of heaven to look down with Him at such a glorious sight. How proud He must have been of his two sons! I imagined that God got so happy He began to dance and jump, and although I can't find scripture to back me up, it is my opinion that this is the reason there was an earthquake in Philippi that opened all the prison cells, and released the iron stocks from their feet! God gets happy when we praise Him in all circumstances!

Sorrow is, of course, just as real an emotion as joy and happiness. The Bible makes it clear that God does experience sorrow. Genesis 6:6 said regarding mankind, "So the Lord was sorry he had ever made them and put them on the earth. It broke his heart" (NLT).

Ezekiel 6 :9 (NLT) regarding Israel's sins: "Then when they are exiled among the nations, they will remember me. They will recognize how hurt I am by their unfaithful hearts and lustful eyes that long for their idols. Then at last they will hate themselves for all their detestable sins." God's heart breaks when He, the most pure and righteous being in the universe, has to witness every sin and the detestable things done by His creation.

Jesus, the promised Messiah of Isaiah 53:3 (NLT) fulfilled prophecy by His response to the sin and rejection of His people. "He was despised and rejected—a man of sorrows, acquainted with deepest grief. We turned our backs on him and looked the other way. He was despised, and we did not care."

When Jesus came, He put the heart of the Father on exhibition for all of us to see, John 1:18 (NLT) says, "No one has ever seen God. But the unique One, who is Himself God, is near to the Father's heart. He has revealed God to us."

In Matthew 23:37 Jesus wept over the city of Jerusalem and weeps for the city saying, "O Jerusalem, Jerusalem, the city that kills the prophets and stones God's messengers! How often I have wanted to gather your children together as a hen protects her chicks beneath her wings, but you wouldn't let me" (NLT).

So often we ask God to understand our hearts and appreciate what we are going through, when in actual fact it is far more important that we understand and have a revelation of God's broken heart over a lost world!

Bob Pierce, founder of World Vision gave us a prayer to pray that I think might be one of the most important prayers any Christian can utter,

> Let my heart be broken
> by the things that break the heart of God.

Today more than ever before in human history we must ask God for a revelation of His broken heart over His world. We need to identify with God and ask Him to give us His broken heart for our fellowman. I believe this to be foundational to anything we would accomplish in

Christian service. God becomes our total focus, putting Him in His rightful place.

"But I, when I am lifted up from the earth, will draw all men to myself" (John 12:32).

Heroes

Heroes are important. I believe our current generation is sadly lacking in the right kind of heroes. When I was a senior in Bible college, David Wilkerson spoke in one of our chapel services and strongly encouraged us to read as many biographies of great men and women of God as we could. I have tried to follow his suggestion and have been greatly blessed and challenged to read many powerful life stories.

Pastor Jim Cymbala of Brooklyn Tabernacle once gave me a book to read regarding the life of Charles Finney. He knew that many of us in YWAM had a great love for Finney, "Nick, here's a new biography of the life of Charles Finney. I think you will enjoy reading it. It tells his life story including all the warts."

I love biographies that tell the true story of these great champions of the faith including their darkest days. It gives me hope for the imperfect creature that I am.

One of my greatest heroes of the faith has been General William Booth, founder of The Salvation Army. In 2005 I led a small team of our YWAM Metro New York staff to London following the terrorist bombings of the five railroad stations in the city. On our only day off in the 10 days we spent there, one of our London YWAM colleagues took us for a trip around London, especially the East End. We saw many famous sites including the birthplace of The Salvation Army and two different statues of General William Booth. Of course, I had to have my photo taken by one of them.

William Booth was loved by the people of London. At his funeral, on August 29, 1912 the procession included 5,000 uniformed Salvationists who marched through the city to the beat of 30 brass bands. The procession was a mile long, with 100,000 Londoners turning out to watch. A large number of the poor and disenfranchised of London marched in the procession to demonstrate their love and respect for this great man of God.

I have read a few books about William Booth, but one in particular gave me pause. It told a story from the later years of Booth's life just after the death of his dear wife and co-founder of The Salvation Army, Catherine Booth. They had always worked together as a team, and so it is today that every Salvation Army church has a husband-and-wife team as pastors, both of equal rank. Catherine was considered the best preacher of the two and actually wrote many of William Booth's sermons. He dearly missed her when she passed on October 4, 1890. General Booth was 61 when she died.

The story is told that General Booth was lovingly cared for by his children after the death of his dear wife, Catherine. One of his daughters was very concerned that her dad was working far too hard for his age. She would often give him lectures about his need for rest and would invite him over to her home to relax and have dinner. Most times he didn't come, caught up in all that he was doing with the Army.

On one particular day, however, his daughter heard a knock at her door in the afternoon and was so pleased to welcome her dad into her home. She quickly escorted him into her parlor, seating him in a soft chair with a footstool under his feet. She said to him, "Please rest and fall asleep, while I prepare dinner. When I am done, I will come and bring you into the dining room." She was so pleased and with great joy began her preparations. After about an hour or so she began to hear some sounds and traced them back to the parlor. She gently opened the door and peeked in. To her disappointment her dad was not sleeping or resting in the chair, but pacing the floor deep in prayer with great tears flowing down his cheeks.

Instead of showing reverence for this holy sight, she was so concerned that her dad had not followed her counsel to rest that she walked into the room and voiced her displeasure. General Booth was doing what came naturally to him, spending time in prayer. He smiled at his daughter and asked her to sit with him on the couch so he could share with her what had just happened to him.

The story I am about to tell you is the best definition of the word *vision* I have ever heard. Christians love to talk about *vision* and we in YWAM often use the word.

William Booth shared that he was resting, but as was his custom, he was also communing with the Lord. As he prayed, the Lord began to lay upon his heart the orphaned children of London. Now Booth was well acquainted with the orphans of his city. He probably knew many of them by name as he often walked the streets. There was already a Salvation Army ministry among them. This was different however; God was giving Booth His perspective of the orphans of London in a way Booth had never experienced before. You could say that God gave William Booth a SECOND TOUCH.

He said to his daughter, "God began to show me the orphan children of London like I have never seen them before."

This is what I believe is the first part of vision, *seeing what God sees!*

Her dad went on to say that when God began to show him the orphan children of London through His eyes, he began to weep.

This I believe is the second part of what vision is, *feeling what God feel!.*

You can't see what God sees without also experiencing His emotions. God was breaking General Booth's heart with the things that broke the heart of God.

He concluded by saying, "Then God showed me what I should do to help the orphan children of London." This is the final part of vision, *thinking God's thoughts!*

See What He Sees and Feel What He Feels

We can call this strategy! The important thing to understand in this story and as a matter of principle, is that before God can give anyone His strategy for ministry and missions, He must be assured that we first *see what He sees* and *feel what He feels.* Then, and only then, are we candidates for God to give us His strategy. When we identify with God's broken heart, He can then entrust us with His plan.

Many churches and ministries seek to know the best strategies for their programs. Too often the way we pursue this is by forming a committee to do research for new and innovative ideas. I like what I once read in an issue of a Reader's Digest magazine, "For God so loved the world He didn't send a committee." It has been my experience in ministry that committees often come up with expensive, complicated ideas that end up spending a lot of money and accomplishing very little.

Our world is too lost for *good ideas*, we need *God ideas*.

God's ideas only come when we earnestly seek the Lord and let Him break our heart with the things that break His. We need to be actively waiting and listening for Him to share with us, just as General William Booth did.

Alan Redpath, a well-known British evangelist, pastor and author said, "We need to be men so possessed by the Spirit of God that God can think His thoughts through our minds, that He can plan His will through our actions, that He can direct His strategy of world evangelization through His Church."

Two Approaches

To date Rozanne and I have served in YWAM for 49 years. If you were to ask me why we continue to serve in this mission, I would say because the strategies in evangelism have come from prayer meetings and not committee meetings! This has made all the difference!

I have identified what I like to call two approaches to world evangelism.

1. The **horizontal approach**. Here we endeavor to gain vision for the lost of this world. We research whatever we can find about them and make those lost people our total focus. The problem with this process is that whatever we come up with is very superficial at best. Theologically, if we just focus on a lost people group, we can begin to think that God is vindictive and the people pathetic. If we believe that, then we cannot ask that group to repent of their sins. This is what I call Christian

humanism! Humanism is bad enough, but Christian humanism is even worse.

Finally, this method provides a very poor motivation for evangelism and missions. When we make people our focus, we set ourselves up for failure and disillusionment. What happens when people don't appreciate our efforts, sacrifices and devotion to them? People can be very cruel and ungrateful for the things that we try to do for their benefit. Like Jesus and the prophets before Him, we may be misunderstood, unappreciated, falsely accused, etc. When people are our focus and this happens, it makes us want to give up as so many in ministry have done. Personally, I know some who were trained with me in Bible College to pastor churches. Today they would not darken a pulpit due to the abuse they received. Instead of receiving a pat on the back they got a kick in the pants and now want nothing more to do with ministry. It is very dangerous to make people our focus no matter how much we may love and care for them.

2. To achieve God's highest and best and gain vision for the lost of this world while ministering to their needs, we must have a **vertical approach**. God becomes our total focus. Only then is He able to give us a perspective of people that no resource could ever provide. He is the creator of every moral being on earth and knows and loves them intimately. Without God's perspective we will never understand mankind's intrinsic value. The burden and compassion He will share with us is far beyond our human understanding. He alone can give us the balance between both the temporal and the eternal.

Only God can give us the proper perspective of the gospel, enabling us to understand that He is guiltless and innocent regarding the plight of any individual. Consequently, we have the authority to present to them their need for repentance and reconciliation.

When God is our focus, we become candidates for His "God ideas" and strategies. We are eligible to receive from Him the deep secrets only He knows, enabling us to reach a person's heart. We become partners with God in the great work of salvation for a lost world, working together with the same mind and heart. The Holy Spirit becomes the *Paraclete*, meaning—the One Who stands beside us and does the work, drawing people to the Father.

Best of all, because our focus is on God Himself, our motivation is to bless Him with our service. It doesn't matter if what we do to reach out to people in need is appreciated or not. They may love us or they may want to kill us. The fact is that we do what we do for Him and Him alone. If we get a pat on the back or a bit lower down, it is still all for Him!

David Brainerd, American missionary to Native Americans, had that passion for God and man, he said, "I care not where I go, or how I live, or what I endure so that I may save souls. When I sleep, I dream of them; when I awake, they are first in my thoughts."

To conclude this chapter, I want to share a life-changing revelation God gave me some years ago on a well-known passage of Scripture.

The setting was Catania, Sicily. I had just arrived to visit with my father's family. My dad was with me and we were staying in my uncle's home. It was my first night in Italy and I was jet lagged, so I rose early in the morning and took my Bible out to the balcony of my uncle's condo for my morning devotions.

My New Testament reading that morning was Luke chapter 15. I first scanned the chapter and found it to be the story of the lost sheep and the lost coin, but the main part of the chapter told the story of the prodigal son.

I prayed, "Lord, I have heard the story of the prodigal son since I was a boy in Sunday School, I've also heard my pastor and a host of other evangelists preach on this text. I have even preached from the passage myself. Please show me something new, a revelation I have never understood before." I marvel at how the Holy Spirit can do this!

He began to unfold the story to me, as if telling how it could have been, or should have been, rather than the way it went. My focus became the older brother, the one who had the bad attitude at the end of the chapter. He was jealous of his brother's reconciliation with his father, and the lavish treatment the prodigal received.

I saw it unfold before me like a movie script. In scene one, the younger brother came before his father and demanded his inheritance. There is a major problem with this request, the father was not yet deceased. There could be no inheritance for either of his sons while he was still living. The father probably had to sell something in order to give his younger son the money. As he watched his brother leave, the older brother noticed tears flowing down his father's cheeks.

In scene two I saw the older son walking past his father's bedroom, stopping and listening to his father in prayer and travail for his rebellious son.

In scene three, the older brother observed his father walking down the road not once, but often throughout the day, peering into the distance, looking for any sign of his son returning home. This was very important since in Jewish law if the elders of the city saw this rebellious son before the father did, they were obligated to stone him to death for his rebellion. Therefore, the reason the father went down the road to search for his son was because he must find him first, and redeem his life from the sentence of death. This act of compassion would have registered with the older son and deeply impacted his mind and heart.

In the final scene of this "movie," the father came out of his bedroom one morning and looking toward the door noticed that there was a bag packed and ready to go. The father looked at his oldest son with a heavy heart, "Are you going to leave me too?"

The older son ran to his father, wrapped his arms around him and began to weep.

"Father, I am leaving today, but not for the same reason as my brother. You see, I have been watching and listening to you since my brother left us. You have demonstrated to me your great love for my brother. You have taught me to love him too. I love you and can't bear to see you suffering any more. Last night I decided I would go and find my brother, and when I do, I will tell him about your great love for him, and how your heart is broken over his rebellion. I will do my best to convince him to come home to you Father, because I know that if I can bring my brother home, I will bring healing to your broken heart!"

I was overwhelmed!

The only reason for evangelism must be because we are so in love with our Father, that we can't bear to see Him suffering anymore and want to bring healing to His broken heart!

Evangelism is an expression of our love relationship with God the Father and Jesus Christ, His Son. Our commitment must be to bring healing to God's broken heart. If this is not our heart motivation, we are working out of obligation and discouragement will be the inevitable outcome.

"Perhaps if there were more of that intense distress for souls that brings us to tears, we would more frequently see the results we desire. Sometimes it may be that while we are complaining of the hardness of the hearts of those we are seeking to benefit, the hardness of our own hearts and our feeble apprehension of the solemn reality of eternal things may be the true cause of our want of success."—Hudson Taylor

Chapter 14

Purpose for Pentecost

It has been said that Calvary is complimented by Pentecost. What was made possible for us at Calvary is made available to us at Pentecost. On the cross Jesus paid the price for our salvation. On the Mount of Olives, He gave His Church His last commandment, and it was at Pentecost that He released the power, energy and enabling to accomplish what His commission required.

To the followers of Jesus, Pentecost absolutely transformed their lives. There seems little to no comparison between the disciples before the cross and the apostles they became after Pentecost.

The words promised by Jesus on the Mount were made possible because of Pentecost. "But you will receive power when the Holy Spirit comes upon you. And you will be my witnesses, telling people about me everywhere—in Jerusalem, throughout Judea, in Samaria, and to the ends of the earth" (Acts 1:8 NLT)

I was privileged to meet Stanley M. Horton, author of several books, at Central Bible College in Springfield, Missouri. He commented on the power of the Spirit this way, "Jesus promised them power which became theirs through the Holy Spirit. *Dunamis* or mighty power, is how the Bible describes the Holy Spirit in Acts 1:8. The meaning or purpose of the baptism of the Holy Spirit is to receive the power and authority to be a witness, and for service."

"Dunamis" Power

The Greek word, *dunamis*, used in Acts 1:8 is often explained as dynamite but is in fact very different. Dynamite explodes, making the earth around it shake, usually causing great damage and often leaving nothing but a huge hole in the ground. I don't think that this was Christ's intent when He promised us "power from on high." Instead, I believe that power was more like the energy produced by a generator to accomplish something constructive.

We are often impressed by things that are loud and visible, like an explosion, but the person of the Holy Spirit, who is promised to every believer, is the power God gives us to accomplish His work. My brother, Carmelo, came home from a church service one evening and was trying to explain to Rozanne and I what the service was like. He kept saying the speaker was powerful. When I pressed him on what he meant by powerful, it became clear that the preacher spoke loudly. Personally, I would much prefer that the power was in the content of the message.

Anyone can stick a bobby pin in an electrical outlet and hold on for a thrill, or they can plug in an electric shaver and actually accomplish something constructive with that power. If I was in a steam locomotive, I could expend all of the built-up steam in the tank just by sounding the horn over and over, or I could put the locomotive in gear and proceed from one station to another.

I often refer to the power of the Holy Spirit as "the energy of heaven." Reaching the world and every creature with the gospel is a formidable task, to make it happen we need the power and energy of His Holy Spirit.

The late, great man of God, Reinhard Bonnke, who did powerful exploits for God in Africa, once shared on the 700 Club. "We have the Great Commission and we have the Holy Spirit. If we have only the

Great Commission or only the Holy Spirit, we have power without purpose or purpose without power. It is a package deal."

In the Old Testament God gave instructions to Moses regarding the consecration of the priests. First the blood of the sacrifice would be applied to the right ear lobe, right thumb, and right big toe. Afterward the anointing oil was placed on the same places. The blood speaks of salvation and the oil speaks of the anointing of the Holy Spirit.

Salvation must always precede the baptism of the Holy Spirit However, on occasion, it happens simultaneously as it did with those in the household of Cornelius in Acts 10:23-48.

The Benefits of the Baptism of the Holy Spirit in Evangelism

1. To Pray God's Prayers

When we intercede, we need to learn how to wait on God for the prayers He wants us to pray. Praying His prayers is the most important and powerful type of praying we can do. When we wait on the Lord, He shares with us the burdens of His heart, we have the privilege of actually praying in the will of God. This also assures us that we have been heard and the answer is on its way.

Sue, a Prayer Station worker, relates how God gave her a prayer to pray over a complete stranger, and how it hit the target.

"Two girls who had received flyers for the Prayer Station, began to pass by me. I asked if they wanted prayer and one girl looked startled. She asked if we were Christians and I said, 'Oh yes, and we pray to Jesus.' She looked relieved and explained that she thought we might be palm readers! I prayed for one of them. The Lord showed me an apartment with lovely wooden floors and windows with sun streaming in. So, I prayed that God would bless this girl with a beautiful apartment, as well as other needs.

"When I finished praying, she gave me her name and address and asked me to have someone from the nearby church get in touch with her. Then she asked how I knew that she had wanted a nicer apartment? I told her, 'God gives me pictures when I pray.' She smiled and nodded, but I knew that God had demonstrated His love and the promise of His blessing in a personal way to this lady."

2. Feeling God's Emotions

In Romans 8:26 (AMP) the Scripture says, "In the same way the Spirit [comes to us and] helps us in our weakness. We do not know what prayer to offer *or* how to offer it as we should, but the Spirit Himself [knows our need and at the right time] intercedes on our behalf with sighs *and* groanings too deep for words." Prayers prayed that are on the heart of God will be accompanied by God's emotions.

When I was a student at Zion Bible Institute, I had a roommate who was very emotional and would often pray with tears. I didn't have the same experience in prayer and was a little envious of his ability to be so broken in God's presence. Eventually I became desperate to the point of going on a fast and spending seasons of prayer earnestly asking God for tears. The more I prayed for this brokenness the more elusive it seemed to become. This brought about a state of depression so bad that I was not fun to be around anymore. My roommates gave me an ultimatum that I needed to stop this behavior or move out.

After one midweek evening meeting I went to a classroom to pray on my own. I stopped praying prayers for tears and focused my total attention on Jesus. God's presence filled that room so powerfully that I broke and began to weep uncontrollably for almost an hour.

God taught me a powerful lesson that evening, to always make Jesus my focus, not some kind of emotional experience. When Jesus becomes our focal point, we will no longer concern ourselves with anything else, but just allow God's presence to fill our hearts and lives and do whatever He chooses to do in us.

3. Go in God's Direction

When we pray and ask the Holy Spirit to guide us, He will.

When Peter was in prayer on the rooftop, God began to speak to him and prepare him for what would become a major paradigm shift for the early church.

God's heart was that the Gentiles receive the gospel and become a part of the body of Christ without first becoming Jews (Acts 10). Paul also received the Spirit's correction while in prayer, to change direction from going toward Asia and head toward Europe instead. So began the westward move of Christianity across the world (Acts 16).

Only the Holy Spirit can give us the direction we need to know the Father's will and plan. We can depend on the Holy Spirit to give us His direction both in major and minor decisions.

Countless times in our life and ministry Rozanne and I have experienced God graciously giving us this kind of direction by the inspiration of the Holy Spirit. The Holy Spirit speaks to us in His still small voice, or, on occasion in what seems to be an audible voice, like when I heard Him call me back to the city of my birth in 1981. Divine guidance is one of the great blessings of the Holy Spirit.

4. Have Boldness

Boldness is a byproduct of the baptism of the Holy Spirit. No matter whether you are a quiet introvert or an exuberant extrovert, there is a great element of courage and fearlessness that God can give you in the work of the Lord. The Holy Spirit will stiffen your spine and give you the "chutzpah" you need to obey Him.

Some who know me well might not believe that in reality I am an introvert. I enjoy privacy and never relish confrontation. I need to be honest and say that whenever I am in the preparation stages for evangelism, I do get butterflies in my stomach and, at times, even a little stress and tension. I find my strength when first, I know I am doing what God would have me to do, and second, by asking the Holy Spirit to give me His grace, peace and boldness.

As a boy, not trained in evangelism and having never read the Bible through once, I knocked on doors with no prepared statement but with the boldness of the Holy Spirit. He was with me then; He is with me now. He has always been faithful and enabled me to share the Good News of the gospel. Sometimes even in places and circumstances that were scary and even a little threatening.

While working for Teen Challenge, the chaplain of the Monmouth County Jail asked me to speak at a Sunday service regularly conducted at the prison. He was going to be out of town and I was going to be on my own with the prisoners. As only a few men attended the meeting I was told there was no need to worry. I brought along one of the residents of the program, Alvin, to give his testimony. We were ushered into the cafeteria of the prison and told to wait there until they were able to bring the prisoners in. Alvin and I prayed asking the Lord to help, direct and anoint us.

The doors of the cafeteria opened and prisoners began pouring into the room in large numbers. Apparently, there was a major bust in the county the night before and everyone wanted to come to the cafeteria to see which of their buddies had just been arrested—not to hear about Jesus! There were a couple of hundred quite fierce-looking characters in the room, roving around high fiving each other and causing quite a ruckus. The prison guards left the room and locked the doors.

I turned to my friend Alvin, "We can either let these guys take over or we get their attention and have our service." I swallowed hard and in the loudest voice I could muster (there was no sound system), I called out to the men to please be quiet! I introduced Alvin and myself and told them that we were there to have a Sunday service with them. They didn't strike me as a crowd that might know the words to "The Old Rugged Cross" or "Power in the Blood," so I took a deep breath and began to preach the gospel.

Immediately the room became quiet, you could have heard a pin drop. I knew I didn't have the luxury of time, so I followed the "KISS" method (Keep It Short, Stupid). After sharing my message, I introduced Alvin and he gave his testimony. Like many of our audience, he had been on drugs and in prison. Alvin was able to share how Jesus had made the difference in his life. I closed by saying that we would be happy to talk with any of them personally, and if anyone wanted prayer to receive Christ into their lives, we would be blessed to pray with them. To our surprise, the men became very friendly and we enjoyed some good personal time with a number of them, praying and even leading some to the Lord.

Holy Spirit boldness makes up for a lot that we might be lacking in our life and preparation. A story told by D.L Moody, one of America's greatest evangelists illustrates this fact.

"I can't help thinking of the old woman who started out when the war commenced with a poker in her hand. When asked what she was going to do with it she said: 'I can't do much with it, but I can show what side I'm on.'"

My friends, even if you can't do much, show which side you belong to!

The words of Acts 4:31 both challenge and encourage me. "After they prayed, the place where they were meeting was shaken. And they were all filled with the Holy Spirit and spoke the word of God **boldly**."

I am often amazed at the lack of boldness in the body of Christ these days among young people, middle-aged or even older. Boldness in general just seems to be lacking unilaterally. At times I wonder if some Christians think that timidity is one of the fruits of the Spirit! It is not!

Second Timothy 1:7 (AMP) says "For God did not give us a spirit of timidity *or* cowardice *or* fear, but [He has given us a spirit] of power and of love and of sound judgment *and* personal discipline [abilities that result in a calm, well-balanced mind and self-control]."

Boldness that is not a product of the Holy Spirit is ugly and does nothing to compliment the character of God. When, however, the Spirit gives us His holy boldness, it is both powerful and godly.

Mom Wilkerson (David and Don Wilkerson's mother) worked with her sons at Brooklyn Teen Challenge. While walking back alone to TC from the subway late one night following ministry in Manhattan, Mom Wilkerson became aware that two men were gaining ground behind her. She prayed, turned around, and facing the men she rebuked them in the name of Jesus! They both took off running in fear from a little lady full of Holy Spirit boldness!

It has been sad but somewhat amusing to me, to watch a group of Christians sing "Christian fight songs" about putting Satan under their feet, and then watch them as we hit the streets. These "mighty warriors" cower, afraid to approach a single person to ask them if they would like to receive prayer. Acting tough within the safety of church walls, but terrified in the marketplace means we lack the boldness of the Holy Spirit.

While on outreach in Cuautitlan, Izcalli, Mexico, just outside of Mexico City, we had set up our Prayer Station with a Spanish banner, aprons, and Gospels of John. I asked one of my Mexican friends to give me the phrase in Spanish for **"May I pray for you?"** I quietly practiced the words "Puedo orar por usted?" In a few minutes a lady approached and I let fly with my version of the *five little words*. The dear lady looked at me in utter horror and started running! To this day I have no idea what I said, apparently it was not "Puedo orar por usted?" I was so embarrassed I wanted to quit, but instead I turned to the Lord asking Him for His encouragement and boldness. He answered, and I had a wonderful day of ministry.

Rozanne continues

Boldness may or may not be in our genes, but I believe it comes from a willingness to obey the Holy Spirit when He speaks, sight unseen.

In the early summer of 1987, we were living in Hauppauge, Long Island, having left the *Anastasis* the year before. Anita was 17 years old, the same age I was when God directed me to leave my homeland and go to New York City, alone. Funny how your life can close your mouth.......

A personal phone invitation from Dale Kaufman, founder of YWAM's King's Kids International, came for Anita. Dale asked our daughter to be a part of the King's Kids International Team that was going to the Philippines that summer. They had been invited to perform at a large Asia and Pacific YWAM Conference and outreach in Manila, the capital city.

I remember standing in the kitchen when Anita walked in and asked me what she should do? "Go to your bedroom and pray," I responded.

She did, and an hour or so later she came out.

"What did God say," I asked.

Her reply was brief, "He said, 'Acts chapter 12.'"

"Any particular part of the chapter?"

"No, just Acts chapter 12."

The next morning, I went to prayer with my Bible open to Acts chapter 12. Not a comforting scripture for a mum whose daughter is considering traveling to the Philippines, alone. Peter was in prison!

Anita had had a pain in her side for about a week which we could not explain. I took her to the doctor and he had no answers. The first thing that "struck" me in Acts 12 was verse 7.

"Suddenly an angel of the Lord appeared and a light shone in the cell. He *struck* Peter on the side and woke him up. 'Quick, get up!' he said, and the chains fell off Peter's wrists."

It became clear to me that we needed to move on this very quickly. We called the airlines and found the flight to the Philippines out of California for the date we needed was filling up very fast. We booked Anita one of the last available seats. After the booking was made, the pain in Anita's side miraculously went away!

My next thought was how could we find a traveling companion for Anita. We knew a number of YWAMers would be flying to the Philippines for the Conference, surely Anita could hook up with one of them in LA. We tried, but failed to find anyone scheduled to fly out at the same time.

Again, I went to prayer and again God answered from Acts 12.

"Who took Peter out of prison?"

"An angel, Lord," I responded.

"I have an angel to travel with Anita," He said.

When I shared this with our daughter, she was scared, "Oh Mum, that's spooky, I don't think I like that."

"Don't worry, hon," I responded, "God's angels come in all shapes and sizes and nationalities."

There were no funds for Anita's trip, no savings account to draw from, but over the few weeks we had to prepare, every need down to the last dollar was provided. I never cease to be amazed at how God does that. Anita prayed too and watched as her airfares, costume, ground fees, a little spending money, clothes, shoes, everything needed was provided. This is how our girls have learned that God is faithful, and whenever and wherever He calls, He always makes a way. Anita had a front row seat to God's faithfulness to her "Yes."

Travel day arrived and Nick and I drove Anita to JFK International Airport, staying with her until she boarded. We knew God had orchestrated this mission, we knew we could entrust our precious girl to His care, but seeing an angel hovering overhead at that point would have been very comforting.

Returning to our car we began to drive home. We hadn't gone far when Anita called from a pay phone to tell us that as they were taxiing out to the runway, they were told there were some mechanical issues with the plane. They had returned to the terminal. We exited the Southern Parkway, changed direction, and headed back.

Anita was waiting for us. We were told the plane needed repairs and the wait time would be significant. Anita shared that in the short time she had been on board she had chatted with the lovely Philippino lady sitting next to her. Anita introduced us.

This sweet woman told Nick and I, "Don't worry, if this delay means that we miss our connection in Japan, I will take care of Anita. Whatever happens I will be with her, don't worry." We knew Anita had her angel, and God had arranged for us to meet her!

They did miss their connecting flight, and were put up in a hotel. Anita's angel took her to dinner, and the next day took her for a tour of Tokyo. They caught the evening flight to the Philippines together. When they arrived Anita could not see anyone in the terminal to pick her up.

"Don't worry," Anita's angel said, "I will stay with you until they arrive," and she did. Eventually Anita saw a man with a Conference sign. She greeted him, turned to hug her friend who she wanted to thank and say good-bye to, but she was nowhere to be found!

Just as God had promised, Anita had her angel.

Anita has been married to her wonderful husband Ron Setran, for 28 years now. They have 3 beautiful children and a daughter-in-law. Anita is the Executive Director of Prayer Stations Inc. working alongside her dad every day which they both enjoy.

Karissa, Anita's oldest daughter, has her mother's boldness and tenacity. One day in middle school science, her teacher asked the class to share their opinion about how the earth came to be? Karissa, without hesitation and with holy boldness and typical dramatic flair, popped her hand up and simply said, "GOD!" The teacher was somewhat taken aback by this and responded, "Well, Karissa, there are many who have other ideas." Karissa knew her "holy boldness" might cost her, but she did not hesitate for a moment to proclaim her faith. In 2019 Karissa traveled to South America with a team from her Christian college. She visited five countries, sharing her faith and even preaching to a large outdoor crowd.

One of our grandsons, Tyler Burd, oldest son of Dan and our daughter Rebecca, was part of a YWAM Joshua Generation outreach in Boston. Tyler had no misgivings as a middle schooler to go with a team to the Harvard University campus and share his faith with the students. I asked him later how that went and he said a number of the students told him that he gave them much to think about!

Our grandkids, Tyler, Caleb, Karissa and Aidan have all been on Prayer Station outreaches with us. We send the intellectuals to Tyler; he always challenges them!

One day I went to pick Tyler up from the secular college he was attending at the time. He walked toward me in a black tee shirt emblazoned with bold white lettering that read, "I AM A CHRISTIAN." I was so blessed by his courage and genuine witness for Christ.

After a Prayer Station outreach in the city, Nick was driving our grandchildren home, and in typical style they were totally stopped on the Long Island Northern State Parkway (sometimes known as the Long Island Parking Lot!). Tyler, who was sitting shotgun, was looking out his window at the young man in the car that was stopped right next to them. "Poppa, shouldn't we ask if we can pray for him?" Nick was surprised at his boldness. "Sure," he said. Tyler put down his window and managed to get the man next to him to do the same. Our 14-year-old engaged him in conversation and witnessed, and then asked if he could pray for him, which he did. I am very sure that young man has never forgotten his encounter with a teenager in the middle of the Northern State Parkway!

Children and young people have the potential to be powerhouses for the gospel. They just need a mission, an opportunity to serve, an example of boldness that assures them that, "All things are possible to him who believes" (Mark 9:23 NKJV).

Prayer Station testimonials in their own words, from young people with God-given boldness...

Taylor
"I could never have imagined myself going up to people and telling them about Jesus. At least not random people on the street. I have been able to minister to my friends, but God gave me a different kind of strength to be able to go up to these people. It was awesome."

Jason
"I loved being brought out of my comfort zone into a place where I can be used by the Spirit to minister."

Laurie
"The Prayer Stations were a big 'stretch' for me. They took me out of my comfort zone and made me bolder about my faith than ever before. I got to pray with so many people. God used me to pray with three people to receive Christ which was the best and most exciting experience ever."

Nicole
"I was impressed and overwhelmed by God's feelings for these people that didn't know Him. It was a great experience! God broke a huge part of the fear of man that I had in my life. I even wanted to keep praying for people on the street after the Prayer Station time had finished. God is so awesome!"

Andy
"God answered my prayers for boldness and courage."

"His voice leads us not into timid discipleship but into bold witness."—Charles Stanley, Senior Pastor of First Baptist Church in Atlanta, Georgia; founder and president of In Touch Ministries and past President of the Southern Baptist Convention

"Catch on fire with enthusiasm and people will come for miles to watch you burn."—Charles Wesley

Nick continues

5. To Do God's Works

The Holy Spirit works through us to do exploits for God. The disciples, who during the time Jesus was with them here on earth, often suffered from unbelief Following Pentecost, signs, wonders, miracles and healings became a daily occurrence in their ministry to the marketplace. "And the disciples went everywhere and preached, and the Lord worked through them, confirming what they said by many miraculous signs" (Mark 16:20 (NLT).

6. For Conviction of Sin

It is always important that we understand what our part is in evangelism and what part the Holy Spirit plays. We are God's agents, which means our choices affect our witness. If we choose not to be prepared and not to make evangelism a serious commitment, our experience won't have the impact it might have had.

A Bible teacher once said, "Winning a soul to Christ is the hardest job in the world."

We need to be prepared and do our pre-evangelism, which involves both knowing God and knowing our fellowman, his or her thoughts, ideologies, philosophies, and religions.

We may not be as successful as we could be because we do not understand the role of the Holy Spirit. It is His job to enlighten, persuade, and convict. We lovingly present truth and He brings illumination. We might be able to bring condemnation, but the Holy Spirit brings conviction which involves His power to draw people to Jesus.

"No one can come to Me unless the Father who sent Me draws him [giving him the desire to come to Me]; and I will raise him up [from the dead] on the last day" (John 6:44 AMP).

The Father's wooing works through the power of the Holy Spirit. An excellent demonstration of this took place after Peter's anointed sermon on the day of Pentecost.

> When the people heard this, they were cut to the heart and said to Peter and the other apostles, "Brothers, what shall we do?"
>
> Peter replied, "Repent and be baptized, every one of you, in the name of Jesus Christ for the forgiveness of your sins. And you will receive the gift of the Holy Spirit" (Acts 2:37-38).

In 1991 we took a team to Ukraine just as the Communist iron curtain was falling and the USSR was crumbling. We didn't know what to expect, but God's Holy Spirit mightily anointed our small band. Each day our street meetings drew hundreds of people. When we preached the gospel and gave the altar call most of the crowd came forward and asked to receive Christ as their Savior. At one meeting I purposefully made the altar call as hard as I could, emphasizing repentance and turning from their sinful lives. They still came in droves.

During that outreach we were invited to speak to soldiers at an army barracks. They marched into the auditorium looking stern and serious, demonstrating no emotion as we shared the gospel with them. One of our team was an army vet and shared his testimony. At the conclusion of our program, we gave an invitation for them to receive Christ and we held our breath. To our amazement the officers came forward first, followed by the rank and file. The Holy Spirit touched their hearts and brought them all to Jesus!

Billy Graham said it best, "It is the Holy Spirit's job to convict, God's job to judge, and my job to love."

7. Speak God's Words

The distance is vast between words that come from our intellect, opinion or frame of reference, and God's wisdom and perspective. Our words, no matter how profound we think they may be, cannot come close to yielding the same results as His. We need always to desire that God give us the right words to speak at the opportune time.

John 12:49 says "For I did not speak on my own, but the Father who sent me commanded me to say all that I have spoken."

If Jesus was committed to sharing only what the Father gave Him to say, how much more must we be intentional about doing the same. Luke 12:12 says "the Holy Spirit will teach you at that time what you should say."

The baptism of the Holy Spirit and the tongue have special relevance right from the beginning and throughout our life. "All of them were filled with the Holy Spirit and began to speak in other tongues as the Spirit enabled them" (Acts 2:4). Not only are we able to speak in other languages, but even the words of our own native tongue will have greater power and authority.

Throughout my life I've been aware when I spoke with God's anointing and when I did not. I have regrets for things I have uttered with my own understanding, but I have never ever regretted saying anything that I knew came directly from God, no matter how it may have been received.

When we speak God's words with the accompanying power of the Holy Spirit, we call that "the anointing."

One professor in my Bible college said something that has always stuck with me. She said, "I don't know whether I can always define what the anointing is, but I sure know when I don't have it."

God desires that we always speak His words, we must be ready to hear, receive and share as He directs. First Peter 4:11 (NET BIBLE) says

"Whoever speaks, let it be with God's words. Whoever serves, do so with the strength that God supplies, so that in everything God will be glorified through Jesus Christ. To him belong the glory and the power forever and ever. Amen."

This marvelous and powerful blessing that God affords us through the Holy Spirit's anointing is invaluable in the process of evangelism. In my first year of serving in YWAM I led a summer evangelism team to work with a church in Buffalo, New York. One afternoon we walked through a park adjacent to a university where many students hung out. My evangelism partner and I came across a student couple walking their dog and we began a conversation with them. The couple were not married but were living together. They kept firing questions at us. They asked about the existence of God, the validity of the Bible, evolution, etc. I had carefully studied all of these arguments and was actually quite proud of the answers I was giving them. After talking for about half an hour and fielding all kinds of questions that were coming like machine gun fire, one after the other, I began to realize that we were getting nowhere fast, (sometimes I have a keen sense for the obvious!).

Finally, at one point, as my partner was speaking, I paused long enough to cry out to the Lord, asking Him, "Where do we go from here?" I realized that their queries weren't really honest questions, but rather a smoke screen to protect themselves because of the way they had chosen to live their lives.

I will never forget God's answer. He reminded me of something I had heard a Bible teacher say years before. God said, "I want you to tell them these words, then thank them for speaking with you both and end the conversation."

So, I said to them in the words of my Teacher, The Holy Spirit, "You know, sometimes our lifestyle dictates our philosophy."

As I spoke, I looked into their eyes and knew immediately that His words had hit their mark. Rather than firing back with another question, it was as if they had been hit with a stun gun. They were silent. I thanked them for speaking with us, shook their hands and said goodbye.

I have prayed for that couple through the years, and I believe that one day we will meet again in Heaven. Perhaps they will even come up to me and say, "What you said to us that day stayed with us until we found our way to God and received Christ as our Savior."

As I shared earlier, success in evangelism depends upon obedience. We need to know what God wants us to say and, equally important, not say, and also trust Him to know when to quit. When we are dependent on the power of the Holy Spirit, God will speak through us and His word will not return to Him empty. "So will My word be which goes out of My mouth; It will not return to Me empty [useless, without result], Without accomplishing what I desire, and without succeeding *in the matter* for which I sent it" (Isaiah 55:11 NASB).

Even if it comes to the point where our life depends on the words we say, God's promise is that He will, in that hour, give us His words.

For I will give you [skillful] words and wisdom which none of your opponents will be able to resist or refute (Luke 21:15 AMP).

When they take you and turn you over [to the court], do not worry beforehand about what to say, but say whatever is given to you [by God] in that hour; for it is not you who speak, but it is the Holy Spirit [who will speak through you] (Mark 13:11 AMP).

Testimonies from Prayer Station volunteers giving examples of the Holy Spirit's power to speak God's words in their witness:

Mary Catherine

"One person stopped and I prayed for him about his relationship with his wife. It was cool because I don't know anything about marriage as a 16-year-old, but God gave me the exact words to say."

Amber

"I talked with one man today who has touched my heart and intrigued me. From the moment we started talking, I realized how scared and insecure he was in his environment. God enabled me to use words and sentences that were so natural. Not once did I feel nervous or panic for the next thing to say. He told me that I was pushing all the right buttons in the things I shared with him about Christ."

Hayley

"I constantly prayed to God that He would give me the words to say because I'm an introvert and He did. I know God sent those people to me and gave me the right words to say. I was much more comfortable than I'd thought I'd be, and it really was an amazing experience."

Jenna

"I was praying with this one lady, and while praying, I asked the Lord to restore to her what the devil had stolen. After I got done praying, she told me a story that went right along with what I had prayed regarding God's restoration."

Danielle

"I prayed not only that God would make me louder, but that people's ears would be open to hear. I was so happy and joyful to pray with the people and God granted me clarity to speak, which is something I often don't have as words elude me. It was a God-filled day. His Holy Spirit was with me."

Beth

"My eyes were opened more than ever to the depth of the pain and needs of the lost. When I prayed, the Spirit gave me the right words. I am learning to rely on God in my weakness and to hear His voice."

8. Power over the Enemy

Satan is not God's counterpart and by no means is he any match for the Holy Spirit. He is only a fallen angel as are his demonic forces as well. The work of the Holy Spirit in evangelism is also to restrain the enemy and take control of the atmosphere. I always try to impress on our teams to first prayer walk the area where they will be ministering.

We call this spiritual warfare, but the warfare is accomplished by the power of the Spirit.

I have been privileged to go into some very interesting but evil environments with the gospel, and I have seen God do exploits bringing the enemy under the control of the Spirit.

In 1990 I took a team into Romania just months after the tyrant, Nicolae Ceaușescu, had slaughtered a number of protestors on the steps of the Romanian Orthodox Church in Timișoara. Ceausescu and his wife were killed by a firing squad shortly after. The city was in great unrest and no one knew what the future held for its citizens. The Spirit of God spoke to us to drive into Timisoara and do open air evangelism on Piata Victoriei (Victoria Square) just a few hundred yards down from the site of the massacre.

We made contact with a local pastor and the pastor's son accompanied us to the square. We were no more than a dozen in number, and we formed a circle in the middle of the square. The Romanian people knew we were Americans, and looked at us tentatively. We began in prayer and in worship singing gospel songs in English. To our surprise, people began to flock around our little circle. Soon there were hundreds. We stopped singing and began to share the gospel. To our knowledge, we were the first group of Christians that had ever done something like this in Romania since the Communist takeover of that country.

The people listened intently and we ended our presentation with an invitation. People came forward to receive Christ. We had the opportunity to talk with many through interpreters and with some who spoke a little English. After about half an hour we repeated our circle of prayer and worship and presented the gospel to a whole new group with similar results.

God the Holy Spirit took control of the atmosphere, heaven came down and touched the hearts of the people. The spirit of death and destruction was overcome by God's love and mercy. "And these signs will accompany those who believe: In my name they will drive out demons" (Mark 16:17).

9. To Bring Unity to the Body of Christ

The baptism of the Holy Spirit is a baptism of Love! If we say we are filled with the Spirit then we should be overflowing with love for our brothers and sisters in the body of Christ irrespective of our differing points of view on non-essential areas of doctrine. The greater truth we have the more tolerant we ought to be of other Christians.

I heard Floyd McClung share years ago that there is a big difference between the unity of the *Spirit* and the unity of the *faith*. I don't believe the body of Christ will ever experience the unity of the faith until we all see Jesus and He makes all doctrine clear. We all have different points of view on non-essential areas. But the Bible does promise us the unity of the Spirit. That means that even though we don't totally agree on every point, we are yet one body.

Rupertus Meldenius, a Christian writer in A.D. 1627 said, "In the essentials unity, in non-essentials liberty, in all things charity."

The Scripture says in John 16:13 "But when he, the Spirit of truth, comes, he will guide you into all the truth..." I believe the way that happens is by God spreading out His truth to the whole body of Christ. Different parts of the body have different understanding of Scripture that others do not. The Holy Spirit guides us into all truth by giving us the humility to bow to the revelation our brother or sister has that we don't and they do the same with us. So, we all come to God's truth.

The most important thing I have learned about evangelism is that without the anointing and power of the Holy Spirit it can't be done. That's why Jesus said to His disciples to "...stay in the city until you have been clothed with power from on high" (Luke 24:49).

"To evangelize is to so present Jesus Christ in the power of the Holy Spirit, that men shall come to put their trust in God through Him, to accept Him as their Savior, and serve Him as their King in the fellowship of His church."—William Temple, former Archbishop of Canterbury

Chapter 15

House of Prayer

The Bible is replete with evidence of God's presence among His creation.

The Old Testament House of Prayer

Beginning with the Book of Genesis:

— God walked with Adam and Eve in the Garden in the cool of the day (Genesis 3:8)

— He appeared to Abraham when he offered his sacrifice before the Lord (Genesis 15)

— For Moses God's presence was manifest through a burning bush (Exodus 3:1-17)

— Then with the pillar of cloud and the pillar of fire (Exodus 13:21)

— On Mount Sinai, in the giving of the Law (Exodus 20:1-21)

— In Exodus 33:11 it says "The Lord would speak to Moses face to face, as one speaks to a friend...." Moses had an intimate relationship with God and spent much time in His presence

In Exodus 20 God gives Moses the Law. Later He gave very detailed directions regarding the building of the Tabernacle. The Tabernacle then became the place where God's presence dwelt, until Solomon built the Temple in 1 Kings 6. The Temple signified the place where God's presence resided until the birth of the Christ child. In these earthly structures people worshipped God, and found forgiveness for their sins. They were "God's House of Prayer."

Jesus Becomes the House of Prayer

When Jesus came to earth, He was the very presence of God dwelling among us. John 1:14 says in the Tree of Life Version, "And the Word became flesh and tabernacled among us." In Young's Literal Translation it says "And the Word became flesh, and did tabernacle among us, and we beheld his glory, glory as of an only begotten of a father, full of grace and truth."

When Jesus died on the cross the Scripture declares in Matthew 27:51 that "At that moment the curtain of the temple was torn in two from top to bottom. The earth shook, the rocks split." This is the veil that separated the Holy place from the Holy of Holies. The veil served as a physical and visual barrier, between the Holy place and the Most Holy presence of the enthroned Lord, Therefore, creating separation between God and man.

Hebrews 10:19-20 says "Therefore, brothers and sisters, since we have confidence to enter the Most Holy Place by the blood of Jesus, by a new and living way opened for us through the curtain, that is, his body."

Jesus not only becomes the Father's House of Prayer as the embodiment of the presence of God for us, but also, through His death, opens the way for us to have access with God through His shed blood and death.

The era of the Tabernacle and Temple has ended and now there is complete access to the Holy of Holies for all of humankind. The House of Prayer is no longer a building but a Person, the Lord Jesus Christ!

Believers Become God's House of Prayer

When Jesus ascended to the Father He promised His followers that He would send them the Holy Spirit to dwell in them, and empower them as they do His bidding. On that day, the day of Pentecost, a new dynamic takes place, a new paradigm shift. Jesus, the House of Prayer from the Father now dwells by His Spirit in every believer and they become "God's House of Prayer for the Nations"!

— Matthew 18:20 "For where two or three gather in my name, there am I with them."

— 1 Corinthians 3:16 "Don't you know that you yourselves are God's temple and that God's Spirit dwells in your midst?"

— 1 Peter 2:5 "you also, like living stones, are being built into a spiritual house to be a holy priesthood, offering spiritual sacrifices acceptable to God through Jesus Christ."

— Ephesians 2:21 "In him the whole building is joined together and rises to become a holy temple in the Lord."

Jesus, the apostles and the early church became walking, talking, HOUSES OF PRAYER to their world! They became living and powerful PRAYER STATIONS! The book of Acts is replete with stories of these early believers bringing the presence of God to their generation and world. Everywhere they went they carried the shekinah presence of God within them.

After you receive Jesus Christ as Savior, you become the temple of the Holy Spirit. 1 Corinthians 6:19 reminds us "Do you not know that your bodies are temples of the Holy Spirit, who is in you, whom you have received from God? You are not your own."

Through the ages of Christendom, the church has been obsessed with buildings and properties. Land and buildings are often treated as if they were sacred. We call our meeting places "the House of God," often spending huge amounts to build, beautify and maintain these houses of worship. Sadly, we can begin to associate these buildings with God's presence and convince ourselves that only when we gather together in these meeting places is God present. That position is simply Old Testament.

Jim Cymbla, pastor of the Brooklyn Tabernacle, said in his message on "The House of Prayer" that "There are no sacred buildings."

Buildings and properties can become the Church's greatest hindrance to bringing closure to the Great Commission. Possessions are that which we have already attained. Former YWAM colleagueKalafi Morla once said, "Too often these possessions are material things."

"Ask me, and I will make the nations your inheritance, the ends of the earth your possession"(Psalm 2:8).

Our inheritance is that which we have not yet attained. The unreached. We have too often been preoccupied with our possessions at the expense of our inheritance.

When we begin to revere buildings and call them sacred, we lose the power God gave the church at Pentecost!

People of the Presence of God

God has called and equipped us to be people of the presence of God wherever we go. This is true of us as a body of believers, but also true of us as individuals. When Peter walked the streets of Jerusalem, he brought with him the presence of God. Acts 5:15 (AMP) says "to such an extent that they even carried their sick out into the streets and put them on cots and sleeping pads, so that when Peter came by at least his shadow might fall on one of them [with healing power]."

Keith Thomas wrote in his book, *If God Is for Us:*

In nineteenth century, America, God touched the life of
Charles Finney. He was a man that gave himself to prayer and

the ministry of the Word of God. The Lord used him greatly in ministry from church to church. The presence of the Spirit was on him to such a degree that people who heard him would come under great conviction of heart and feel cut to their very inner being. On one occasion Finney was preaching in a school house, Suddenly an awful Solemnity fell upon the assembly and the people fell from their seats crying for mercy. Finney said, "If I had had a sword in each hand, I could not have cut them off as fast as they fell. I think the whole congregation was on their knees or prostrated in two minutes." The crying and weeping of the people was so loud that Finney's exhortation of God's mercy could not even be heard. Finney seemed so anointed by the Holy Spirit that people were often brought under conviction of sin just by looking at him. When holding meetings in Utica, NY, he visited a large factory. At the sight of him, one of the workers and then another and then another broke down and wept under the sense of their sins and finally so many were sobbing and weeping that the machinery had to be stopped while Finney pointed them to Christ.

These stories should not only be of historical figures like Peter and Charles Finney, but also of Christians today, Spirit-filled vessels bringing the presence of God wherever they go.

The first martyr of the Christian Church, Stephen, standing before the Sanhedrin said in Acts 7:48 "However, the Most High does not live in houses made by human hands..." We are to be the embodiment of the Spirit of God and the presence of God to everyone we meet.

The most important asset of the Christian church should be prayer. It is more essential for change in our world and society than anything else we do.

"To be a Christian without prayer is no more possible than to be alive without breathing."—Martin Luther

Pastor Cymbla also said the following: "Preaching, music, reading of the Word, are all good, but God called His House, a House of PRAYER!"

"The Church should be a place of prayer more than anything else. Many churches have everything but prayer."

"On the day of Pentecost, the Christian Church was formed not where people were preaching but where they were praying! Prayer is what will change the world."

"Every historical revival began with prayer."

Prayer Is Primary

The Scripture makes it very clear in 1 Timothy 2:1, "I urge, then, first of all, that petitions, prayers, intercession and thanksgiving be made for all people." Prayer is primary and of the highest priority so that the apostle Paul says to Timothy, "FIRST OF ALL."

God puts a very high value on the prayers of His people. He tells us in Revelation 5:8-9 "The four living creatures and the twenty-four elders fell down before the Lamb, each having a harp, and golden bowls full of incense, which are the prayers of the saints. And they sang a new song, saying: 'You are worthy to take the scroll, and to open its seals; for you were slain, and have redeemed us to God by your blood out of every tribe and tongue and people and nation.'"

Our motto for Prayer Stations has always been "Prayer Changes Things." We don't know who said it originally, but it is true and very Biblical. We need to know and believe that our prayers are powerful and effective. James 5:16 (NLT) says "Confess your sins to each other and pray for each other so that you may be healed." The earnest prayer of a righteous person has great power and produces wonderful results.

We are not just observers of all God is doing in the world, but participators. The great Bible teacher Derek Prince wrote a book that was entitled *Shaping History through Prayer and Fasting*. It made clear that prayer is powerful enough to actually shape history.

Another great book *Reese Howells: Intercessor*, is the story of this great man of faith and prayer who rallied the Christians of Britain at the critical time of the Battle of Britain. It was the prayers of these men and women of God that saved that great nation and the world from tyranny.

Norman Grubb said, "How thankful we are that God had this company of hidden intercessors, whose lives were on the altar day after day as they stood in the gap for the deliverance of Britain." Prime Minister Winston Churchill famously said regarding the Royal Air Force, "Never has so much been owed by so many to so few." It is true that those brave RAF pilots in their Spitfires did so much to save Britain from being invaded by the Nazis. I also believe that the real battle, fought on the knees of those faithful intercessors raised up by Reese Howells, made the biggest contribution to the victory of the Battle of Britain.

The Christian's Personal Prayer Life

Effective prayer begins in our personal prayer life. Some call it their quiet time, devotions, the war room, or the prayer closet but nevertheless it is the foundation and core of our intercession.

Here we pray both prayers of supplication (for ourselves, our family and those that are close to us) and also prayers of intercession where we stand in the gap for others. If we have no personal prayer life, we have no other access with God. Access with God comes through salvation, given to us at Calvary, and power with God comes through the work of the Holy Spirit given to us at Pentecost.

One of my dear professors at Zion Bible Institute, Marie King, said something in one of her classes that I shall never ever forget. It is a principle I have used to pattern my walk with God and especially my ministry. She said, "Service is born out of communion." It is that sweet communion with God that gives us both access and power.

Beginning with my time as a student at the YWAM School of Evangelism in Hurlach Germany, my life has been infused with the importance of intercessory prayer. I have prayed alone, together with family, with colleagues and friends, in all manner of situations and places. Many times with an intercessory prayer partner, most often Rozanne, but also other fellow laborers. It has been in times like these that God has spoken to us, and has granted us victory for the battle we were about to face. It is in the place of prayer that the real battle is fought and won. I love the balance in the Word of God between praying and doing. They are in sync together, but praying always comes first.

Intercessory Prayer

Results of intercession:

- God gives us the power to accomplish His work
- God gives us His guidance, what to do, when, and how
- God prepares the hearts of those to whom we will minister
- Spiritual warfare takes place and the enemy is bound and defeated

There is a difference between praying FOR people and WITH people. When we pray for people, we may be praying for individuals, groups, cities, nations, people groups, etc. A Bible teacher once said, "No one comes into the Kingdom who isn't prayed in first!" Perhaps you don't know that anyone prayed for you before you came to Christ. The fact is they may not have even known your name, but I guarantee that when you get to heaven the Lord will introduce you to the person or persons that helped pray you into the kingdom. If there was no earthly intercessor the Bible says in Romans 8:34 that Jesus ever lives to make intercession for us.

Prayer Walking

There is a story I read in a book called *Prayer Walking* by Steven C. Hawthorne. It was one of many exciting prayer walking stories Steven related. A couple began to prayer walk through their neighborhood. As they did, God kept giving them a deep burden for whoever lived in a particular home just down the block from theirs. They didn't know who lived there. They had never seen anyone in the course of their prayer walks, but each time they passed that home God asked them to pray for the residents, specifically that they would come to Christ.

After doing this for some months, one day for the first time, they saw a man and woman standing in front of the home. Without hesitation they went over and introduced themselves.

After a good conversation the Christian couple began to speak of spiritual things. At that point the couple shared that they had not been very spiritually minded until some months ago when they turned to each other and said, "Let's buy a Bible and begin to read it together." As they read their new Bible the Holy Spirit began to speak to them and soon after they gave their lives to Christ! They were now a part of a Bible-believing church. The Christian couple did not know them, or even their names when they began to pray, but God heard their prayers and drew this man and woman to Himself.

Praying For and Praying With

Praying FOR someone is great and effective but there is something very dynamic that can happen when we actually pray WITH an individual. The encouragement value can be off the charts!

While serving as the director of YWAM Concord, New Hampshire back in the early '80s, I received some very bad news about our ministry's finances, or rather the lack thereof. I was actually overwhelmed by what I had just been told and felt like everything was being upended. I walked sullenly from the ministry center to the home our family was living in. Bursting into our living room I found Rozanne was counseling one of our staff. I walked quickly past them and upstairs to our bedroom where I paced the floor in deep depression. I took a moment to write a very short, very to the point, note, and went back downstairs and handed it to Rozanne. Rozanne scanned it and quickly finished the session with prayer, then ran upstairs to see what could possibly have happened that was so urgent. Realizing the state I was in, she immediately called for one of the leaders of the ministry to come over to our home and pray with us. David DeFebbo and Rozanne prayed WITH me and I felt the weight of the world come off my shoulders. God miraculously helped us through that crisis, but what I will never forget is how very thankful I was that they just didn't pray FOR me but WITH me!

This is what prayer in the market place is all about. One Prayer Station volunteer, Carlenie, put it this way, "Prayer Stations give the ability to reach out and touch the lives of people right where they work, live or visit."

People are deeply touched when we pray with them. It touches their hearts and brings about a softening of their attitude and sensitivity to the Holy Spirit.

Steve, who worked at a Prayer Station at Ground Zero said, "I loved joining with people and leading them before God in faith, knowing His love was at work in us. The Prayer Station experience was awesome! Heaven opened over us at an altar on the sidewalk."

We are God's house of prayer and we bring God's presence wherever we go and to whomever we meet. They don't need to come to a church structure to meet with God. He is with us and when we meet people who don't know Him. God is revealed to them through our lives, our conversation and especially our prayers.

Lisa, a Prayer Station volunteer with a Ph.D. shared, "I most enjoyed the fact that we were taking truth and life-altering prayer outside the walls of the church building."

We are the Gospel According to Us! We become what Oral Roberts used to call "the point of contact."

It is the heart of God to bring the message of His love, mercy and forgiveness to the people, where they are, and draw them to Himself. We are that conduit for the love of God!

Charles Spurgeon said, "Love your fellow man, and cry about them if you cannot bring them to Christ. If you cannot save them, you can weep over them. If you cannot give them a drop of cold water in hell, you can give them your heart's tears while they are still in this body."

The Fire Engine and the Ambulance

Imagine that you are a fireman in your city. What should you do to be of service to your community? You could just keep the fire engine in the fire house, clean it, polish it, gather around it and sing fire engine songs, perhaps hear speeches about firefighting. All of this while there are fires burning all around us. Or we can take that fire engine to the fires and save lives, buildings and property. The same would be true if we were EMTs and in charge of the community ambulance. The best thing for that ambulance to do is to go to where sick people are and bring them to the emergency room to save their lives. Its destiny is not to just stay clean and shiny in the garage.

The Scripture in Isaiah 56:7 (AMP) ends by saying that the house of prayer is FOR ALL PEOPLES! "All these I will bring to My holy mountain and make them joyful in My house of prayer. Their burnt offerings and their sacrifices will be accepted on My altar; For My house will be called a house of prayer for all the peoples." We are to be His house of prayer for everyone with no exceptions, all ethnicities, languages, cultures, races, EVERYONE! This is the ALL in the Great Commission.

It is our commission to present the gospel to everyone. We can accomplish this through prayer. Praying for their felt needs, absolutely, and then for their real need. Their need of a Savior!

Pastor Willy Bobe, assistant pastor at the Manhattan Bible Church, in New York City has used Prayer Stations extensively in his evangelistic outreaches. He said, "Prayer eliminates long-winded and fruitless theological debates with atheists and others. Prayer attracts people who want to know God. These people believe in God and need help. Prayer Stations are by far the most effective evangelism tool I have used in my 26 years of ministry. I have been involved with almost every other form of evangelism, mass evangelism, street evangelism, tract evangelism—you name it and I have done it."

Prayer Changes Things! Prayer Changes Lives!

Could a mariner sit idle
if he heard the drowning cry?
Could a doctor sit in comfort
and just let his patients die?
Could a fireman sit idle,
let men burn and give no hand?
Can you sit at ease in Zion
with the world around you damned?

—Leonard Ravenhill, an English Christian evangelist and author who focused on the subjects of prayer and revival

Chapter 16

Sold Out

Rozanne and I have not known any higher call than to give our lives completely to Jesus, to do our utmost to be obedient to Him at any and all cost. We certainly have made mistakes in the process, but our hearts have always been totally committed to the advancement of the kingdom of God. I don't say this to boast, but only to testify that as far as we are concerned there is no other way to live. In the words of Joshua, "As for me and my house, we will serve the Lord" (Joshua 24:15).

We have never sought either affirmation or pity, truth be told, we have had the time of our lives serving Jesus! God has been so good to us, and though at times the road has been challenging, and the temptation to quit has been real, but "we know that all things work together for good to those who love God, to those who are the called according to *His* purpose" (Romans 8:28 NKJV, italics added).

I love to speak to children and young people in Christian schools and churches, encouraging them to live their best life with no regrets.

The only way to do that is to walk daily in obedience to Jesus and follow His will for our lives.

After Rozanne and I were married we compared notes on our early years and discovered that interestingly enough we both came to Christ the very same year on two different sides of the world. Rozanne at age seven in New Zealand and me at age nine in New York.

God, I Don't Have a Testimony!

When I was at Bible college there were a number of young people attending who had come from desperate backgrounds. Some even came from years of addiction to drugs and alcohol. When it was testimony time, they would bring the house down with praise to God as they shared their stories of deliverance. By comparison, I felt that I did not have an exciting testimony. This became an obsession with me.

One night after dark I went to the altar at the college auditorium. Laying prostrate on my face before the Lord I complained, "Lord, I don't have a testimony! When I tell people I came to Christ as a young boy partly because of a Vacation Bible School, they say something like, 'Oh isn't that sweet.'"

God spoke so clearly to me that night, "Nick, their testimony is that I delivered them from sin, and your testimony is that I am so powerful I can keep someone from sin."

I love to encourage Christian children being raised in a Christian home and church with that true story.

Gerald Kauffman, was the pastor of Love Gospel Assembly in the South Bronx. Jerry was a heroin addict for over 12 years and raised in a Jewish home. He had a marvelous and powerful conversion and became a powerhouse for God in New York City. He was respectfully referred to as the "Bishop of the Bronx." Jerry had a radio program and interviewed me for a special segment. When he asked about my background, I shared how different his story was from mine, but how both stories spoke of God's might, power, mercy and grace. Jerry then said to his audience, "I firmly believe that Nick's testimony is actually greater than mine." Jesus saves, keeps and satisfies!

Rozanne and I were both raised in solid Bible-believing churches and sensed early in our lives that we were called to Christian service. We even discovered that we could have met at least four years before we did. Both of us had heard Loren Cunningham share about an outreach he was planning in the Caribbean in 1965. Both of us, on opposite sides of the globe, gave serious thought to attending that outreach, but in the end neither of us did.

Spiritual Compatibility

Although our ethnic cultures could not have been more opposite, our Christian spiritual culture was totally compatible. When we met and began to talk about our lives and vision, it was amazing how we were both on the same page. What made us so in sync was that we had "sold out" to Jesus in our youth and were committed to a life of Christian service, even if we didn't always understand what lay ahead or what being "all in" was going to look like.

My dear father-in-law, Alan Brett, who was one of the great mentors of my life and ministry, would often say when it came to understanding the will of God, "It is much easier to guide a moving vehicle than one that is standing still."

Rozanne and I have always kept moving in the direction we felt God was leading, and He has given us the on-course corrections necessary to reach our spiritual destiny.

It has been my observation that when it comes to effectiveness in life and ministry being passionately sold out to Jesus makes all the difference in the world. Makes me think of the title of Oliva Newton-John's song, "Hopelessly Devoted to You." That should be the testimony of every Christian regarding their relationship with God.

Radical Christianity

From the very beginning Christianity has always been a radical religion! The disciples, Paul, the early church, they were all radicals, obedience was not optional; they were sold out! Unfortunately, some of today's Christianity has been modified to the point of, dare I say, lukewarm? Jesus spoke to the church of Laodicea in Revelation 3:16 (AMP), "So because you are lukewarm (spiritually useless), and neither hot nor cold, I will vomit you out of My mouth [rejecting you with disgust]."

I have always loved what General William Booth once said, "I like my religion like my tea, strong and hot."

Rick Warren, pastor of the Saddleback Church in Southern California spoke a message at the Anaheim Stadium in 2005 to Christian young people. He urged them to be as dedicated as were the Hitler youth!

In that meeting of 30,000 people, he said such things as, "Only radicals change the world." "Everything in the world is done by passionate people. Moderate people get only moderately nothing done and moderation will never slay the global giants." He challenged his church with three goals for the next 25 years: 1. Global expansion of the kingdom of God. 2. Total mobilization of His church and 3. The dream of a radical devotion of every believer.

Pastor Warren continued, "In 1939 they packed a stadium in Munich, Germany with young men and women in brown shirts to hear a fanatical man standing behind a podium. His name was Adolf Hitler. They formed a sign with their bodies that said, 'Hitler, We Are Yours.' And they nearly took the world!"

He talked about Lenin, who once said, "Give me 100 committed, totally committed men and I will change the world," and he nearly did it!

He then said, "Some years ago they took the sayings of Chairman Mao Se Tung and put them in a little red book and committed them to memory. They put them in their minds and they took that nation by storm."

Then he asked his church, "What would happen if just the Christians in this stadium would say, 'Jesus we are yours'?"

I believe our only hope for the future of this world is that Christians become the same radical followers of Jesus as were those of the early church. That means we trade moderation for radicalization. To do that we must first come to a point of desperation. We must be sold out to

Christ and committed to the point where our cause, the cause of Christ, means more to us than anything else in life. Even more than life itself.

Marching in the Same Parade, but to the Beat of a Different Drum

Jesus must be our first love and our priorities need to be focused on God's agenda for this world, not our own. Yes, we are in this world, even marching in the same parade, but to the beat of a very different drum. Our lives need to be marked by sacrifice, obedience and holiness.

I want my life to be so radical for Jesus that if ever the government changes for the worse in this country, and believers are persecuted, may there be more than sufficient evidence to convict me!

My pastor, Virginia Impellizzeri, shared with me when I was quite young in the ministry, "Nick, you need to live your life in such a way that when you get up in the morning all hell will say, 'Oh no, he's up!'"

D.L. Moody, the great American evangelist said it best, "The world has yet to see what God can do through a person who is totally given to Him."

What Is God's Vision for the World?

We must become men and women of vision, embracing not our own vision but God's vision for this world which is given to us.

The first time I flew between Honolulu, and Kona, Hawaii was in 1983 when our family arrived to attend the Leadership Training School. One of the YWAM leaders picked us up and drove us to the YWAM University of the Nations campus. As we drove along the highway our driver introduced himself to me as a retired Air Force officer. He asked if I remembered how high our plane was over the water during our short flight. I didn't know just how high we were but remarked that it was a considerable distance above the ocean. He informed me that we flew at about 10,000 feet above the surface, adding, "Did you know that from the surface of the water to the bottom of the ocean in the area you just flew over, was the same distance, 10,000 feet?" I was impressed to say the least!

The oceans cover two-thirds of the surface of the earth, and in places the bottom of the ocean has yet to be fathomed. I was reminded of Habakkuk 2:14 (KJV) "For the earth shall be filled with the knowledge of the glory of the Lord, as the waters cover the sea. *That's God's vision!* We need to embrace His HUGE vision for our world.

No Compromise

A sold-out person for Christ is one of undivided purpose. There is no compromise or question regarding their priorities.

In Hebrews 12:1-2 (AMP) we read "Therefore, since we are surrounded by so great a cloud of witnesses [who by faith have testified to the truth of God's absolute faithfulness], stripping off every unnecessary weight and the sin which so easily *and* cleverly entangles us, let us run with endurance *and* active persistence the race that is set before us, [looking away from all that will distract us and] focusing our eyes on Jesus, who is the Author and Perfecter of faith [the first incentive for our belief and the One who brings our faith to maturity], who for the joy [of accomplishing the goal] set before Him endured the cross, disregarding the shame, and sat down at the right hand of the throne of God [revealing His deity, His authority, and the completion of His work]."

There are two things that the writer of Hebrews speaks of here that can distract us and disqualify us from God's destiny for our lives.

Sin Is a Disqualifier

The first has to do with sin, the things that we know in essence are wrong and contrary to God's law. Obviously, sin has no place in our lives and is always a disqualifier.

He also says that we must lay aside anything that will hinder us in any way. Often these things are not sinful in essence, but simply do not fit the call God gave us. I remember someone giving me a gospel tract that was meant for an audience of Christians that was entitled "Others Can but You Cannot." When you understand what God has called you to do, you need to consider carefully the things of this life that either sensitize that calling or desensitize it. C.S. Lewis once said about distractions, "Do not allow any temporary excitement to distract you from the real business."

Paul spoke of his destiny as "the heavenly vision' in Acts 26:19 (NET), "I was not disobedient to the heavenly vision." Paul kept his focus on what God had called him to do and put aside all other distractions. Philippians 3:14 says, "I press on toward the goal to win the prize for which God has called me heavenward in Christ Jesus."

We live in a world today where pluralism is thought of as a positive character trait. Some Christians are one person at church and another in the life they live Monday through Saturday.

I have often recalled the story of the deacon who lived in the Pittsburgh area and worked in a steel mill. At church on Sunday, he was respected as a man of God, but when at work he was one of the boys, he used the same language as his workmates and told some of the same off-color jokes. One day a fellow worker had a terrible accident and lay on the floor of the mill with his life ebbing away. The deacon felt the need to tell his friend about Jesus and ask him to receive Christ into his life. As he thought about sharing the gospel with the man and leading him in praying the sinner's prayer, he realized that "his life had sealed his lips."

The word *integrity* means *one*, whole and undivided. If you are a man or woman of integrity, you are one person regardless of where you are or whose company you are in.

What Are Encumbrances?

Hebrews 12:1 in the King James Version speaks of "encumbrances." Encumbrances are things that are legitimate, but they don't fit our calling and are inconsistent with who we are in Christ. As such they distract us from our focus.

Early in my YWAM career, when we were based in New Ringgold, Pennsylvania. I was invited to speak in a Discipleship Training School in Arkansas. It was the fall and not being familiar with the weather in Arkansas, I wasn't sure how to pack. I decided to take clothes for all possibilities. As I filled my luggage, I kept hearing a still small voice say to me, "Go light, Nick." Instead, I ended up with two suitcases and my carryon bag. In my travels I had to fly two different carriers through four airports. I ended up carrying all my luggage from one gate to another through different terminals. This was before wheeled luggage. I labored with my bags trying not to miss the next flight, but having to stop periodically to rest my hands and aching fingers. I thought I might end up with permanent grooves from the handles on my luggage.

During that process God spoke to me and gave spiritual application to my predicament. He said, "You see, Nick, that is why some people give up the walk, because they are carrying excess baggage."

Baggage God never intended us to carry. We may desire some things of this life that are inconsistent with our calling, and end up laboring between the journey or "call" and the baggage. At some point we make a decision to either give up the baggage or abandon the call!

When I finally arrived at my destination. I went to collect my checked luggage and found that it didn't come in with my flight. I was escorted to the YWAM base and my host said he would go back to the airport to see if my bags came in on the later flight.

I made the mistake of packing the notes regarding the messages God had given me to teach that week in my checked bags! My friend reported to me later in the evening the bad news that my bags did not come in on the later flight either.

I remember praying and saying to the Lord, "What do I do about speaking to the students tomorrow morning since I don't have my teaching notes?" As I began to quiet myself to hear God's voice, I heard Him say, "Speak on the subject of excess baggage."

He began to pour His thoughts into my mind and a "life message" was born. I have since taught it to many young people training for missions, relating it to their call into Christian service.

We can be carrying bags of attachment to things, relationships or wrong priorities. In each case we need the Holy Spirit to do inventory and reveal which are consistent and which are inconsistent with His plan and purpose for our life.

Regarding things, Jesus said in Luke 12:15 (AMP), "Watch out and guard yourselves against every form of greed; for not even when one has an overflowing abundance does his life consist of, *nor* is it derived from, his possessions."

The question is not how wealthy you may be, but how distracted you are by what you own. How much can God entrust you with before you become preoccupied and sidetracked?

Relationships, Blessing or Curse?

Relationships can be a major distraction! There is an essential subject we need to understand having to do with rights and privileges. I came to a critical juncture in my 20s, when I gave up my right to marriage and having a family. It is all about Jesus being number one in our lives, and understanding that everything else must serve that primary relationship. I didn't make that commitment with ulterior motives, I fully expected God to take me up on it. Instead, He gave me the privilege of receiving Rozanne as my wife. No one else could have been a more perfect fit for me. God gave me the one, the lady He had chosen to help me be faithful to the heavenly calling upon my life.

Rozanne and I often reflect back and glorify God for all the ways He has orchestrated our lives. He has been faithful, blessing us beyond measure. We have no regrets, complaints or issues with all the ways God has led us. There were times we wondered how we could cope with what appeared as mountains, loss of parents, siblings, relatives, co-workers and friends, finances, ministry struggles, and the day-to-day issues of our lives and ministry. In retrospect we see not only how God's plan was flawless and incredibly benevolent to us both, but also to our children, grandchildren and those who have worked faithfully alongside us.

The Great Commission comes with just one guarantee, "And surely I am with you always, to the very end of the age" (Matthew 28:20).

This is our testimony. He has never forsaken us, even when we've blown it, made mistakes, messed up. He was there, picked us up, dusted us off, and entrusted us with the next thing. What a privilege to serve, to go, to give. Our children have seen God's faithfulness throughout their lives, and each of them are now obeying God's call. They are visionaries who, along with their children, are world changers in their sphere of influence.

Our Brothers' Keepers

At one juncture of our lives, as previously noted, God gave us the privilege and the responsibility of caring for my two brothers and a cousin, each one mentally disabled. We did so in the middle of one of the most intense seasons of ministry. Even some of our colleagues were concerned that our commitment to my brothers and cousin would sidetrack us from God's call, some counseling us to consider other options. God's word to us however, was clear and we never questioned it. For 23 years we lived, loved, laughed, occasionally cried, and always were grateful for the privilege of having Angie, Junior and Sonny in our lives. In God's perfect time, He called them home one by one, and again we marveled at His grace and mercy. Yes, I trust we were a blessing to them, but they gave so much, taught us so many things about ourselves, some good, some not so good. Through those years our daughters loved their uncles deeply and in return were loved back unconditionally. We cherish those memories. The stories we could tell! Enough to fill a book with love, laughter and tears! Angie, Sonny and Junior were never a distraction. Their generous hearts have left us with precious memories we wouldn't have missed for anything. The grace of God was abundant during that time, so much so that often people would say things like, "I don't know how you do it." To them it was monumental, but to us, we just loved them and received so much more in return. Someone put it this way, "God will never lead you where His grace cannot keep you."

Burning Our Bridges Behind Us

Early in our life together God taught us to fully commit ourselves to the next thing He had for us to do and to never have a Plan B or an escape hatch. We moved ahead with both feet and tried to leave no drag marks behind us. What an exciting adventure it has been! Not always easy for sure, but oh, so worth every tear and every battle scar.

Often when we obey the Lord, we don't see immediate fruit, which reminds me of a missionary story I heard a number of years ago. Even now it brings tears to my eyes.

The story is of a man by the name of Frank Arthur "Bones" Jenner, better known as "the little white-haired man on George Street."

At a church in South London as the service was closing, a stranger stood up in the back and asked the pastor if he could share his testimony: "A few weeks ago, I was visiting a relative in Sydney, Australia and was walking down George Street. A little white-haired man stepped outside of the doorway of a shop and asked me, 'Excuse me, sir, are you saved? And if you died tonight, would you go to Heaven?' I was astounded at his words; nobody had ever asked me such a thing. All the way back to England on British Airways, I pondered his words. I called a friend about it; he was a Christian and led me to Christ. I want to fellowship here with you, and everyone clapped at his conversion. That pastor flew to Adelaide, Australia the next week to speak at a conference at a church. A woman asked to speak with him and before he would hear her story, he wanted to know if she had given her heart to Christ. She said, "I was visiting friends in Sydney and doing some last-minute shopping on George Street. A little white-haired man stepped outside of the doorway of a shop and asked me, 'Excuse me, madam, are you saved? If you died tonight, would you go to Heaven?' I was greatly disturbed by those words. When I got back to Adelaide, I came to this church and sought out the pastor, and he led me to Christ. Twice in two weeks he heard about this little man on George Street. He then flew to Perth to speak in a church. After the service, a leading member of the church took him out to eat, and he asked him how he came to Christ. I grew up in the church and never really followed Christ, but because of my business ability, I was given a place of influence in the church. I was on a business outing in Sydney, walking down George Street and a little white-haired man stepped outside of the doorway of a shop and asked me, 'Excuse me, sir, are you saved? If you died tonight, would you go to Heaven?' I was infuriated and told him I was an elder in the church. I flew home and told my pastor what had happened, thinking he would sympathize with me. The pastor told me he had been disturbed for years about my spiritual condition, and my pastor led me to Jesus." The pastor flew home to London and was speaking in a minister's conference in Kesick and shared the story of the little white-haired man. four elderly pastors came up to him after the service and told him that they got saved between 25 and 30 years ago, respectively, through that little man on George Street. He next was speaking at a convention in the Caribbean to a group of missionaries from his denomination and shared the story about the little white-haired man. three missionaries came up to him and said, "We got saved through him 15 to 20 years ago, respectively." He continued on to Atlanta, Georgia, and spoke at a Naval Chaplain's convention. After three days of speaking, the Chaplain General took him out to a meal. The pastor asked him how he gave his life to Christ. "When I was a young sailor, living a very sinful life, I was aboard a ship in the South Pacific, and we stopped in Sydney Harbor for replenishments. I got blind drunk, got on the wrong bus, and was dropped off on George Street. A little white-haired man stepped outside of the doorway of a shop and asked me, 'Excuse me, sir, are you saved? If you died tonight, would you go to Heaven?' The fear of God shook me. I was shocked sober and went back to the battleship, sought out the Chaplain, and he led me to Christ." Six months later the pastor flew to India to do a convention for 5,000 Indian missionaries. The leader of the missionaries took him to his home to eat and the pastor asked him, "How did you, as a Hindu, come to Christ?" "I was in a very privileged position. I worked for the Indian diplomatic mission, and I travelled the world. I am so thankful for Jesus and the forgiveness of my sins. I would be very embarrassed if people knew how dark of a life I was living. I was in Sydney, Australia doing some last-minute shopping, laden with gifts that I was bringing home to my wife and children. A little white-haired man stepped outside of the doorway of a shop and asked me,

'Excuse me, sir, are you saved? If you died tonight, would you go to Heaven?' I was disturbed, and when I returned home, I sought out my Hindu priest. He told me to satisfy my curiosity and go and talk to the Christian missionary. That missionary led me to Christ; I abandoned Hinduism and soon began to study for ministry. I left the diplomatic mission and am today the head of these missionaries. We have led tens of thousands to Christ." Eight months later, the pastor was speaking in Gamier, a southern suburb of Sydney, and he asked the pastor if he knew about a little man who witnessed on George Street. He said he did, and the man's name is Mr. Jenner. He doesn't do it any more as he is too old and frail. The pastor asked if he could meet him, and two nights later they went to Mr. Jenner's apartment, and this frail little old man opened the door. He made them tea and was so frail that he kept spilling his tea as his hand shook. The London preacher told him of all the accounts of the past few years. He began to cry and said, "My story goes like this: I was working on a warship and at a time when my life fell apart, I went to a Christian man whom I had treated horribly. He led me to Christ and my life changed from that day forward. I was so grateful to God that I would share Jesus with at least 10 people every day. I wasn't always able to do it; I wasn't paranoid about it, but did my best to fulfill my promise. I have done this for over 40 years, and in my retirement years the best place was on George Street, as there are hundreds of people there. I got a lot of rejections, but a lot of people listened to me, and in 40 years of doing this I have never heard of one person coming to Jesus from doing this, until today." The Pastor told him he estimated 140,000 who had come to Christ through those he had influenced. two weeks later Mr. Jenner died. Can you imagine his reward when he got to heaven? Nobody but a handful of people in Sydney knew Mr. Jenner, but his name is famous in heaven.

The last estimate I heard was that there were now probably more than 400,000 people who have come to Christ as a result of Mr. Jenner's faithfulness and perseverance to share the gospel, and the number continues to increase because of multiplication. What an incredible story of commitment to Christ and perseverance, even when there were no signs of fruitfulness for over 40 years!

I remember when I was about 18 years old, I used to go to the Farmer's Market in Bay Shore, New York. with a dear brother from my church. We would stand among the wares and give out tracts all evening. We must have given many hundreds of tracts during that summer. Next to the Farmer's Market was a theatre. One evening we saw long lines standing outside waiting to buy tickets for the show. My friend and I positioned ourselves in front of the line and started to give out tracts to all the people. I am sure many thought it had something to do with the movie and happily took the gospel tract. I don't know of any that we actually led to Christ during those summer nights, but I expect to hear some testimonies in heaven when I get there.

A scripture that has deeply encouraged me over the years is found in 1 Corinthians 15:58 (NLT)—"So, my dear brothers and sisters, be strong and immovable. Always work enthusiastically for the Lord, for you know that nothing you do for the Lord is ever useless."

Obedience and Evangelism

I have learned that obedience is what counts in evangelism. Link that with perseverance and you get results, even when you don't see them immediately with your own eye.

"Then He said, 'The kingdom of God is like a man who throws seed on the ground; and he goes to bed at night and gets up every day, and [in the meantime] the seed sprouts and grows; how [it does this], he does not know. The earth produces crops by itself; first the blade, then the head [of grain], then the mature grain in the head. But when the crop ripens, he immediately puts in the sickle [to reap], because [the time for] the harvest has come'" (Mark 4:26-29 AMP).

I would rather do what I believe God tells me to do in evangelism for as long as He tells me to do it, than to believe what some "evangelism expert" says works or doesn't work. My father-in-law, Alan Brett, used to say that an expert is someone who, is an "X" which means nothing and then a "pert" which means next to nothing. SAY what He tells you to say, GO where He tells you to go, and DO what He tells you to do.

Rozanne continues

My brother, David Brett, was a missionary who knew the voice of God and obeyed in any and all situations. David loved cars. He knew what car to buy, how to fix it up and sell it for a profit. He used his hobby to fund most of his mission trips around the world. (Over 90 border crossings into China alone.) David's favorite car was the Jaguar.

On one occasion David was under doctor's orders to go away and rest for at least a month. Well, that lasted a week and David was going a little stir-crazy. He checked the local paper for "Cars for Sale."

A Jaguar caught his eye and he decided to check it out. After traveling a few miles to the address listed and spotting the Jaguar in the driveway, David was not at all impressed and he continued past the house.

"Go back."

"I don't want that car, Lord; it needs too much work."

"Go back."

David obediently turned around and pulled in behind the Jag in the driveway. He knocked on the door, waited a little while, but there was no answer. He thought about walking away, but then he remembered Who sent him there, so he kept knocking. After knocking for some considerable time, a large scruffy man, who obviously did not want visitors, came to the door.

"Yeh, what do you want!?"

David told the simple truth, "God sent me."

The man looked shocked, but responded, "Well, then I guess you had better come in."

They sat down on shabby furniture in a small front room and the man began to pour out his heart to David.

"I was leaning over my bathroom sink with a razor blade in my hand when you began knocking on my door. I thought you would just go away, but you didn't, you kept knocking."

He shared how his wife had left him, that he was broke and about to lose everything. He was desperate and didn't want to live anymore.

David shared the love of Jesus with him and led him to Christ.

Even although he really didn't want the man's car, David bought it in order to help him out.

Nick continues

Ecclesiastes 11:5-6 helps us understand the principle of obedience in evangelism, "As you do not know the path of the wind, or how the body is formed in a mother's womb, so you cannot understand the work of God, the Maker of all things. Sow your seed in the morning, and at evening let not your hands be idle, for you do not know which will succeed, whether this or that, or whether both will do equally well."

If you are sold out to Jesus you will live only for the applause of heaven. One of the things folks who use Facebook are generally interested in, is how many of their friends "LIKE" whatever they posted. We all want to be liked by everyone. For some people, all that matters is:

- Popularity

- Fame

- Applause

- What do other people think of me?

- How do I look to everybody else?

Image is everything! The Scripture warns us about being liked by everyone: "Woe *to you* when all the people speak well of you *and* praise you" (Luke 6:26 AMP).

Big Evangelism Challenge—Fear of Rejection

A major reason for not engaging in evangelism is the fear of rejection. We need to understand whose approval we are most concerned about, God or man?

Solomon said in Proverbs 29:25 (AMP) that "The fear of man brings a snare, but whoever trusts in *and* puts his confidence in the Lord will be exalted *and* safe." Jesus said that some hid their faith "for they loved the approval of men more than the approval of God" (John 12:43 AMP). Paul the apostle said in Galatians 1:10, "Am I now trying to win the approval of human beings, or of God? Or am I trying to please people? If I were still trying to please people, I would not be a servant of Christ."

When I train a team for a Prayer Station outreach, I remind them, "It's not about you. No matter whether we are laughed at, rebuffed, or rejected. It's all about JESUS and never about us!"

Taking Risks

A great part of being a sold-out Christian is being a risk taker! One of my Bible heroes has always been Caleb. When the children of Israel traveled toward the Promised Land, they picked up various groups and clans. One such individual was Caleb, a Kenizzite, an Edomite. He was a descendant of Esau rather than Jacob. Caleb and his clan became part of the tribe of Judah. Despite all of this, Caleb became prominent among the tribes of Israel.

The people of Israel decided to set up a committee to do a feasibility study regarding the Promised Land. "Let's send twelve spies into the land to search out the best route"—is the story in Numbers 13 and 14. Remarkably, the one they chose to represent the tribe of Judah was a Gentile—Caleb! He would have been about 45 years old when he joined the 11 other spies.

As one Bible scholar put it, "Ten of the spies measured the giants of the land against themselves. 'There's no way we can defeat the occupants of the land,' they said, 'They are much stronger than we are, we're like grasshoppers compared to them!'"

Interestingly enough the spies went to Hebron. It was in Hebron that Abraham received the promise of the land of Canaan (Genesis 13:18). Apparently, none of this was on their minds and hearts, all they could see were high walls and giants in the land.

Only Caleb and Joshua "measured the giants against God!"

Even after 40 years in the wilderness, Caleb's spirit was still strong, "Give me this mountain," he said to Joshua. Caleb was now 85 years old. The inheritance he desired was the hilliest part in the Promised Land, and it was dominated by giants; the enemy was strong there. It was the most challenging part of the entire Promised Land, and Caleb at 85 said, "Give me that mountain."

I have observed that risk takers have certain characteristics:

- They resist discouragement.
- They refuse to see obstacles or difficulties, instead seeing opportunities and challenges.
- They are people of faith and hope. "Faith laughs at impossibilities and cries, 'It shall be done'" (Charles Wesley).
- They endure ridicule and criticism.
- Hard work does not scare them.
- They are not preoccupied with their possessions at the expense of their inheritance.

Years ago, I heard of a survey taken of retired men of God.

They were asked, "If you had it to do all over again, what would you have done differently?"

"Take more risks!" Was the number one answer.

As we write this book Rozanne and I are in our '70s. Our heart's cry is still with Caleb.

"Now therefore, give me this mountain…" (Joshua 14:12 KJV).

Chapter 17

"Understanding The Times"

Discerners of the Times

More than any other people on the face of the earth, the Church of Jesus Christ needs to be discerners of the times! In 1 Chronicles 12:32 (AMP) the Scripture speaks regarding the tribe of Issachar and says "Of the tribe of Issachar, men who understood the times, with knowledge of what Israel should do."

We are living in an unparalleled time of crisis that affects all areas of our lives physically, morally, and spiritually. Never in my lifetime have I experienced such a time of total moral decadence as this. Truly as I once heard a speaker say, "The tide of God's judgment is beating against the dam of God's mercy."

At the writing of this book, we are still under the scourge of the COVID-19 virus outbreak in the world. It is reminiscent of an Old Testament plague.

"When I shut up the heavens so that there is no rain, or command locusts to devour the land or send a plague among my people, if my people, who are called by my name, will humble themselves and pray and seek my face and turn from their wicked ways, then I will hear from heaven, and I will forgive their sin and will heal their land" (2 Chronicles 7:13-14).

One of the judgments God spoke of was a plague sent among His people. In verse 13 and immediately following, He says, "If my people." That confirmed what I, and others, had been sensing. In order to be rid of this terrible plague the Church needs to come to a place of repentance and call on God in prayer for His forgiveness and deliverance.

Some Christians may blame the plague on the ungodly for their wicked acts, but I believe that as Peter said in 1 Peter 4:17, "For it is time for judgment to begin with God's household; and if it begins with us, what will the outcome be for those who do not obey the gospel of God?" Before God can deal with the ungodly, He must first deal with His children.

Survival Mentality

When I assess the days in which we live, I find that the Body of Christ often responds to what is happening around them in different ways. There are those who are given to what I call the survival mentality, preparing for the worst, storing up food, moving to places where they can live without dependence on the support systems we are all accustomed to. This is an isolationist and withdrawal mindset. Their patron saint is Joseph of the Old Testament. He did not, however, save the food selfishly, but in order to preserve the then known world. This is a totally defensive posture and reminds me of a story I heard many years ago.

A group of pacifists after World War 1 were smart enough to see the signs of another impending world war coming. These were intelligent and learned men and women. They gave themselves to research looking for a "war free zone" somewhere in the world. A safe place they could move to in order to escape the coming catastrophe of global war. After much time spent in research and study they decided to move to Okinawa! Any student of World War ll would of course recognize this as the site of the fiercest battle of the Pacific Theatre. Often when we try to hide, we can put ourselves in the most vulnerable position of all.

Pessimists Mentality

There are also Christians who ascribe to another frame of mind which I will call the pessimists mentality. These speak only of gloom and doom. Their counsel is to cut back, downsize, and maintain the status quo. It reminds me of the story of an uneducated immigrant that came to the US and found out American's love hot dogs. Having little funds, he put together a makeshift hot dog stand in front of his home and began to do a roaring trade. With the income he received he built a bigger and better hot dog stand and business was even better.

The man did so well he was able to afford to send his son to college to study business. His son came home after his freshman year. The most dangerous person in the world is a college freshman. When his father told him how the business was breaking all previous records and that he was planning to build an even better restaurant his son said to his dad, "No, Dad, don't do that. Things are not good for business right now and you will lose your money." The dad thought, "My son is a college man, he knows." So, he cut back instead of moving ahead and guess what? His business went down and he did not do as well as before. All because he was not as aggressive as he was earlier but became pessimistic and followed pessimistic advice.

Gazing Mentality

Other Christians I have encountered ascribe to what I call the gazing mentality. Their favorite verse is Revelation 22:20 (KJV), "Even so, come, Lord Jesus." Those on the Mount of Ascension saw Jesus disappear into the clouds going up to be with the Father. They stood there gazing into heaven hoping He would come back. The angels appeared and reminded them of Christ's command. Some Christians still spend most of their time gazing into heaven consumed with the second coming. Like those disciples on the mount, they're not getting on with His commandment to "Go into all the world" It is right to anticipate the return of the Lord, but not to be so obsessed with the second coming that we forget what Jesus said in Matthew 24:14—"And this gospel of the kingdom will be preached in the whole world as a testimony to all nations, and then the end will come."

No Response Mentality

Finally, some in the Church seem to embrace a no response mentality. Perhaps they could be called, "the days of Noah people," Jesus said in Matthew 24:37-38, "As it was in the days of Noah, so it will be at the coming of the Son of Man. For in the days before the flood, people were eating and drinking, marrying and giving in marriage, up to the day Noah entered the ark." In other words, some just carry on "business as usual," having little or no regard for what is happening around them or understanding its relevance to what God is doing in the world.

None of the above positions are where we ought to be as Christians living in this age. None of these mentalities represent what God would have us embrace in our thoughts, acts and conduct. We need to be like the sons of Issachar and understand the times to know what we as the Church of Jesus Christ ought to be doing.

Therefore, the question for the Church is, "What time is it?" How can I/we be discerners of the time in which we live?

Crisis—Danger and Opportunity

No Christian I know would argue with the fact that we live in a time of crisis. Normally most of us think of "crisis" as a negative. It is interesting that in both the Chinese and Korean languages the word used for crisis is actually two characters. One stands for "danger," which is what most of us would consider a crisis to be and the other character stands for "opportunity."

Every crisis has both danger and opportunity. Unfortunately, many, perhaps most of us, only see the danger and miss the opportunity.

When I lived in New York and traveled into the city by train, I would come up from the subways on a rainy day and find more than one person selling cheap umbrellas. Some New Yorkers would curse the rain, but others saw the opportunity to profit and sold umbrellas.

In every crisis there is opportunity not just to selfishly profit, but to do what Paul the apostle suggested in Ephesians 5:16, "making the most of every opportunity, because the days are evil."

In Isaiah 60: 1-3 the Scripture says, "Arise, shine, for your light has come, and the glory of the Lord rises upon you. See, darkness covers the earth and thick darkness is over the peoples, but the Lord rises upon you and his glory appears over you. Nations will come to your light, and kings to the brightness of your dawn."

We live in a very dark world, and yes, the darkness is thick. Our duty however, is not to curse the darkness but to shine the light of Christ. Even if all the light we have could be compared with the flicker of a single candle, that would be enough to overcome thick darkness.

Our family was invited to a July 4th celebration at the home of some YWAM friends in Washington DC. It was a gloriously sunny day, not a cloud in the sky. While we chatted in the backyard it became apparent that the neighbors must have had money to burn, literally. They chose to shoot off their rockets into the blue sunlit sky. We only knew this because of the small explosion as they launched and some barely visible smoke. It was far too clear and sunny to enjoy the splendor of bright colors and beautiful sparkles in the sky.

Later that evening we enjoyed the beauty of fireworks in a black velvet sky. When things are dark, our light shines brighter! "Don't curse the darkness, but instead, light a candle."

Being raised in church, Rozanne and I have heard one ominous phrase all of our lives, "We are living in the last days," or "The End Times." I much prefer looking at the great opportunities God is affording us as, "the Church's finest hour" or "the grand finale." The greatest part of any musical is always the finale. That's when they pull out all the stops, turn up the music, pour on the energy and give it all they've got!

I'm not denying that hard times are upon us, perhaps more persecution of believers than we have ever known in our lifetime, even in the United States, but with that will come some of the greatest opportunities for revival and evangelism. This was the essence of David Wilkerson's vision in the 1980s. He spoke of great calamity ahead (some of which has been fulfilled during COVID), followed by a powerful and historic ingathering of souls!

At the time of the Great Depression of the 1930s there were people committing suicide, but many others found Christ during that time of crisis which changed the course of their lives. Today we need to be "Christian entrepreneurs" and make the most of every opportunity for the sake of His kingdom.

Since 1992 Prayer Stations have been on the frontlines in times of crisis. The greatest example of this, as mentioned earlier, was 9/11 at Ground Zero in Manhattan.

When you search through church history you find that the finest moments for the Church of Jesus Christ were when they faced a crisis squarely and came to the rescue of those in trouble. God fashioned us to be this way, because God Himself is present in every crisis. He gives us courage and selfless compassion to respond to human need and be a part of His answer.

Army or Audience

There is no doubt today that we are in a battle for the souls of men and women in our world. As the body of Christ, we are the army of God in this battle. King Solomon saw this back in Song of Solomon 6:10 when he prophetically spoke of the Church of Jesus Christ,

"Who is this that looks down like the dawn, Fair *and* beautiful as the full moon, Clear *and* pure as the sun, As majestic as an army with banners?" (Song of Solomon 6:10 AMP).

We are an army and not an audience! We are called soldiers and should not become sissies! Not a nursery, but an armory! The Church of Jesus Christ is not a cruise ship, but a battleship! The war we fight is not against flesh and blood, but principalities and powers. We fight with God's weaponry. "The weapons we fight with are not the weapons of the world. On the contrary, they have divine power to demolish strongholds" (2 Corinthians 10:4).

As an army we should always be on the offensive. In my short-lived football career in high school, I do remember one thing my coach said to us, "The best defense is a good offense." For some reason when I read Matthew 6:18 (KJV) as a young Christian, "Upon this rock I will build my church; and the gates of hell shall not prevail against it," I saw the Church in the fortress, and the enemy was trying to batter down the gates of the fortress and defeat us. Actually, the Church is the offensive force assailing the fortresses of the enemy and the promise of the scripture is that "the gates of hell will not prevail against us!"

Our children or grandchildren may well be the generation that launches the last great offensive against the enemy on planet earth. Jesus said in Matthew 11:12 (KJV) that "And from the days of John the Baptist until now the kingdom of heaven suffereth violence, and the violent take it by force." The Church of Jesus Christ is always at its best when it is on the offensive. Our decisions regarding militancy are far more important than those of the Communist, secularist, anarchist, or Muslim extremist.

A few months ago, I was discussing these thoughts with Rozanne and she suggested I listen to Steve Camp's song, "Run to the Battle." When I did, I was so excited with the lyrics and the message it shared. Inspired by the quote of the great British missionary to China, India and Africa, C.T. Studd, who said, "Some want to live within the sound of church or chapel bell; I want to run a rescue shop, within a yard of hell."

Some people want to live
Within the sound of chapel bells
But I want to run a mission
A yard from the gates of hell

And with everyone you meet
I'll take them the gospel and share it well
And look around you as you hesitate
For another soul just fell, let's run to the battle
Run to the battle
(go to youtube for the lyrics and musice to *Run to the Battle*
by Steve Camp)

I believe God is looking for those who are willing to "run to the battle." It is a time for us to come to the frontlines with an attitude of "whatever it takes" to bring a message of redemption to a very sin-cursed world. We do not do that with physical force or measuring out hate for hate, but with the love of God and the power of the Holy Spirit. He has sent us into the world to be saviors and not judges. The world does not need another indictment, but redemption. We, the Church, need to have a redemptive attitude!

It all begins in the place of prayer. We need to pray the prayer of Daniel in Daniel 9:5-6 (NLT), "But WE have sinned and done wrong. WE have rebelled against you and scorned your commands and regulations. WE have refused to listen to your servants, the prophets, who spoke on your authority to our kings and princes and ancestors and to all the people of the land (emphasis added)."

Daniel did not say that the people alone had sinned, his prayers included himself. Likewise, our prayers too should identify with our fellowman. We should repent on behalf of all.

Changing God's Mind Regarding Judgment

In the course of Biblical history two things have changed God's mind regarding impending judgement. One is repentance and the other is intercessory prayer. Those prayers need to be for the people and with the people!

Prayer is the foundation of action! When we come to God in repentance and with intercession, He will give us His marching orders!!

David Adams, our close friend who served as associate director of our ministry, loved to quote the great coach Lou Holtz when he said, "When all is said and done, much more will be said than done."

We are beyond the time to pontificate here in America, it is time to act! The terrorists know this, and the forces of evil know this, but all too often the Church continues talking!

The famous German pastor, who was killed by the Nazis, because of his faith and his outspoken support of what was right, Dietrich Bonhoeffer, said in his book *The Cost of Discipleship*, "One act of obedience is better than one hundred sermons."

We need to be like the tribe of Issachar in 1 Chronicles12:32 and "understand the times." If we do not wake up and seize the moment God is giving us, we will miss our "hour of visitation." Jesus rebuked the Pharisees and Sadducees in Matthew 16:3 when He said to them "You know how to interpret the appearance of the sky, but you cannot interpret the signs of the times."

Taking a stand for Jesus in many places around our world could mean signing our death warrant. We need to come to that place of total abandonment if we aspire to be a candidate to change our nation and our world. Charles Colson, former attorney and political advisor to President Nixon, and the founder of Prison Fellowship, said in one of his books that he saw a picture of a college demonstrator holding up a sign that read, "Nothing is worth dying for." "But," Colson wrote, "if nothing is worth dying for, then nothing is worth living for either."

Prayer Station First Responders

On July 7, 2016 there was a terrible shooting in Dallas, Texas that ended with five policemen being killed by a deranged sniper. As I watched the horror of that shooting from my living room, I clearly heard the Lord say to me, "Nick, I want you to work on a strategy where you can get a Prayer Station on site of a man-made or natural disaster, within 48 hours of the incident."

This gave birth to a new game plan for us called Prayer Stations First Responders. This is not totally new to us as we quickly responded to the tragedy at 9/11 in New York City in 2001. Then in 2005 to the railroad station bombings in London, as well as to the disaster of Hurricane Katrina in New Orleans that same year. We sent a team to the Virginia Tech shooting in 2007 and to the Stoneman Douglas High School shooting in Parkland, Florida on February 14, 2018. We were present following the Pittsburgh synagogue shooting that same year, and also sent a team to the Virginia Beach municipal building shooting in 2019.

If the body of Christ is God's army, then I feel that those of us who work with ministries like Prayer Stations are the Special Forces division. Our vision for Prayer Station First Responders is to raise up units who would be ready to respond on short notice. Their assignment would be to get to the site of a disaster promptly to pray, to assess the need and to do whatever is required. Their goal being to bring comfort, peace, and hope to a community, city or town through prayer, through action, and especially through a witness of the love of Jesus and His saving grace.

1966 Rozanne saying goodbye to her Mum, before leaving for New York

Rozanne and a co-worker at
Teen Challenge in Brooklyn, New York

1968 Nick becomes a pastor

Teen Challenge Center, Long Branch, New Jersey

Courting

January 25, 1969

Home of our first DTS at Blue Mountain
Christian Retreat, Pennsylvina

Nick, CEO and Anita, the future
Executive Director of Prayer Stations

The Shaddock Inn, Jaffrey, New Hampshire

Youth With A Mission, Concord, New Hampshire

Dave and Tammy Adams and Family

Rozanne speaking through an interpreter in Mexico

The M/V Anastasis

Family on The Bridge of The Anastasis

Hotel in Elizabeth, New Jersey

Linda Cowie, Alan Williams and Nick, "Cross Across Manhattan"

The very first Prayer Station 1992

Our daughter Rebecca
at a Prayer Station in New York

Linda Cowie, Tammy Adams and Rozanne,
2001 9/11 outreach

Prayer Station in Mexico

Nick with Pastor Juan Ramirez

YWAM Smithtown, New York Campus

Nick at a Prayer Station

Ron Setran – Director of Operations
Anita Setran – Prayer Stations Executive Director

Nick's parents, Carmelo and Anna Savoca

Rozanne's parents, Rev. Alan and Margaret Brett

Nick's Cousin & his Brothers Sonny, Angelo & Carmelo

Rozanne with her Brother, Rev David Brett

The Savoca Family

Nick & Rozanne at a Prayer Station

PRAYER STATI⊙NS

Prayer Changes Things

The Classic Prayer Station

The NEW Prayer Station Flag

Prayer Changes Things

MAY I PRAY FOR YOU?

Five Little Words can *change a life.*

- ✓ Prayer Stations are being used all over the world.
- ✓ We now have the PRAYER STATION banner in 11 different languages.
- ✓ Almost a thousand Prayer Stations have shipped globally since 1992.
- ✓ There are Prayer Stations on almost every continent in the world.
- ✓ Tens of thousands of people have participated in the Prayer Station ministry.
- ✓ Literally thousands of lives have come to Christ because of the Prayer Station Ministry.

Get one of the fastest growing and most effective evangelism tools being used today!

PRAYERSTATIONS.ORG

PRAYER STATIⓄNS

A Prayer Station consists of a table and tall red banner with the words PRAYER STATION emblazoned on it. That, combined with the aprons the Prayer Station workers wear make for a formidable spiritual force that can be used anywhere in the world. The full Prayer Station package comes with a training kit that you can use to train the people that are interested in taking part in the Prayer Station ministry.

We now have a new Prayer Station Flag available for shipping that makes it much easier to transport and have high visibility. Make sure to check them out in the Prayer Station online store!

Tens of thousands of churches, teams and individuals have used Prayer Stations globally, offering people of all cultures and communities the opportunity to be prayed for, and to learn more about Jesus Christ and His wonderful message of Salvation.

Five Little Words can *change a life.*

PRAYER STATIONS
info@prayerstations.org
888-686-5550
Jupiter, Florida

Chapter 18

Five Little Words

In this final chapter we want to share just a few of the hundreds of testimonies shared by some who have participated in the ministry of Prayer Stations over the years.

May God use these stories to bless, encourage, uplift, challenge and motivate you to take prayer beyond your closet and church, out into the market place!

All of the testimonials are from real people, in their own words, unedited and uncensored. Only first names have been given with no other personal information.

I would suggest you have tissues on hand. I cannot read them without getting emotional. God is at work in our streets and neighborhoods.

Prayer truly can change a life!

Prayer Station Testimonials

April

"Prayer Stations gave me the opportunity to share God's love to hurting people. It offers hope to people and lets them know someone <u>really cares</u>."

Drew

"I think Prayer Stations are a great way to get youth out on the streets ministering to the people. It's easy to get close with the people in a short time."

Rev. Pace

"I want to do this in my area with my youth group. Thanks, YWAM."

Amy

"I enjoyed seeing people's reactions to finding out I wanted to pray with them. I felt like God used me to penetrate their hearts with His love."

Callie

"I got to see people walk away happy after prayer when they came distressed. People walked off with a smile and a spring in their step."

Will

"As a youth pastor, it was such a joy to see my teens giving and praying. They didn't realize that they had it in them. I watched all of them step out in boldness and love to hundreds of lives. This was great training and ministry for our youth."

Kari

"It was great being able to bless people in such a simple way—just praying for them. I prayed with two women about finding jobs, with a man about his life, with a woman for her friend's father who was very sick in the hospital, with a woman for a relationship she was in, with a man and his children for healing and for a number of Christians as well."

Valerie

"On this day we had the challenge of heavy rains so we took our Prayer Station down into the subway station. We prayed with so many people and some of them gave their lives to God. During the time there were people literally lined up waiting to be prayed for. It was a most wonderful experience which I will never forget."

Ezra

"Prayer Stations is an awesome way to open the door to share my faith."

Julie

"The joy a simple prayer can bring to broken hearts."

Laura

"It was so easy, so many times I had trouble starting a conversation with someone but this made it so easy."

Latonya

"It was wonderful loving the people, sharing Christ with them and watching their eyes when they realized He is genuine."

Danny

"I love how the power of prayer changes the whole countenance of people. More than they need my words, they need a touch from God and He touches them every time."

Gary

"I was blessed to see the openness of people. Many would cry and some would come to the Prayer Station without being urged."

Michael

"I am an executive businessman who normally does not get the opportunity to minister one on one. These two days of Prayer Station ministry afforded me a unique opportunity that I truly cherished. I had the experience of sharing God's love with non-believers and believers alike. We hope to get a Prayer Station of our own and extend this experience to our home town."

Nora

"I found what impressed a lot of people was that our Prayer Station team was not selling anything nor accepting donations."

Paul

"As a team leader I cannot describe what I felt as I saw my team test the Prayer Station idea, tentatively at first and then with 'gusto' and abandon. We loved the idea of blessing people with prayer and the overall response was positive. We were able to lead between ten to fifteen people to the Lord. This has been a time for us to experience God working in others' lives, but just as much in our own."

Randall

"We were a little nervous at first, but as time went on, we started enjoying it. The people were very open to praying. At the end of the day some of us didn't want to quit."

Ronald

"This was my first time witnessing. I enjoyed it and will do it again."

Justin

"It's amazing how many people need prayer."

Martha

"This has been the most wonderful experience of my life."

Betsy

"This is an experience that young people will never forget."

Scott

"After prayer there is hope in the other person's eyes. The Lord opened my eyes to the needy. The person on the street needs and wants prayer."

Tilly
"This ministry is powerful and anointed."

Gayle
"Prayer Stations impressed me with the interest people had in knowing God. People stopped to thank us for praying for them. It was great to have the opportunity to hear how to pray God's heart for individuals."

Maggie
"I like the Prayer Stations a lot more than approaching people on the streets. I prayed for so many and two received Christ. It was great."

Drew
"I think Prayer Stations are a great way to get youth out on the streets ministering to the people. It's easy to get close with the people in a short time. I prayed with about 10 people today."

Ryan
"I love Prayer Stations because I saw God change lives."

Angela
"We brought Christ to people that otherwise would not have made it another day without a touch from the Lord!"

Melissa
"I enjoyed actually getting to pray with people and seeing how much they appreciated that someone would care about them."

Lyn
"I thank the Lord for enlarging my territory and showing me more compassion for the lost souls of this world."

Michael
"I was able to lead an entire family to Christ today!"

Jesse

"Thank you for introducing me to the most exciting and effective ministry I have experienced in my 81 years. We are doing Prayer Stations in Eugene, Oregon and I am attempting to get other churches in our state involved in this ministry."

Naomi

"A man came rushing towards me with a 'Stop for Prayer' flyer in his hand. I asked him if there was anything I could pray with him about and he said, 'Yes, I want to get my life back together.' He shared what he was going through and said he wanted to know God more and I asked him if he wanted to receive Jesus in his heart and he said, 'Absolutely.' He received prayer and accepted Jesus as his Lord and Savior. I know he felt a change and was awe inspired."

Allen

"Harold came out of the train station and said 'My life is a mess and I need help.' I asked what I could pray for and he said 'A job.' I prayed for God's blessing and provision for the right kind of job. I prayed several things that the Lord seemed to be telling me to pray as a blessing to him. Harold was touched and thanked me, ready to leave. I asked if he knew the Lord wanted to bless him as His precious child. He said 'Not really.' 'Would you like to?' 'Yes, I would.' I then shared with him the booklet 'Steps to Peace with God' and he was very responsive and said he understood it and prayed to receive Christ."

Nicholas

"I was able to share with a gentleman named Stanley. We prayed for his education, he wanted to go back to school. I asked Stanley if he knew the Lord and he said he did as a child. I then asked if he would like to re-dedicate his life to Jesus Christ, Stanley did and we prayed together."

Salvatore

"My partner and I prayed for a man and then shared the tract 'Steps To Peace With God.' He read the prayer aloud to himself and without even praying he began to cry. Then he prayed it with us and his eyes filled with joy and he ran off with the Bible we gave him saying that he was going to make a rap song out of the sinner's prayer. It really encouraged me and touched my heart that I helped God change this man's life."

Christy

"I had the thrill of praying the sinner's prayer with 2 people. In both cases I was amazed when I got to the prayer at the positive response to people wanting to receive Jesus. I thought I was going to have to talk them into it, but it was evident that God had already prepared the hearts of these people. All I had to do was pray with them. It almost seemed too easy.

One of the people received the Lord and it was easy simply talking to him and going through the booklet 'Steps to Peace With God.' He almost came to tears and I could see him fighting it. God's Spirit had really gone ahead of our conversation. I certainly didn't feel I had said anything so special."

Katie

"I was at the Prayer Station for one minute at the most and I had someone ask me for prayer. I told him I would pray for him and we prayed and he ended up receiving the Lord into his heart. It was a huge thing for me only because I have never done anything like this before."

Neil

"A backslidden man by the name of Andre had just prayed on the train for God to help him and when he came out of the station, Boom! We were there with the Prayer Station. He was so broken and contrite, acknowledging his need for help to be free from addictions to alcohol, and nicotine. It was precious!"

Angela

"Today two ladies told me they received jobs after coming to a Prayer Station previously and being prayed for."

William

"There have been so many people just being grateful! One lady named Joy said her job was in jeopardy. She had to put her house on the market, and I was able to share how God had done the same thing in my life and because of that accomplished great things in me. She came back later and thanked me."

YWAM Lebanon Leader

"It was 10 minutes to 5, and our Prayer Station was going to end at 5 p.m. I was walking back toward the Prayer Station and could see it in the distance. As I got to within a couple blocks of the Prayer Station, I saw a car pull over in front of our Prayer Station which was being manned by some other people from YWAM. A woman and a boy got out and I could see them talking to our people. Later when I got back to the Prayer Station, they were excited, and they told me what happened. The lady had been driving down the road talking to her son who was sitting in the backseat. They were talking about her getting a new job and she was saying to her son that she hadn't got a new job yet, and that maybe they needed to pray about it more. Just at that moment they happened to be driving past our Prayer Station, and right on cue the young boy said to his mother, 'Hey, there's a Prayer Station right there. Let's pray now.' So, she swung in really quickly in front of the Prayer Station and they got out and right on the spot our crew was able to pray for the lady to get a job."

Barbara

"I prayed for a man sitting with his hardhat looking weary. He was at Ground Zero since day 3 of the disaster. He asked for prayer mostly for those who were finding the bodies of those who had been killed."

Mindy

"I met a chaplain on his way to Ground Zero who said when I asked him if I could pray for him, 'Please, I don't get prayed for very often.'"

Tom

"I prayed with one of the paramedics who had been rescued from the ruins of the WTC. Though already a believer, he knows it was God's grace that saved his life and has been instrumental in the process of healing from injuries to his back and legs."

Danielle

"We set up our Prayer Station right across from the Criminal Courthouse and a few policemen came to us and said that we shouldn't be there, but they would try their best to keep us there. God was giving us His favor! Towards the end of the day a man came up to us and said that he was the sergeant and that many of the police involved in the WTC were in that area. He also said many of the officers were hurt and there were only a few Christians among them. The Christians had been praying and asking God why the Prayer Stations were everywhere but not there. He thanked us and said that the cops needed us! He then said that he would not cry, but his eyes were filled with tears."

John

"One of the greatest blessings of the night was the time when 4 or 5 police officers actually serenaded us with a number of Christian songs like 'Amazing Grace' and 'Jesus Loves Me.' They took it upon themselves to watch over us and were really blessed by what we were doing."

Tim

"I saw a man coming toward me in full dress uniform. He was tall and stoic with a stone face. I stepped alongside him as he was walking past me and asked him if I could pray for him. He was with another uniformed officer. He looked at me and said 'yes.' His other friend said, 'I'll meet you over there' and kept walking. I asked him his name and I began to pray for him and his family for protection. His prayer request was that God would help him release the pain he held inside. I asked God to help him know it was OK to let out his pain and grief. He then began to weep and when I ended the prayer, he smiled at me and I knew he felt better. I found out later he was a fireman working in rescue and recovery at Ground Zero."

Brenda

"I prayed with a lady who was working on the 27th floor of the WTC and got out in time. She had tears in her eyes and took literature in Spanish to give to her mother. She so appreciated us praying for her."

Leigh Ann

"I prayed with a woman named Alice that had visited a Prayer Station before. At that time, she asked for prayer for her sick mother. Her prayer was answered and her mother is now out of the hospital. She has many emotional, physical and financial needs and she felt like the Prayer Station prayers were better than her own, because she was not worthy. This gave me an opportunity to share scripture and bring her closer to receiving Jesus Christ as her Savior."

Sharon

"Learned that a woman with a skin disease where her skin started peeling off was completely healed after being prayed for at a Prayer Station."

Heather

"I was standing at the bottom of an escalator when a man came up to me and told me how he had seen us last year. He had dangerously high blood pressure. He had someone pray for him and he has been fine ever since. He wanted an opportunity to thank us for praying for his healing. I told him God deserves all the glory and so he said, 'Praise God!'"

Kris

"A man from Estonia came to the Prayer Station who is trying to bring his family into the US. I prayed for him and his family and he hugged me and thanked me for reminding him that Jesus loved him and there was hope."

C. Wagner
"A passerby told us that a Prayer Station he stopped at last week turned his life around."

Elizabeth
"I enjoyed how many people were really encouraging us to 'Keep up the good work.'"

Whitney
"A lady came up to us and had one of our pieces of literature and had read it and loved it, so she asked for a Bible. She said she was going home to go ask Jesus in her heart."

A Long Island Pastor
"We came to the Prayer Station 9/11 outreach with a group of 30 students from our Christian school. We were able to distribute literature and pray with passersby. Students reported meeting people of varied backgrounds, some seemed to have facial expressions of listlessness and when approached, it was exciting to hear how many accepted the literature.

"I was able to speak and pray with a couple from Italy and also with US Army personnel patrolling the entrance to the Brooklyn Bridge. The factor of no charge for the literature came as a surprise to many. Some came seeking literature and were delighted to receive New Testaments both in English and Spanish."

Kathy
"I had a lengthy and meaningful conversation with a young woman, Wendy, from Kansas City, who had not been raised in church and had never opened a Bible. I gave her a Gospel of John and asked her to read it and email me what she thought. I feel it was a great 'seed planting' experience and I hope it will bear fruit someday."

Romeo
"This was definitely an awesome time of evangelism and ministry to people's life by sharing the love of Jesus. I'd say that the most important

thing to me was being able to sow a seed to the lost. It was definitely a stepping stone for the next level of my walk with God."

Sarah

"I met two pastors from the only legalized church in the United Arab Emirates. They told me all kinds of stories about tragedies and hardships they face every day that we can't ever imagine. Being arrested for public prayer and worship, etc. We prayed for them and encouraged them."

Autumn

"I found other brothers and sisters who really encouraged us. Some people came up to me and prayed for our Prayer Station. That was a blessing!"

Debbie

"A woman said to me 'I've been trying to pass by here three times and God won't let me go, I walked by and something said to go back, So here I am.'"

Susan

"I just wanted to say thank you for giving us the opportunity to minister with your ministry in New York City. We enjoyed it very much. Our young adult ministry will never be the same. I told the group I didn't know how many people were going to want prayer, but to believe God for divine appointments. It was awesome, we had so many people that wanted prayer. I was especially blessed to see God bring three deaf people to our Prayer Station. We had deaf young people on our team. God is so faithful. May God bless all of you with YWAM. My prayer was that these young adults would see how easy it is to take the gospel to the streets and there are so many hungry people wanting someone to care. Thanks again."

Suri and Tammy

"We asked the Lord for divine appointments. He gave us one today! A woman came for prayer for her daughter who was on the seventy-ninth floor of the WTC when it was hit. Her daughter's name was Tammy, her daughter lost both of her legs from the waist down and is still recovering. We prayed together and the woman just broke down in tears. She said that this was the first time since 9/11 that she came down to Ground Zero. She went to the WTC and afterwards felt drawn to come to our specific street, she said. She felt 'something draws her to this street.' I felt led to give the woman a CD and a Bible for her daughter. She again began to cry and kept hugging and thanking us. We believe that God has grabbed hold of her heart and won't let go until He has all of her."

Harry

"I had the opportunity to lead three people to the Lord. Two of the people were a married couple. The man's father was a Pentecostal pastor. What seemed very strange to me was what happened when our teams first came out of the subway. I asked our leader, 'Where do we set up the Prayer Station?' He looked at the directions and said, 'by the blue fence with no posting signs on it across the street from Macys.' We were standing at 6th Ave and 34th St. and we couldn't see any blue fence because it was at the other end of the block closer to 7th Ave. As soon as I heard our leader say 'blue fence' I knew exactly where it was and what it looked like

"Five months earlier, I was on my way home from working as a security guard at a construction site, as I passed the blue fence on 34th St. I was daydreaming about how I would like to have the job of providing security at this location. Little did I know that five months later, I would be doing security work at the blue fence. Eternal Security!"

Donna

"I was particularly blessed to pray with a Ukrainian woman named Ludmilla. I know the Lord sent her to me as I had just returned from a missions' trip to Ukraine. We had a real connection and she sort of told me her life story. I was able to share the gospel with her and prayed over her. She then said that I taught her how to pray. She now knows that she can just speak from her heart to God."

Karen

"God took over and even brought truly seeking and needy people right to us. Then to have the privilege of listening to them and praying for them was awesome. To have some that were open to the gospel and prayed to receive Jesus was such a highlight and honor."

Justin

"I spent 25 minutes speaking with a man stricken with fear and anxiety, who just lost his job and is overcoming a heroin addiction. He knows a lot about God, but his heart is hard to God's grace and His redemption for sins. I prayed with him and sent him off with some literature and he is expecting to hear from someone to help him find a church."

Katherine

"The power of God was evident to me when I prayed with people. The people were peaceful and grateful afterwards and were changed or at least touched by the fact that someone cared enough to do this for them."

Paul

"I'm so physically tired and can't hardly move, but at the same time I'm so spiritually filled from what I saw and experienced. I want to grasp on to this and remember it forever."

Rev. Najem

"This morning as we were setting up the Prayer Station about ten people came and said, 'Can we pray for you? We are an intercession team.' They stayed two hours behind us praying for us. The same thing happened yesterday at our Prayer Station with another group of intercessors."

Ann

"For me personally, I think this outreach meant more to me growth wise then those that I talked to. It has given me boldness, and strength to trust God more fully."

Abigail

"My favorite memory is a woman who came back and asked me to pray for her. I did and when I opened my eyes, she was weeping. She said, 'I've got to go, but now I know why I took a different train this morning.' Isn't God good? So many times, this week, I've been staggered and undone by the Sovereignty of the Lord we serve. Every seed planted, conversation shared and compassion shown was divine. I benefitted more than anyone I talked or prayed with."

Nichole

"My experience at the Prayer Station was wonderful. I had to keep myself from crying several times because I felt the Spirit of God with me."

Susan

"I did feel a lot better after having left the Prayer Station. I walked away with a great sense of comfort."

Lydia

"I talked with a man who kept stressing how great it was to just speak with a person who cared. He said he hadn't spoken with a Christian for a long time and he was encouraged that Christians would come out to reach the people of NYC after the 9/11 tragedy."

Douglas

"I was praying for people on Wall Street. Two Wall Street types were looking at the literature on the table, so I asked the one man if he would like prayer and he said, 'You can pray for him,' pointing to his buddy. The other man said his problem was drugs and he began to cry. I prayed for him. He walked away and came by later and gave me a thumbs up."

Stefanie

"I was approached by a Native American woman. I talked to her about God and she said she prayed to the Great Spirit, and asked, 'It's all the same thing, right?' She seemed very unsure and insecure about her beliefs. I explained sin, Jesus's death, His Blood, heaven, etc. and she said, 'Well, what do I do? I want to go to heaven.' I wasn't sure if the conviction was really there or she just wanted to cover her bases so I explained things again. I felt like I stumbled my way through, but then felt the power of the Spirit and the words flowed out. She began to weep and said again that she wanted to know what to do. I prayed with her and gave her a Bible."

Mark

"It was a thrill to pray for a Jewish lady named Anita. She was in tears and she had already been prayed for, but after talking was open to more prayer. She talked about living more comfortably with Christians in times of trouble than with her own. We shared the plan of salvation and she received our gospel literature."

Two Teenagers 17 and 18

"We met 2 pastors from the only legalized church in the United Arab Emirates. They told us that we are so fortunate to live in a country where we can practice Christianity freely. They were strongly against the Islamic religion because it is the law where they are from which keeps them from practicing Christianity. They told of tragedies and hardships they face every day that we can't even imagine. Being arrested for public prayer, worship, band practice, etc. The girls encouraged them to remember that we are against the evil one and not people. They agreed that we should try to show love instead of hate. We prayed together and were blessed."

Shawn York

"A guy came and shared that his prayer had been answered from another Prayer Station."

Mike

"A gentleman named Steve just started talking to me about how he stopped a few weeks before to pray with someone at a Prayer Station.

The person who prayed for him asked him, 'If God would do one thing for you, what would that be?' He said 'Watch over my children.' They prayed for his family and later found out that at the very same time they prayed, the babysitter started beating his baby. The baby was OK. He stopped to thank us, because if they hadn't prayed, things could have been so much worse. We prayed for his children again and thanked God together for His protection."

Alvin
"A young lady walked behind me and asked if she could pray with me, and then she told me how her mother had just come out of the hospital 3 days ago after she had prayed with someone at a Prayer Station for her mom. She also shared that when her mom was discharged, she committed her life to Jesus."

Megon
"One woman came up to me with her two children and asked me to pray for some general family needs. So, we prayed and she thanked me and left. Three hours later she came back crying and tried to give me some money. God had worked a miracle in her life when she left, and she was just so thankful."

Tammi
"I prayed with a lady who needed direction in her job, and her marriage. She was so touched that she went and got her friend and tracked me down in the sushi restaurant, so that I could pray for her. We prayed right in the middle of the restaurant."

Grace
"I talked to a man named Gabriel, who was a security guard in the building next to our Prayer Station. He shared that he had been having problems with the IRS for several years. He told me that yesterday someone from one of our Prayer Stations had come up to him and asked

if he wanted prayer. They prayed and this morning, the IRS contacted him to say everything was fine."

Angela

"Today two ladies told me they came to a Prayer Station previously and were prayed for. One lady said her nephew was in critical condition in the hospital. After receiving prayer at a Prayer Station, he was released in two days."

Phyllis

"One gentleman came for prayer due to an answered prayer at a Prayer Station last week. His sister had been in the hospital very ill and has since improved."

Sasha

"The highlight of this ministry for me was on the last day when I had a girl come up to me and thank me for praying for her a few weeks ago. She said that my prayer had been answered."

Gabriella

"In July of this year a woman came across a Prayer Station on 34th St. in Manhattan by Macy's department store. She had two girls pray for a financial need of $500 she had to pay for tests she was to take for medical school. The two girls agreed with her in prayer for the needed funds. She said that it was within two or three days that she received a phone call from her mother, unexpectedly, saying that she wanted to give her the $500 for her test fees. She was so impressed that she has been looking for another Prayer Station so that she could share how God supplied her need and strengthened her faith."

John

"It's meaningful that although our team felt lots of rejection from busy people, they didn't give up."

Barbara

"As we prayed for people, a woman named Carol and her daughter Venus were passing by. My daughter, Debbie, and I asked them if they needed prayer for anything and Carol responded very quickly saying that she was just talking to Venus about getting out to church. We prayed for her for a job which she needed. We then began to share with them the 'Steps To Peace With God' tract. Venus began to repeat the sinner's prayer which softened her mother's heart as she joined in and also began to pray. Both were genuine prayers and they felt so much of the love of Jesus."

Lauren

"I was surprised to see people come up to me wanting to be prayed for. I felt God was doing amazing things through us to reach people we were meeting right then and there."

Rosa

"Before we even got the Prayer Station set up, we were swamped by people wanting us to pray for them. We were encouraged and emboldened by this response."

April

"The fact that people actually came up to us to ask for prayer, instead of us going to them was so encouraging."

Katrina

"It was very good. At first, I was a little shy, then after about a half hour I really got into it."

Nancy

"It was a day that has shaken me from my comfort zone. Praise God!"

Kaey

"I really enjoyed stepping out of my comfort zone and being forced to go up to people (strangers) and just ask them to pray with me. I really felt the power of the Holy Spirit there."

Heidi
"In the beginning, I was scared and nervous. As I was filled with boldness the fear went away and more people responded."

Steve
"I was afraid at first, but I realized that I needed to put my heart into my job. I believe that God gave me the strength and the encouragement to be bold."

Janey
"I enjoyed watching my group excited to share Jesus. One girl from our group was full of fear before we came, so we prayed for her. When we arrived, she received boldness that was contagious. She had a smile the whole time we were there."

Rev. Steve and Leanna
"Our youth grew and came out of their shell through this experience."

Erica
"It's amazing the way that God gives us courage and boldness to speak into the lives of hurting people."

Hillary (Did Prayer Stations for a month and a half)
"Prayer Stations gave me a lot of experience doing street ministry and taught me much boldness. Stepping out more in my faith. At first, I was very timid and it was hard for me to approach people, but over time God gave me the boldness to speak out and approach people, even those in my own culture. I learned a great deal about spiritual warfare and the power of intercession as well. It was a good experience overall; there were harder and easier times, but the Lord taught me that He is the same no matter how I feel that day and that I must persevere no matter what the circumstances."

Kristine

"I thought it was an awesome step out of my comfort zone, and God actually made me feel comfortable doing it."

Sarah

"What stuck out to me was God's power over all. I was always a shy person since I was born, but He used me even though. He blessed me by having people actually come up and ask me for prayer. He is awesome and powerful."

Donna

"This was such an awesome experience for me. The Lord gave me the boldness and wisdom I prayed for."

Gail

"The Lord drew me out of my comfort zone. He allowed me to step out and actually fish for mankind. Every opportunity to pray drew me closer to Him and helped me to rely on Him and put my trust in His grace. It is not about us, but all about Him!"

Heidi

"This is an awesome ministry! What I like is just being able to come out of my comfort zone and just be able to be hope and joy and a smile to people who are hurting."

Martha

"Watching my 12-year-old boldly pray for people and seeing how touched they were by her sincere prayers will stay in my mind and heart forever as a cherished blessing."

Margie

"I was deeply moved by hearing the children in our group praying with and for adults and interacting with strangers."

John

"I was a Prayer Station warrior watching 6 children hand out gospel tracts. We watched a police officer constantly reading the tract one of our children gave him. After a while we went over and he admitted he was a backslidden Christian. We prayed with him and he recommitted his life to Christ."

Krista

"An 11-year-old boy named Andy accepted the Lord today at the Prayer Station!"

Bill

"I began my day walking around the corner to find an elderly woman who was looking at the WTC site and told me she sees this every day. She was visiting from Jerusalem. I read to her from Amos 9:10-14 the promise of God for Israel that they would never again be rooted out of the country God gave them, and as I read her husband came near to listen and their faces beamed. By the way, her husband's name was Amos."

Doug

"When I first got to the Prayer Station, we had not even got the table up or anything ready and a woman came up in tears needing prayer. I was able to pray for her about her family. Also, a girl came up and was just there and didn't know why she was, but I was able to share the gospel with her and it seemed like a divine appointment."

YWAM Lebanon, Pennsylvania. In Tremont, Pennsylvania at a Christian picnic / Prayer Station outreach in a park

"A haggard-looking man walked up to us and asked if we would pray for him. He looked like an alcoholic who'd lived a tough life. We prayed a simple prayer over him, and when it ended, he looked at us and said, 'I haven't had a prayer like that prayed over me in 30 years.' You could tell he was pretty excited. Later in the day he brought his young son, maybe

13 years old, over. His name was Andrew, and he said 'Can you pray for Andrew too?' I could tell Andrew wasn't really into it but his dad was insisting that we pray for him, so we prayed for Andrew also. Still later in the day there was a drawing for bicycles. I think there were three different bicycles for three different age groups. And they had the drawing and I noticed after a few minutes that Andrew won the drawing and he received a new white bicycle, a really pretty looking one. I was walking from the stage area back to the Prayer Station and as I did, I looked over to the side and I saw the dad and Andrew standing by the bicycle. The dad beckoned me to come over. As I did, I could hear the dad saying to Andrew, 'See what happens when people pray. See what God does when people pray,' and he was just so excited. That was a pretty cool story about the Prayer Station."

Cindy
"Prayer Stations were set up in downtown Canton, Ohio. A husband and wife showed up for prayer. They were living a pretty hard life. They lived in another state and had come to Canton to visit a parent that had surgery. It was their plan to stay with the parent, but there were complications and the parent had lost all of their memory, even the memory of who their children were, so that meant they did not have a place to stay.

"They had been staying outside in an undesirable location until they felt it was safe to leave their parents. They actually preferred to live together under the stars rather than separate in male and female shelters. They didn't know anyone to ask for a place to stay so asked for prayer. The Prayer Station leaders, Brad and CeCe prayed for them. They then invited them to come back later to share a pizza. Even though they said they didn't want to intrude or take a hand-out, Brad and CeCe insisted, so lunchtime rolled around and they returned and shared a pizza. CeCe noticed a gentleman across the way in the pizza restaurant staring at them while they were eating. They thought maybe he was hungry or just trying to get up the nerve to come and ask for prayer. It turned out that the man recognized the homeless husband and wife from a connection many years previous. He came to announce himself and reconnect and when he found out about the plight of the couple, he insisted they come and stay with him. Why? Because when he was down and out, these folks helped him in a time of need."

Urban Harvest Ministries—Detroit, Michigan

"A lady leaves work in fear for her life, crying out to God, 'If You are there, help me!' She turns the corner and sees a Prayer Station, parks her car and finds the peace she longed for."

"May we pray for you?"

"For this reason I kneel before the Father, from whom every family in heaven and on earth derives its name. I pray that out of his glorious riches he may strengthen you with power through his Spirit in your inner being, so that Christ may dwell in your hearts through faith. And I pray that you, being rooted and established in love, may have power, together with all the Lord's holy people, to grasp how wide and long and high and deep is the love of Christ, and to know this love that surpasses knowledge—that you may be filled to the measure of all the fullness of God.

Now to him who is able to do immeasurably more than all we ask or imagine, according to his power that is at work within us, 21 to him be glory in the church and in Christ Jesus throughout all generations, for ever and ever! Amen."
—Paul's prayer in Ephesians 3:14-21

Now
Who can you encourage today with just Five Little Words?
May I pray for you?